The United States and Genocide

There exists a dominant narrative that essentially defines the US' relationship with genocide through what the US has failed to do to stop or prevent genocide, rather than through how its actions have contributed to the commission of genocide. This narrative acts to conceal the true nature of the US' relationship with many of the governments that have committed genocide since the Holocaust, as well as the US' own actions. In response, this book challenges the dominant narrative through a comprehensive analysis of the US' relationship with genocide.

The analysis is situated within the broader genocide studies literature, while emphasizing the role of state responsibility for the commission of genocide and the crime's ancillary acts. The book addresses how a culture of impunity contributes to the resiliency of the dominant narrative in the face of considerable evidence that challenges it. Bachman's narrative presents a far darker relationship between the US and genocide, one that has developed from the start of the Genocide Convention's negotiations and has extended all the way to present day, as can be seen in the relationships the US maintains with potentially genocidal regimes, from Saudi Arabia to Myanmar.

This book will be of interest to scholars, postgraduates, and students of genocide studies, US foreign policy, and human rights. A secondary readership may be found in those who study international law and international relations.

Jeffrey S. Bachman is Professorial Lecturer in Human Rights and Director of the Ethics, Peace, and Global Affairs MA Program at the American University's School of International Service, USA.

Routledge Studies in Genocide and Crimes against Humanity
Edited by Adam Jones
University of British Columbia in Kelowna, Canada

The *Routledge Studies in Genocide and Crimes against Humanity* series publishes cutting-edge research and reflections on these urgently contemporary topics. While focusing on political-historical approaches to genocide and other mass crimes, the series is open to diverse contributions from the social sciences, humanities, law, and beyond. Proposals for both sole-authored and edited volumes are welcome.

For more information about this series, please visit: www.routledge.com/Routledge-Studies-in-Genocide-and-Crimes-against-Humanity/book-series/RSGCH

The Structural Prevention of Mass Atrocities
Understanding Risks and Resilience
Stephen McLoughlin

Constructing Genocide and Mass Violence
Society, Crisis, Identity
Maureen Hiebert

Last Lectures on the Prevention and Intervention of Genocide
Edited by Samuel Totten

Perpetrating Genocide
A Criminological Account
Kjell Anderson

The United States and Genocide
(Re)Defining the Relationship
Jeffrey S. Bachman

The United States and Genocide
(Re)Defining the Relationship

Jeffrey S. Bachman

LONDON AND NEW YORK

First published 2018 by Routledge

2 Park Square, Milton Park, Abingdon, Oxfordshire OX14 4RN
52 VanderbiltAvenue, New York, NY 10017

Routledge is an imprint of the Taylor & Francis Group, an informa business

First issued in paperback 2019

Copyright © 2018 Jeffrey S. Bachman

The right of Jeffrey S. Bachman to be identified as author of this
work has been asserted by him in accordance with sections
77 and 78 of the Copyright, Designs and Patents Act 1988.

All rights reserved. No part of this book may be reprinted or reproduced
or utilised in any form or by any electronic, mechanical, or other
means, now known or hereafter invented, including photocopying and
recording, or in any information storage or retrieval system, without
permission in writing from the publishers.

Notice:
Product or corporate names may be trademarks or registered trademarks,
and are used only for identification and explanation without intent to
infringe.

British Library Cataloguing in Publication Data
A catalogue record for this book is available from the British Library

Library of Congress Cataloging in Publication Data
A catalogue record for this book has been requested

ISBN: 978-1-138-04795-2 (hbk)
ISBN: 978-0-367-19496-3 (pbk)

Typeset in Times New Roman
by codeMantra

To my Mom for all of her love and support. May she rest in peace.

And to the victims of US foreign policy, past, present, and future.

Contents

	Acknowledgments	ix
1	Introduction: (re)contextualizing the US relationship with genocide	1
2	Redefining genocide	19
3	Cultural genocide: *nullum crimen sine lege*	56
4	Conspiracy to commit genocide in Indonesia	78
5	Complicity in genocide in Bangladesh and Guatemala	97
6	A history of genocide in Iraq	123
7	Genocide in Vietnam	156
8	Again and again: the US relationship with genocide	175
	Index	203

Acknowledgments

I would like to take this opportunity to thank those who helped make this book possible. First, I thank my wonderful loving partner, Jeannie Khouri. Through her role as my unofficial editor, Jeannie has helped to spare me the embarrassment of submitting documents full of typos and questionable grammar. Because she will not be editing this particular entry, I can only hope that I catch them all on my own.

I also want to thank, of course, my family for their patience and support. I have gone incommunicado a number of times during this process, but they have always been there when I resurfaced. I have received additional support from my friends and colleagues at American University's School of International Service, who have also witnessed my vanishing act.

Finally, I want to thank Routledge, series editor Adam Jones, Lydia de Cruz, Nicola Parkin, and Lucy Frederick for working with me to bring this book to publication.

1 Introduction

(Re)contextualizing the US
relationship with genocide

In 2013, Win/Gallup International published the results of a massive survey that asked more than 66,000 people in 65 countries to identify which country posed the greatest threat to world peace. The results were overwhelming. The US received 24 percent of the vote. Pakistan was closest to the US, receiving a mere 8 percent of the vote, followed by China at 6 percent, and Afghanistan at 5 percent.[1] There is a reason for this. In the post-World War II era, the US "has been far and away the most belligerent and destructive of the world's nations, internationally speaking."[2]

A little more than three years after Japan surrendered, ending World War II, the United Nations General Assembly adopted the Convention on the Prevention and Punishment of the Crime of Genocide on December 9, 1948, which then entered into force two years later on January 12, 1951.[3] Since then, the US has been involved in a near-continuous stream of violence and atrocities. From 1950 to 1953, in response to North Korea's invasion of South Korea, the US "carpet-bombed the north for three years with next to no concern for civilian casualties."[4] During the Korean War, the US dropped 635,000 tons of bombs and 32,557 tons of napalm on the Korean Peninsula—more than the entire amount used against Japan during World War II. Upwards of three million civilians were killed, most of them residing in the North.[5] In an interview with the Office of Air Force History, Curtis LeMay, head of Strategic Air Command during the war, recalled, "Over a period of three years or so, we killed off—what—20 percent of the population of Korea as direct casualties of war, or from starvation and exposure?"[6]

During the 1960s and 1970s, the US engaged in a war of aggression against the Vietnamese people. From 1965 to 1975, the US dropped more than seven million tons of bombs and other munitions on South and North Vietnam, equaling the explosive force of approximately 640 atomic bombs like the one used on Hiroshima.[7] As Adam Jones stresses, "This was more than was dropped by all countries in all theaters of the Second World War."[8] The US also used eight million tons of other ordnance and 400,000 tons of napalm, an incendiary weapon.[9] Throughout the duration of this aggressive war, as many as three million people were killed. As the aggressor in an illegal

2 *Introduction*

war, the US is responsible for every death in Vietnam that would have been avoided had the US never attacked the people of Vietnam.

In 1965, the US conspired with Indonesian officials to kill communists in Indonesia. Soon after a coup brought General Suharto to power, mass killings of members of Indonesia's Communist Party and its sympathizers began.[10] From late 1965 to early 1966, over a period of six months, the Indonesian Army and its civilian proxies murdered hundreds of thousands of people. Benedict Anderson puts the minimum number of people killed at 600,000, with the possibility of upwards of two million deaths.[11] During this time, in addition to material and diplomatic support, the US also systematically compiled a list of as many as 5,000 Indonesian Communist leaders, which was delivered to Indonesian officials. The US allegedly checked off the names of individuals as they were killed.[12]

For nine months, beginning in March 1971, Pakistan conducted military operations in Bangladesh (then East Pakistan), killing at least one million people, and forcing another ten million to seek refuge in India.[13] The violence was preceded by contentious elections in 1970 that resulted in the Awami League, based in East Pakistan, winning 167 of 313 seats in Pakistan's National Assembly and becoming the majority party. Yahya Khan, Pakistan's President and Chief Martial Law Administrator, viewed the Awami League's electoral victory as a threat to Pakistan's territorial integrity, and refused to seat the newly elected government. On March 25, 1971, as tensions mounted, Pakistan launched 'Operation Searchlight,' a massive military assault on the East's capital city of Dhaka.[14] Prior to and while Pakistan was killing its own people, the US provided Pakistan with material and diplomatic support. Regional interests and Pakistan's role as intermediary between the US and China were too important to allow "a little matter of genocide" to interfere.[15]

Similarly, the US provided Guatemala with material and diplomatic support while it was committing genocide against its Mayan population. From 1979 to 1983, the Guatemalan military viewed Guatemala's Mayans as a support base for leftist rebels, labeling them "enemies" of the state. During this time, "massive and indiscriminate aggression" was directed against Mayan communities "independent of their actual involvement in the guerilla movement and with a clear indifference to their status as a non-combatant civilian population."[16] The peak of the killings came following General Efraín Ríos Montt's military coup in March 1982. During his eighteen months in office, Ríos Montt oversaw the murder of as many as 80,000 Guatemalans.[17]

In 1987 and 1988, when Iraq was gassing members of its Kurdish population, the US was once again providing a government killing its own people with material and diplomatic support. In what is known as the Anfal Campaign, Iraq killed between 50,000 and 100,000 people over a seven-month period.[18] Only three years later, the US initiated a war with Iraq under the pretense of protecting Kuwaiti sovereignty. In August 1990, Iraq invaded Kuwait, which was followed by the initiation of a brutal sanctions regime.

Introduction 3

In January 1991, the US launched 'Operation Desert Storm'. In the process of ejecting Iraq from Kuwait, the US intentionally attacked Iraq's civilian infrastructure, including electricity and sanitation facilities.[19] The sanctions that were implemented following Iraq's invasion and occupation of Kuwait were maintained even after Iraq was expelled. Though the sanctions were administered by the UN, there is general agreement that the US was primarily responsible for drafting the sanctions and ensuring they were maintained and enforced.[20] The combination of damage to the infrastructure and the enforcement of a sanctions regime described as the most comprehensive in history caused a precipitous decline in public health in Iraq.[21] By 1998, more than one million Iraqis died from circumstances connected to the sanctions, including as many as 500,000 children.[22]

The sanctions continued until the US once again invaded Iraq in 2003. The US claimed the invasion was necessary for reasons including Iraq's alleged connections with al-Qaeda, its alleged "WMD" program, and its treatment of members of its own population. A Physicians for Social Responsibility (PSR) report published in 2015 cited a Lancet study which found that 655,000 Iraqis were killed between 2003 and 2006. Further, PSR notes,

> should the number of Iraqis killed from the 2003 U.S. invasion until 2012 actually be around one million, as the analysis of the existing scientific studies presented in the present study suggests, this would represent 5% of the total population of Iraq—a number which additionally indicates the extent of the corresponding damage inflicted upon society and the infrastructure.[23]

In addition to the people killed in the US war of aggression and those killed as a result of the war, cultural sites were destroyed. Iraq also experienced a looting of cultural artifacts on a scale not seen since the Mongol's invaded Baghdad in 1258.[24]

In addition to its foreign exploits, the US maintained policies at home designed to strip indigenous youth of their cultural identity. These policies included, among others, the forcible transfer of children from their families, prohibition of the use of their language, and the destruction of historical or religious monuments or their appropriation for other use. Individually and collectively, these policies represent acts of cultural genocide. Importantly, during the Genocide Convention's drafting process, the US aggressively opposed the inclusion of cultural genocide, even threatening to undermine the treaty's adoption if the final text included cultural genocide. For example, during negotiations the US issued a thinly veiled threat:

> Were the Committee to attempt to cover too wide a field in the preparation of a draft convention for example, in attempting to define cultural genocide—however reprehensible that crime might be—it might well run the risk to find some States would refuse to ratify the convention.[25]

4   *Introduction*

Problems of definition

Despite all the above, the US has largely been excluded as a focus of genocide studies. There are three interconnected reasons for this: problems of definition, the associated limitations on cases selected for analysis, and the culture of impunity that surrounds US policies worldwide. According to Benjamin Lieberman,

> No other branch of history or field of inquiry centered on historical events is so dependent on a definition as genocide studies. Studies of war, politics, wealth and poverty, society, culture, men and women, and a host of other topics have all given rise to detailed analysis of terms and definition; but no other field depends for its very existence upon the invention and definition of a single term.[26]

The legal definition of genocide, codified in the Genocide Convention, has proven inadequate, which has contributed to the proliferation of dozens of scholarly definitions.[27] Some scholars, nonetheless, continue to rely on the legal definition. For example, in his important work, *Genocide: Its Political Use in the Twentieth Century*, Leo Kuper declares,

> I shall follow the definition of genocide given in the [UN] Convention. This is not to say that I agree with the definition.... However, I do not think it helpful to create new definitions of genocide, when there is an internationally recognized definition and a Genocide Convention which might become the basis for some effective action, however limited the underlying conception.[28]

This is consistent with the deliberative school of thought on human rights. Central to this school is the belief that "there are no human rights beyond human rights law."[29] For deliberative scholars, in an international system still dominated by state actors, efforts to evaluate state actions using a set of requirements unrecognized by states would be an exercise in futility.

Yet, the legal definition of genocide was not determined by an objective process. Instead, through a process that began with the development of the initial Secretariat Draft of the treaty, the Genocide Convention was shaped by states negotiating on behalf of their interests. The Secretariat Draft was replaced by the Ad Hoc Committee Draft, which was ultimately superseded by the final adopted text. All the while, negotiating parties were able to determine the treaty's specific language and provisions, including both treaty obligations and prohibitions. As Beth Van Schaack aptly notes, examination of the Genocide Convention's preparatory works

> reveals the way in which political bodies may attempt to limit their obligations under international law when they reduce customary law

norms to positivistic expression in multilateral treaties. In this case, the Convention had to respond to the tragedy of the Nazi Holocaust. At the same time, however, the Convention could not implicate member nations on the drafting committee.[30]

The legal definition of genocide, then, is a political one. Employing the legal definition thus imposes political limitations on the scholarly study of genocide. As Gérard Prunier notes, adhering strictly to the legal definition "runs the risk of falling into largely abstract formalism and of not *seeing* [emphasis in original] the realities on the ground because it insists on their being framed by pre-defined and inapplicable conditions."[31] More explicitly, Israel Charny declares, "Insofar as there is ever a major discrepancy between the reality of masses of dead people and our legal-scholarly definitions, it is the latter which must yield and change."[32] Central to Prunier's and Charny's critiques of the legal definition is its inapplicability to most mass death-producing events. However, Charny goes further, asserting that scholarly definitions, too, may not adequately encompass all the acts that ought to be recognized as genocide. Thus, like the legal definition, scholarly definitions must yield and change to encompass reality.

Ultimately, whether legal or scholarly, a narrow definition of genocide will apply to only a small number of cases. In fact, William Schabas counts the Tutsi genocide in Rwanda as the only post-Jewish Holocaust case of genocide, as determined by the legal definition.[33] This exemplifies the need for an alternative definition of genocide. Contributions to genocide studies have been extraordinarily interdisciplinary. Early contributions to the field of genocide studies came from historians, legal theorists, political scientists, moral philosophers, and sociologists. Newer contributions have come from the disciplines of anthropology, indigenous studies, and gender studies.[34] This further demonstrates the diversity in genocide studies and its continued scholarly relevance. Jones writes that the "all hands on deck" approach to the study of genocide has left "the field in a constant state of evolution, exploration—and confusion."[35] As a result, Jones concludes it is best to accept that genocide "will forever be an 'essentially contested concept.'"[36] A contested concept of genocide has ripple effects on the study of genocide. The definition of genocide determines which acts within which contexts are relevant to genocide studies. Therefore, there exists a direct link between the definition of genocide a scholar uses and the cases selected for analysis. Put differently, if genocide is a contested concept, then so too are suspected cases of genocide. Hence, as it relates to the study of the US relationship with genocide, if US actions do not fit within a particular definition of genocide, the lack of case analysis involving the US could be justified on those grounds.

Yet, it is possible that the definitions themselves have been influenced by unconscious and conscious biases. In other words, the relationship could be an inverse one. Rather than definitions of genocide determining the cases

6 *Introduction*

studied, the selected cases could also influence how scholars define genocide. Levon Chorbajian argues that political agendas have greatly complicated how scholars define and analyze genocide. "Indeed," according to Chorbajian,

> these agendas often masquerade as legitimate scholarly disagreements since it is more efficacious and seemly and because, unfortunately, apologists who specialize in the concealment of developing or ongoing genocides and the denial of past ones are not unknown in academia.[37]

Similarly, Charny argues that political pressures have inevitably influenced the development of scholarly definitions of genocide. According to Charny, there are "insidious types of political pressure on the definition of genocide that issue from entirely respectable intellectual circles. The subject of genocide draws intense political fire over which events of mass murder are to be considered bona fide genocides."[38]

My definition of genocide is as comprehensive as it will be controversial. I define genocide as the attempt to eliminate, in whole or in part, a national, political, social, ethnic, racial, cultural, or socioeconomic group with the purpose of destroying it as such or achieving a particular political, social, or economic objective. Membership in any of the aforementioned groups may be assigned by the group's members or by the perpetrators. The methods through which genocide can be carried out include killing members of the group; deliberately imposing conditions that are likely to cause the deaths of members of the group; and enacting policies that seek to erase the group's cultural identity, also known as cultural genocide. Genocide may occur in times of peace and war, with aggressive war sharing a nexus with the crime of genocide. Furthermore, both unarmed and armed—noncombatant and combatant—members of the targeted group qualify as victims of genocide. As compared to other definitions in the field of genocide studies, the most controversial elements of my definition are its moderated intent requirement; the inclusion of cultural genocide and "indirect" genocide; its nexus between aggressive war and genocide; and the inclusion of armed individuals as potential victims of genocide.

The controversial nature of my definition of genocide and its impact on my study of the US relationship with genocide requires that the definition be conceptually sound and rigorously defended. It brings within the scope of genocide cases that other scholars might categorically exclude. Thus, in Chapter 2, I offer a point-by-point defense of my definition, situated in the genocide studies literature. In addition to broadening the definition of genocide, I also emphasize the importance of state responsibility for genocide and its ancillary crimes—including conspiracy to commit genocide, complicity in genocide, and failure to prevent genocide. I provide readers with a brief explanation of what state responsibility is under international law, along with a summary of what I refer to as the "Bosnia v. Serbia Precedent."

Introduction 7

In subsequent chapters, I apply my definition of genocide and the Bosnia v. Serbia Precedent regarding state responsibility for genocide to numerous cases that involve the US. In addition to those cases in which the US was directly responsible for atrocities, the analysis of US responsibility for genocide using the Bosnia v. Serbia Precedent is significant in that it redirects the attention in genocide studies away from whether the US could do more to prevent genocide to what role the US has played in connection to the actions of other states when they have committed genocide.

A culture of impunity

It is unlikely that scholarly definitions alone can explain why the US has been largely excluded from genocide studies. The general absence of US cases in the study of genocide would seem to indicate something more— a belief among genocide scholars that cases involving the US are distant enough from the concept of genocide that they do not warrant widespread exploration in genocide studies. Jones coined the term "democrisy" to refer to "the stain of hypocrisy that attaches to regimes that are avowedly democratic in character, that allow comparative freedom and immunity from naked state violence domestically, but that initiate or participate in atrocious actions beyond their borders."[39] For many, the US cannot be hypocritical in its actions, because the US only uses force as a last resort and with the right intentions. When the US does kill "innocent" people, as opposed to the "guilty" people it "justifiably" kills, it is the result of "tragic mistakes." Those who dare suggest the US is responsible for atrocious acts are "viewed as intemperate or ungrateful at best, dangerous or extremist at worst."[40] As Jones notes,

> The result is an effective 'culture of impunity,' in which the atrocities committed by Western states and their allies are systematically ignored, explained away, defined out of existence, or openly celebrated— anything to preserve them from serious and objective criticism.[41]

Chorbajian argues that objections to genocide accusations against the US are "not so much from skittishness at implicating the US in genocide," but from a determination that US actions amounted to something other than genocide.[42] However, Denis Halliday, who resigned as UN Humanitarian Coordinator in Iraq in 1998 in protest over the economic sanctions, stated later that he was made to feel as though he "had crossed an invisible line of impropriety" for daring to describe the impact of economic sanctions as "genocide."[43] Halliday notes, "Perhaps for most, the term 'genocide' is too emotive and too intimate to our democratic obligation to accept responsibility for even the most disagreeable actions undertaken by our respective governments."[44] R.J. Rummel's study of democide—"the murder of any person or people by a government, including genocide, politicide, and mass

8 *Introduction*

murder"—exemplifies the role bias can play in the study of genocide and other mass atrocity crimes. In his research, Rummel focused intensively on the crimes committed under Stalin, Mao, and Pol Pot, but "was far less persuasive in addressing (or rather, failing to address) the politically tinged slaughters inflicted and abetted by capitalist and ostensibly democratic polities, notably his own country, the United States."[45] In the context of the US war on Vietnam, Rummel claimed that "the U.S. democide in Vietnam seems to have killed at least 4,000 Vietnamese civilians, POWs, or enemy seeking to surrender, maybe as many as 10,000 Vietnamese. A prudent figure may be 5,500 overall."[46] Thus, according to Rummel's utterly implausible calculations, out of the more than two million Vietnamese who were killed during the US war on Vietnam, all except a few thousand deaths were attributable to some other actor or were justified.

The "Samantha Power Effect"

Perhaps no contemporary figure has done more to contribute to US impunity in the study of genocide than Samantha Power. Power's book *"A Problem from Hell": America and the Age of Genocide* is the most widely read and influential in the history of genocide studies.[47] The publisher promotes *"A Problem from Hell"* as a "convincing and definitive interrogation of the last century of American history and foreign policy."[48] In 2003, it won the Pulitzer Prize for General Non-Fiction. Yet, *"A Problem from Hell"* does not live up to its description. Instead of truly interrogating the US relationship with genocide, Power overstates the role of US leadership in the creation of the Genocide Convention, omits cases of genocide in which the US was involved, and understates the US role in the cases she does include.

According to Power, the US took on a leadership role in drafting the Genocide Convention and seeing it through to its adoption by the General Assembly. Power claims, "The UN passage had been an American effort in many respects."[49] The US was even the first state to sign the Genocide Convention on December 11, 1948. However, the US failed to ratify the treaty until November 25, 1988. Thus, writes Power, "The early U.S. leadership on the genocide treaty largely evaporated in the months and years that followed."[50] The use of "leadership" to describe the US role in drafting the Genocide Convention has an obvious positive connotation. It portrays the US as having guided the other members of the international community on the path to outlawing a crime that shocked the conscience of humankind not once, but twice in the first half of the 20th century. If it were not for American leadership, a treaty prohibiting the crime of genocide might not have been realized.

While there is truth to this, it paints an incomplete picture. The US did play an active role in the drafting process, and it did consistently engage in the negotiations that concluded with a draft of the treaty that was unanimously adopted on December 9, 1948. However, what it ignores is the

Introduction 9

impact of US "leadership" on the language of the Genocide Convention. Ward Churchill rightly refers to US participation in drafting the Genocide Convention as "gutting the convention."[51] Churchill argues,

> When it came time for the drafting of the actual genocide convention, however, the United States conducted itself in what can only be described as a thoroughly subversive fashion. This began with its response to the initial draft instrument, a document which sought to frame the crime in a manner consistent with accepted definition.[52]

Foremost among Churchill's criticism of the US is the role it played in the exclusion of cultural genocide from the Genocide Convention. As already noted, the US aggressively argued against the inclusion of cultural genocide, even threatening to undermine the entire treaty, while conducting policies that would have been defined as cultural genocide and prohibited by the Genocide Convention had the US not succeeded in winning cultural genocide's removal. Yet, the subject of cultural genocide is essentially excluded from Power's *"A Problem from Hell."*

Power's book also omits or disregards a number of cases of genocide. These include genocide in Indonesia from 1965 to 1966, Bangladesh in 1971, and Guatemala from 1979 to 1983. In each case, the US held significant influence over the governments responsible for the atrocities. Further, as previously noted, in the case of Indonesia, the US provided the names of individuals to be killed. Yet, as Edward Herman and David Peterson note, Power devotes only one sentence to Indonesia, "ignoring entirely the mass killings of 1965–1966, mentioning only its invasion-occupation of East Timor in 1975 and after."[53] It would be easy to use the omission of political groups from the Genocide Convention to explain the absence of Indonesia's genocide in *"A Problem from Hell,"* except that Power writes extensively about the Cambodian genocide. In Power's words,

> The exclusion of political groups from the convention made it much harder in the late 1970s to demonstrate that the Khmer Rouge were committing genocide in Cambodia when they set out to wipe out whole classes of alleged 'political enemies'.[54]

Thus, Power did not let the omission of political groups deter her from devoting considerable space to the Cambodian genocide.

It is also worth noting that Power severely downplays the role of the US in the rise of the Khmer Rouge. In her passing mention of US bombing raids on Vietnam's border with Cambodia, Power claims, "U.S. B-52 raids killed tens of thousands of civilians.... American intervention in Cambodia did tremendous damage in its own right, but it also indirectly helped give rise to a monstrous regime."[55] While it was secretly bombing Cambodia, the US dropped 2,756,941 tons of munitions. As Taylor Owen and Ben

10 *Introduction*

Kiernan note, "Cambodia may well be the most heavily bombed country in history."[56] In many cases, Cambodian villages were mercilessly attacked with dozens of B-52 payloads over a period of hours, resulting in "near-total destruction."[57] At a minimum, the US killed 50,000 people. However, it is likely the US killed more than 100,000 people.[58] Power's description of "tens of thousands" of deaths is simply inadequate. Additionally, whereas Power describes the rise of the Khmer Rouge as an "indirect" consequence of US attacks on Cambodia, Owen and Kiernan describe it as "unintended." The two terms are not interchangeable. The US bombing of Cambodia, in fact, played a direct, even if unintended, role in the rise of the Khmer Rouge. As Owen and Kiernan explain, the "bombs drove ordinary Cambodians into the arms of the Khmer Rouge, a group that seemed initially to have slim prospects of revolutionary success."[59] The damage caused by the B-52 bombings was a main theme of Khmer Rouge propaganda, which, according to the CIA, was quite "effective."[60]

While Power labels what happened in Bangladesh as genocide, it receives little more than half of a page of text in a book that is more than 600 pages long. Power cites between one and two million people killed by Pakistani troops, along with the rape of 200,000 girls and women. Yet, on the US role, Power merely states, "The Nixon administration, which was hostile to India and using Pakistan as an intermediary to China, did not protest."[61] It would be generous to call this an understatement. The US provided Pakistan with material and diplomatic support prior to and throughout the duration of the genocide, including active obstruction at the Security Council. What Power describes as lack of protest, I argue amounts to complicity in genocide.

Power fails to mention Guatemala altogether—an astonishing oversight. Years before *"A Problem from Hell"* was published, the Commission for Historical Clarification, a UN-supported body, issued its report "Guatemala Memory of Silence." The Commission found that 83 percent of Guatemala's victims were Mayan, concluding that "agents of the state committed acts of genocide against groups of Mayan people."[62] Herman and Peterson categorize the Guatemalan Genocide as "benign," because the perpetrator of the genocide was an anti-communist US client state.[63] They argue that the number of people killed in Guatemala, along with the fact that the overwhelming majority of the victims were members of the Mayan population, makes the period in Guatemala between 1981 and 1983 a clear case of genocide under the Genocide Convention.[64] Greg Grandin may have identified why Guatemala is not included in Power's influential text. Grandin summarizes Power's overarching thesis—"the problem is not what the United States does…but what it doesn't do; act to stop genocide."[65] Grandin continues,

> In the Guatemalan case however, genocide was not a result of state decomposition but rather state consolidation, the first step in the military's plan of national stability and return to constitutional rule. And

Introduction 11

it certainly was not the result of Washington's negligence but rather a direct consequence of its intervention.[66]

Power does include a chapter on Iraq in her book, but limits her focus to Iraq's Kurdish genocide, ignoring the US sanctions regime during the 1990s altogether. Additionally, whereas I argue that the US was complicit in the Kurdish genocide, Power leaves readers with the false impression that the US chose not to get involved, essentially turning a blind eye, due to geostrategic interests and a lack of "perfect information."[67] Power acknowledges that the US provided Iraq with military intelligence, but not that the US sold Iraq weapons, including chemical agents.[68] The latter claim simply does not hold up under scrutiny. The US transferred weapons to Iraq through third parties and directly sold Iraq "civilian" equipment that was used for military purposes. Further, the US sold Iraq chemicals that were incorporated into Iraq's chemical weapons program.[69] According to Power, in choosing to back Iraq in the Iran–Iraq war, the US refrained from protesting Iraq's genocide. Rather than "send a strong message that genocide would not be tolerated—that the destruction of Iraq's rural Kurdish populace would have to stop—special interests, economic profit, and a geopolitical tilt toward Iraq thwarted humanitarian concerns."[70] Thus, writes Power, "The Reagan administration punted on genocide, and the Kurds paid the price."[71]

There is a clear pattern in the way Power, as well as others, defines the US relationship with genocide. It presents the US relationship with genocide as one of a bystander that simply needs to find the political will and exert the necessary leadership to take preventive action, meaning intervene militarily. It whitewashes the essential role the US has played in facilitating the conditions in which genocide has been committed and ignores entirely the possibility that the US could be directly responsible for the commission of genocide. It creates a narrative that must be challenged, because of its practical impact. As Carol Rittner, John Roth, and James Smith explain in the introduction to their edited volume *Will Genocide Ever End?*, "Calling—or refusing to call—acts of violence genocidal can make huge differences in… historical memory and its legacies."[72]

The dissident strand

In his own contribution to the dissident strand of literature on US foreign and domestic policy, Jones states that interventions that seek to challenge the culture of impunity are now more necessary than ever.[73] With this book, I hope to join Jones, Churchill, and Herman and Peterson, as well as Noam Chomsky, in making a significant contribution to the dissident strand of literature on US foreign and domestic policy. My book is not meant to be a direct response to Power's *"A Problem from Hell."* However, Power's book, along with the broader treatment of the US in genocide studies, necessitates a response that involves a critical interrogation of

12 *Introduction*

the US relationship with genocide. Until there is an honest account of the US' relationship with genocide, and human rights more broadly, the US will continue to commit international crimes and aid others in doing so, all while operating within a culture of impunity. This is what I seek to do with this book—create the space required to have a more truthful, and hopefully fruitful, conversation, all while actively engaging with my genocide studies peers.

The book from here

The remainder of this book is dedicated to the study of the US relationship with genocide. However, before delving fully into this endeavor, I must first define the parameters within which I assess this relationship. Therefore, in Chapter 2, I defend my definition of genocide. I also explain the principle of state responsibility for violations of international law and summarize the Bosnia v. Serbia Precedent, due to its direct relevance to determining state responsibility for genocide.

In Chapter 3, I present detailed evidence regarding the role the US played in the exclusion of cultural genocide from the Genocide Convention. I then contextualize US opposition to the inclusion of cultural genocide by juxtaposing it with US treatment of its indigenous populations. In Chapters 4–7, I apply my definition and the Bosnia v. Serbia Precedent to a range of cases in which I allege US involvement in genocide, whether as the state directly responsible for the commission of genocide or as a state that shares responsibility for engaging in one or more of genocide's ancillary crimes.

Chapter 4 analyzes the role the US played in the genocide committed by Indonesia against communist members of its population from 1965 to 1966. In Chapter 5, I evaluate the US' relationship with the Pakistani and Guatemalan governments at the time each committed genocide against members of their own populations. Chapter 6 is dedicated to the role of the US in genocide in Iraq. It begins with the Kurdish genocide and then moves to the US-imposed sanctions. In Chapter 7, I seek to determine whether the US is responsible for genocide during its war of aggression perpetrated against the people of Vietnam.

The final chapter brings readers to the present day, providing evidence that little has changed. Currently, the US is providing material support for Saudi Arabia's indiscriminate war and blockade on Yemen, so far leaving as many as 10,000 dead and millions diseased and malnourished. The US has also significantly strengthened its ties to the government in Myanmar, even as human rights organizations have identified precursors to genocide against Myanmar's Rohingya population. I conclude with a brief summary and comment on US legal and scholarly impunity, both of which contribute to the perpetuation of the culture of impunity in which the US acts at home and around the world.

Introduction 13

Notes

1 Cited in Meredith Bennett-Smith, "Womp! This Country Was Named the Greatest Threat to World Peace," *Huffington Post*, www.huffingtonpost.com/2014/01/02/greatest-threat-world-peace-country_n_4531824.html (accessed June 1, 2017).
2 Adam Jones, *The Scourge of Genocide: Essays and Reflections* (London: Routledge, 2013), 70.
3 The full text of the Genocide Convention can be accessed at www.ohchr.org/EN/ProfessionalInterest/Pages/CrimeOfGenocide.aspx.
4 Bruce Cumings, *The Korean War: A History* (New York: Random House, 2011), 149.
5 Mehdi Hasan, "Why Do North Koreans Hate Us? One Reason—They Remember the Korean War," *The Intercept*, https://theintercept.com/2017/05/03/why-do-north-koreans-hate-us-one-reason-they-remember-the-korean-war/(accessed June 24, 2017).
6 Richard H. Kohn and Joseph P. Harahan, *Strategic Air Warfare: An Interview with Generals Curtis LeMay, Leon W. Johnson, David A. Burchinal, and Jack J. Catton* (Washington, DC: Office of Air Force History, 1988), 88.
7 Adam Jones, *Genocide: A Comprehensive Introduction*, 2nd ed. (London: Routledge, 2011), 74–75; Jonathan Neale, *A People's History of the Vietnam War* (New York: The New Press, 2003), 75.
8 Jones, *Genocide*, 2nd ed., 74.
9 Brian S. Wilson, "Bob Kerrey's Atrocity, the Crime of Vietnam and the Historic Pattern of US Imperialism," in *Genocide, War Crimes & the West*, ed. Adam Jones (London: Zed Books, 2004), 167.
10 Douglas Kammen and Katharine McGregor, "Introduction: The Contours of Mass Violence in Indonesia, 1965–68," in *The Contours of Mass Violence in Indonesia, 1965–1968*, eds. Douglas Kammen and Katharine McGregor (Honolulu: University of Hawaii Press, 2012), 2.
11 Benedict Anderson, *Violence and the State in Suharto's Indonesia* (Ithaca, NY: Cornell University Press, 2009), 9.
12 Kathy Kadane, "Ex-Agents say CIA Compiled Death Lists for Indonesians," *San Francisco Examiner*, www.namebase.net/kadane.html (accessed December 2, 2015).
13 Simon Chesterman, *Just War or Just Peace?: Humanitarian Intervention and International Law* (Oxford: Oxford University Press, 2003), 72.
14 Ben Kiernan, *Blood and Soil: A World History of Genocide and Extermination from Sparta to Darfur* (New Haven, CT: Yale University Press, 2007), 575.
15 Ward Churchill satirically titled his examination of genocide in the Western Hemisphere *A Little Matter of Genocide.*
16 Commission for Historical Clarification. "Guatemala Memory of Silence," www.aaas.org/sites/default/files/migrate/uploads/mos_en.pdf (accessed May 15, 2016), 23.
17 Stephen Rabe, *The Killing Zone: The United States Wages Cold War in Latin America* (Oxford: Oxford University Press, 2016), 177.
18 Human Rights Watch, *Genocide in Iraq: The Anfal Campaign against the Kurds*, www.refworld.org/cgi-bin/texis/vtx/rwmain?page=printdoc&docid=47fdfb1d0 (accessed May 10, 2016).
19 Roger Normand, "Sanctions against Iraq: Is It Genocide?" *Guild Practitioner* 58 (2001), 27.
20 See, among others, Joy Gordon, "When Intent Makes All the Difference in the World: Economic Sanctions on Iraq and the Accusation of Genocide," *Yale Human Rights and Development Journal* 5, no. 2 (2014); George E. Bisharat,

14 Introduction

"Sanctions as Genocide," *Transnational Law & Contemporary Problems* 11 (2001); John Tirman, *The Deaths of Others: The Fate of Civilians in America's Wars* (Oxford: Oxford University Press, 2011); Geoff Simons, *The Scourging of Iraq: Sanctions, Law and Natural Justice* (London: Palgrave Macmillan, 1998); Jones, *Genocide*, 2nd ed.

21 Gordon, "When Intent Makes All the Difference in the World," 71; Bisharat, "Sanctions as Genocide," 406–407; Denis J. Halliday, "The Impact of Sanctions on the People of Iraq," *Journal of Palestine Studies* 28, no. 2 (1999): 30.

22 Tirman, *The Deaths of Others*, 208. Ramsey Clark estimates 1.5 million Iraqi deaths, including 750,000 children. Cited in Ramsey Clark, "Documents 2 and 3: Criminal Complaint against the United States and Others for Crimes against the People of Iraq (1996) and Letter to the Security Council (2001)," in *Genocide, War Crimes and the West: History and Complicity*, ed. Adam Jones (London: Zed Books, 2004), 271. Similarly, Richard Garfield cites a figure of 750,000 deaths among children under five-year-old by mid-1998. Cited in Richard Garfield, "Morbidity and Mortality among Iraqi Children from 1990 through 1998: Assessing the Impact of the Gulf War and Economic Sanctions," www.casi.org.uk/info/garfield/dr-garfield.html (accessed May 1, 2016).

23 Physicians for Social Responsibility, "Body Count: Casualty Figures after 10 Years of the 'War on Terror'," www.psr.org/assets/pdfs/body-count.pdf (accessed June 19, 2017).

24 Eleanor Robson is quoted in Frank Rich, "And Now: 'Operation Iraqi Looting'," *New York Times*, www.nytimes.com/2003/04/27/arts/and-now-operation-iraqi-looting.html (accessed July 1, 2017).

25 William Schabas, *Genocide in International Law: The Crime of Crimes* (Cambridge: Cambridge University Press, 2000), 181.

26 Benjamin Lieberman, "From Definition to Process: The Effects and Roots of Genocide," in *New Directions in Genocide Research*, ed. Adam Jones (London: Routledge, 2012), 3.

27 See Jones, *Genocide*, 2nd ed., 16–20, for reproduction of many of these definitions.

28 Leo Kuper, *Genocide: Its Political Use in the Twentieth Century* (New Haven, CT: Yale University Press, 1982), 39.

29 Marie-Bénédicte Dembour, "What Are Human Rights? Four Schools of Thought," *Human Rights Quarterly* 32, no. 1 (2010): 6.

30 Beth Van Schaack, "The Crime of Political Genocide: Repairing the Genocide Convention's Blind Spot," *The Yale Law Journal* 106, no. 7 (1997): 2268.

31 Gérard Prunier, "Darfur: Genocidal Theory and Practical Atrocities," in *Confronting Genocide*, eds. René Provost and Payam Akhavan (New York: Springer, 2011), 46.

32 Israel W. Charny, "Toward a Generic Definition of Genocide," in *Genocide: Conceptual and Historical Dimensions*, ed. George J. Andreopoulos (Philadelphia, PA: University of Pennsylvania Press, 1997), 64.

33 William Schabas, Interview, 17 September 2011.

34 Adam Jones, "Editor's Preface: The Present and Future of Genocide Studies," in *New Directions in Genocide Research*, ed. Adam Jones (London: Routledge, 2012), xxi.

35 Jones, *The Scourge of Genocide*, 5.

36 Ibid., 5–6.

37 Levon Chorbajian, "Introduction," in *Studies in Comparative Genocide*, eds. Levon Chorbajian and George Shirinian (London: Palgrave Macmillan, 1999), xiv.

38 Charny, "Towards a Generic Definition of Genocide," 68.

39 Adam Jones, "Introduction: History and Complicity," in *Genocide, War Crimes & the West*, ed. Adam Jones (London: Zed Books, 2004), 9.

Introduction 15

40 Ibid., 11.
41 Ibid.
42 Chorbajian, "Introduction," xvii.
43 Denis J. Halliday, "US Policy and Iraq: A Case of Genocide?" in *Genocide, War Crimes and the West*, ed. Adam Jones (London: Zed Books, 2004), 264.
44 Ibid., 264–265.
45 Jones, *The Scourge of Genocide*, 69–70.
46 R. J. Rummel, *Death by Government* (London: Transaction Publishers, 1994), 277.
47 Jones, *The Scourge of Genocide*, 5.
48 Quoted from Harper Collins review of Samantha Power's *"A Problem from Hell": American and the Age of Genocide*. www.harpercollins.com.au/9780007346981/#sm.0001n4wzh29j7f5hple1kiq2jigz1 (accessed June 24, 2017).
49 Samantha Power, *"A Problem from Hell": American and the Age of Genocide* (New York: Harper Perennial, 2002), 65. Similarly, Peter Ronayne writes, "Shocked into action by the horror of the Holocaust, members of the world community responded to American leadership and created a document that defined a new international crime and declared an intention to prevent its future occurrence." Peter Ronayne, *Never Again?: The United States and the Prevention and Punishment of Genocide since the Holocaust* (New York: Rowman & Littlefield, 2001), 7.
50 Ronayne, *Never Again*, 64. Lawrence LeBlanc questions why it took so long for the U.S. to ratify the Genocide Convention. According to LeBlanc, "It is ironic that the issue should ever have become so controversial. The U.S. delegation to the United Nations participated actively in the negotiations that led to the convention's adoption, and, whatever misgivings they might have had about any of its provisions, they shared in the broad consensus on the instrument as a whole." Lawrence LeBlanc, *The United States and the Genocide Convention* (Durham, NC: Duke University Press, 1991), 5.
51 Ward Churchill, *A Little Matter of Genocide: Holocaust and Denial in the Americas 1492 to the Present* (San Francisco, CA: City Lights, 1997), 364.
52 Ibid.
53 Edward S. Herman and David Peterson, *The Politics of Genocide* (New York: Monthly Review Press, 2010), 17–18.
54 Power, *"A Problem from Hell"*, 71.
55 Ibid., 94–95.
56 Taylor Owen and Ben Kiernan, "Bombs Over Cambodia: New Light on US Air War," *The Asia Pacific Journal* 5, no. 5 (2007): 3.
57 Ibid.
58 Ibid.
59 Ibid.
60 Ibid.
61 Power, *"A Problem from Hell"*, 82.
62 Commission for Historical Clarification, "Guatemala Memory of Silence."
63 Herman and Peterson, *The Politics of Genocide*, 93.
64 Ibid.
65 Greg Grandin, "Politics by Other Means: Guatemala's Quiet Genocide," in *Quiet Genocide: Guatemala 1981–1983*, ed. Etelle Higonnet (New Brunswick, NJ: Transaction Publishers, 2009), 13.
66 Ibid.
67 Power, *"A Problem from Hell"*, 208.
68 This is evident in Power's discussion of possible responses to the gassing of Kurds. According to Power, France had a "thriving arms business with Iraq" and Germany "nonchalantly sold insecticide and other chemicals to Baghdad."

16 *Introduction*

Meanwhile, a key issue for the US was its "military intelligence liaison relationship" with Iraq. Power, *"A Problem from Hell"*, 222.

69 Mark Phythian, *Arming Iraq: How the U.S. and Britain Secretly Built Saddam's War Machine* (Boston: Northeastern University Press, 1997). See Table 2.3 on page 44. See also Donald Riegle and Alfonse M. D'Amato, "The Riegle Report: U.S. Chemical and Biological Warfare-Related Dual Use Exports to Iraq and Their Possible Impact on the Health Consequences of the Gulf War," www.gulfweb.org/report/riegle1.html (accessed May 11, 2016).

70 Power, *"A Problem from Hell,"* 173.

71 Ibid., 172–173.

72 Carol Rittner, John K. Roth, and James M. Smith, "Part I: What Is Genocide?" in *Will Genocide Ever End?*, eds. Carol Rittner, John K. Roth, and James M. Smith (St. Paul, MN: Paragon House, 2002), 22.

73 Jones, "Introduction: History and Complicity," 11.

Bibliography

Anderson, Benedict. *Violence and the State in Suharto's Indonesia*. Ithaca, NY: Cornell University Press, 2009.

Bennett-Smith, Meredith. "Womp! This Country Was Named the Greatest Threat to World Peace." *Huffington Post*. Accessed June 1, 2017. www.huffingtonpost.com/2014/01/02/greatest-threat-world-peace-country_n_4531824.html.

Bisharat, George E. "Sanctions as Genocide." *Transnational Law & Contemporary Problems* 11 (2001): 379–425.

Charny, Israel. "Toward a Generic Definition of Genocide." In *Genocide: Conceptual and Historical Dimensions*, edited by George J. Andreopoulos, 64–94. Philadelphia, PA: University of Pennsylvania Press, 1997.

Chesterman, Simon. *Just War or Just Peace?: Humanitarian Intervention and International Law*. Oxford: Oxford University Press, 2003.

Chorbajian, Levon. "Introduction." In *Studies in Comparative Genocide*, edited by Levon Chorbajian and George Shirinian, xv–xxxv. London: Palgrave Macmillan, 1999.

Churchill, Ward. *A Little Matter of Genocide: Holocaust and Denial in the Americas 1492 to the Present*. San Francisco, CA: City Lights Books, 1997.

Clark, Ramsey. "Documents 2 and 3: Criminal Complaint against the United States and Others for Crimes against the People of Iraq (1996) and Letter to the Security Council (2001)." In *Genocide, War Crimes and the West: History and Complicity*, edited by Adam Jones, 270–275. London: Zed Books, 2004.

Commission for Historical Clarification. "Guatemala Memory of Silence." Accessed May 15, 2016. www.aaas.org/sites/default/files/migrate/uploads/mos_en.pdf.

Convention on the Prevention and Punishment of the Crime of Genocide. Accessed May 1, 2015. www.ohchr.org/EN/ProfessionalInterest/Pages/CrimeOfGenocide.aspx.

Cumings, Bruce. *The Korean War: A History*. New York: Random House, 2011.

Dembour, Marie-Bénédicte. "What Are Human Rights? Four Schools of Thought." *Human Rights Quarterly* 32, no. 1 (2010): 1–20.

Garfield, Richard. "Morbidity and Mortality among Iraqi Children from 1990 through 1998: Assessing the Impact of the Gulf War and Economic Sanctions." Accessed May 1, 2016. www.casi.org.uk/info/garfield/dr-garfield.html.

Gordon, Joy. "When Intent Makes All the Difference in the World: Economic Sanctions on Iraq and the Accusation of Genocide." *Yale Human Rights and Development Journal* 5, no. 2 (2014): 57–84.

Grandin, Greg. "Politics by Other Means: Guatemala's Quiet Genocide." In *Quiet Genocide: Guatemala 1981–1983*, edited by Etelle Higonnet, 1–16. New Brunswick, NJ: Transaction Publishers, 2009.

Halliday, Denis J. "The Impact of Sanctions on the People of Iraq." *Journal of Palestine Studies* 28, no. 2 (1999): 29–37.

Halliday, Denis J. "US Policy and Iraq: A Case of Genocide?" In *Genocide, War Crimes and the West*, edited by Adam Jones, 264–269. London: Zed Books, 2004.

Hasan, Mehdi. "Why Do North Koreans Hate Us? One Reason—They Remember the Korean War." *The Intercept.* Accessed June 24, 2017. https://theintercept.com/2017/05/03/why-do-north-koreans-hate-us-one-reason-they-remember-the-korean-war/.

Herman, Edward S., and David Peterson. *The Politics of Genocide.* New York: Monthly Review Press, 2010.

Human Rights Watch. *Genocide in Iraq: The Anfal Campaign against the Kurds.* Accessed May 10, 2016. www.refworld.org/cgi-bin/texis/vtx/rwmain?page=print doc&docid=47fdfb1d0.

Jones, Adam. "Editor's Preface: The Present and Future of Genocide Studies." In *New Directions in Genocide Research*, edited by Adam Jones, xix–xxvi. London: Routledge, 2012.

Jones, Adam. *Genocide: A Comprehensive Introduction*, 2nd ed. London: Routledge, 2011.

Jones, Adam. "Introduction: History and Complicity." In *Genocide, War Crimes & the West*, edited by Adam Jones, 3–30. London: Zed Books, 2004.

Jones, Adam. *The Scourge of Genocide: Essays and Reflections.* London: Routledge, 2013.

Kadane, Kathy. "Ex-Agents Say CIA Compiled Death Lists for Indonesians." *San Francisco Examiner.* Accessed December 2, 2015. www.namebase.net/kadane.html.

Kammen, Douglas, and Katharine McGregor. "Introduction: The Contours of Mass Violence in Indonesia, 1965–68." In *The Contours of Mass Violence in Indonesia, 1965–1968*, edited by Douglas Kammen and Katharine McGregor, 1–24. Honolulu, HI: University of Hawaii Press, 2012.

Kiernan, Ben. *Blood and Soil: A World History of Genocide and Extermination from Sparta to Darfur.* New Haven, CT: Yale University Press, 2007.

Kohn, Richard H., and Joseph P. Harahan. *Strategic Air Warfare: An Interview with Generals Curtis LeMay, Leon W. Johnson, David A. Burchinal, and Jack J. Catton.* Washington, DC: Office of Air Force History, 1988.

Kuper, Leo. *Genocide: Its Political Use in the Twentieth Century.* New Haven, CT: Yale University Press, 1982.

LeBlanc, Lawrence. *The United States and the Genocide Convention.* Durham, NC: Duke University Press, 1991.

Lieberman, Benjamin. "From Definition to Process: The Effects and Roots of Genocide." In *New Directions in Genocide Research*, edited by Adam Jones, 3–17. London: Routledge, 2012.

Neale, Jonathan. *A People's History of the Vietnam War.* New York: The New Press, 2003.

18   *Introduction*

Normand, Roger. "Sanctions against Iraq: Is It Genocide?" *Guild Practitioner* 58 (2001): 27–31.

Owen, Taylor, and Ben Kiernan. "Bombs Over Cambodia: New Light on US Air War." *The Asia Pacific Journal* 5, no. 5 (2007): 1–6.

Physicians for Social Responsibility. "Body Count: Casualty Figures after 10 Years of the 'War on Terror'." Accessed June 19, 2017. www.psr.org/assets/pdfs/body-count.pdf.

Phythian, Mark. *Arming Iraq: How the U.S. and Britain Secretly Built Saddam's War Machine*. Boston, MA: Northeastern University Press, 1997.

Power, Samantha. *"A Problem from Hell": American and the Age of Genocide*. New York: Harper Perennial, 2002.

Prunier, Gérard. "Darfur: Genocidal Theory and Practical Atrocities." In *Confronting Genocide*, edited by René Provost and Payam Akhavan, 45–56. New York: Springer, 2011.

Rabe, Stephen. *The Killing Zone: The United States Wages Cold War in Latin America*. Oxford: Oxford University Press, 2016.

Rich, Frank. "And Now: 'Operation Iraqi Looting'." *New York Times*, April 27, 2003. Accessed July 1, 2017. www.nytimes.com/2003/04/27/arts/and-now-operation-iraqi-looting.html.

Riegle, Donald W., and Alfonse M. D'Amato. "The Riegle Report: U.S. Chemical and Biological Warfare-Related Dual Use Exports to Iraq and Their Possible Impact on the Health Consequences of the Gulf War." Accessed May 11, 2016. www.gulfweb.org/report/riegle1.html.

Rittner, Carol, John K. Roth, and James M. Smith. "Part I: What Is Genocide?" In *Will Genocide Ever End?*, edited by Carol Rittner, John K. Roth, and James M. Smith, 21–22. St. Paul, MN: Paragon House, 2002.

Ronayne, Peter. *Never Again?: The United States and the Prevention and Punishment of Genocide since the Holocaust*. New York: Rowman & Littlefield, 2001.

Rummel, R. J. *Death by Government*. London: Transaction Publishers, 1994.

Schabas, William. *Genocide in International Law: The Crime of Crimes*. Cambridge: Cambridge University Press, 2000.

Simons, Geoff. *The Scourging of Iraq: Sanctions, Law and Natural Justice*. London: Palgrave Macmillan, 1998.

Tirman, John. *The Deaths of Others: The Fate of Civilians in America's Wars*. Oxford: Oxford University Press, 2011.

Van Schaack, Beth. "The Crime of Political Genocide: Repairing the Genocide Convention's Blind Spot." *The Yale Law Journal* 106, no. 7 (1997): 2259–2291.

Wilson, S. Brian. "Bob Kerrey's Atrocity, the Crime of Vietnam and the Historic Pattern of US Imperialism." In *Genocide, War Crimes & the West*, edited by Adam Jones, 164–180. London: Zed Books, 2004.

2 Redefining genocide

The Genocide Convention defines genocide as the attempt "to destroy, in whole or in part, a national, ethnical, racial or religious group, as such."[1] Genocidal acts include

> killing members of the group; causing serious bodily or mental harm to members of the group; deliberately inflicting on the group conditions of life calculated to bring about its physical destruction in whole or in part; imposing measures intended to prevent births within the group; and forcibly transferring children of the group to another group.[2]

As noted in Chapter 1, the Genocide Convention developed through a process of negotiation that included two formal drafts—the Secretariat and the Ad Hoc Committee—that preceded the final text.

During the drafting process, states negotiating the treaty decided the treaty's specific language and provisions. Notably, during this process, protection for political groups and cultural genocide were excluded from the Genocide Convention. The former has been widely criticized by genocide scholars, while the latter has increasingly garnered attention in genocide studies.[3] Along with the Genocide Convention's specific intent requirement, the omission of political groups and cultural genocide complicates the legal recognition of genocide in three ways. First, without proof of specific intent, acts that contain the other elements of genocide—prohibited acts committed against a protected group—cannot be recognized as genocide.[4] Second, any of the prohibited acts committed against a political group, even with specific intent to destroy the group, does not qualify as genocide. Third, acts that constitute cultural genocide committed against the culture of a protected group with the intent to destroy the group as such, also cannot be recognized as genocide.

In highlighting the Genocide Convention's limited utility, only four years after the Genocide Convention entered into force, Lassa Oppenheim declared, "It is apparent that, to a considerable extent, the Convention amounts to a registration of protest against past misdeeds of individual or collective savagery rather than to an effective instrument of their prevention

20 *Redefining genocide*

or repression."[5] The legal definition of genocide was shaped and agreed upon via a political process that so limited the term's applicability that William Schabas believes the only post-Jewish Holocaust case it applies to is the Tutsi genocide in Rwanda.[6] As part of an effort to advance the study of genocide beyond the Genocide Convention's constraints, genocide scholars have made two important advances. First, many have moved beyond another conceptual constraint—the predominant role of Holocaust studies in the field of genocide studies. For a time (one that continues for some), the Jewish Holocaust was treated as the archetypal case of genocide, greatly restraining the comparative study of genocide. Thus, as David Moshman put it, the challenge for genocide scholars was not

> to replace the Holocaust with some other genocide as the measure of all genocides, but rather to replace a Holocaust-based concept of genocide with an alternative conception that relates all genocides to each other via a set of formal criteria.[7]

Second, and relatedly, genocide scholars have developed dozens of alternative definitions of genocide, which have been applied to the comparative study of genocide.

In response to the proliferation of definitions of genocide, Levon Chorbajian argues that "rather than assume that genocide can have a fixed, definitive though elusive, meaning, it may be more productive to consider genocide as a *core concept* [emphasis in original] with widely accepted and uncontroversial meanings only at its center."[8] Chorbajian continues,

> The further we move from the center into the wider historical and semantic field, the greater the ambiguity and controversy we engender, and the less satisfactory efforts to apply hard and fast, necessary and sufficient characteristics of agents, victims, and historical contexts are likely to be.[9]

The problem with Chorbajian's position is that genocide's widely accepted meanings are nearly as constraining as those found in the legal definition. The biggest difference between most scholarly definitions of genocide and the legal definition is that scholars expand the groups protected to include political groups and other social groups. Many scholars also impose on the concept of genocide limitations beyond even those found in the Genocide Convention, such as limiting genocide to mass killings/murder. Thus, within the field of genocide studies, genocide's core meanings might include an expansion of the groups protected, while limiting the means through which perpetrators can commit genocide. In an impassioned proclamation, Israel Charny declared the need for a definition of genocide that matches "the reality of masses of dead people."[10] In my definition of genocide, I seek to satisfy this call, while maintaining the rigor that is required of such an undertaking.

I define genocide as the attempt to eliminate, in whole or in part, a national, political, social, ethnic, racial, cultural, or socioeconomic group with the purpose of destroying it as such or achieving a particular political, social, or economic objective. Membership in any of the aforementioned groups may be assigned by the group's members or by the perpetrators. The methods by which genocide can be inflicted include killing members of the group; deliberately imposing conditions that are likely to cause the deaths of members of the group; and enacting policies that seek to erase the group's cultural identity, also known as cultural genocide. Genocide may occur in times of peace and war, with aggressive war sharing a nexus with the crime of genocide. Furthermore, both unarmed and armed—noncombatant and combatant—members of the targeted group qualify as victims of genocide.

My definition of genocide includes four principal elements: protected groups, victims, methods of genocide, and intent. Additionally, based on how I define these four principal elements, I also establish a nexus between aggressive war and genocide. My inclusion of armed victims, cultural genocide, "indirect" genocide, a moderated intent requirement, and a nexus between aggressive war and genocide situates my definition of genocide well outside the "uncontroversial" center. The controversial nature of my definition and its impact on my study of the US relationship with genocide, therefore, requires that the definition be conceptually sound and rigorously defended. What follows is a detailed defense of my definition of genocide, divided into each of the four principal elements, followed by a discussion of the nexus between aggressive war and genocide, and a brief explanation of what state responsibility is under international law, along with a summary of the Bosnia v. Serbia Precedent. In each section, I reiterate the relevant element of my definition of genocide, compare it to that of other genocide scholars, and explain the implications of my definition for the study of genocide and, in particular, the study of the US relationship with genocide.

Protected groups

The Genocide Convention includes protection for national, ethnic, racial, and religious groups. I add political, social, cultural, and socioeconomic groups to my definition of genocide. Most genocide scholars expand on the limited number of groups included in the Genocide Convention. Scholarly definitions range from those that incorporate a broadly inclusive list of identifiable groups to those that abjure any group specification. As Damien Short notes, "Many social scientists now formulate their definition of genocide to include any group, be it a political, economic or cultural collectivity, with such groups being defined...by perpetrator selection."[11] For example, Kurt Jonassohn and Frank Chalk incorporate all identifiable groups, including those "that have no verifiable reality outside of the minds of the perpetrators."[12] Jonassohn and Chalk defend their general group definition by arguing that "none of the major victim groups of those genocides that

22 *Redefining genocide*

have occurred since its [the Genocide Convention] adoption falls within its restrictive specifications."[13] They argue that the Genocide Convention must prohibit "the planned annihilation of any group, no matter how that group is defined and by whom."[14]

I believe Jonassohn and Chalk are too loose in their group definition. Importantly, under Jonassohn and Chalk's definition, an attempt to kill everyone with autism would qualify as genocide. This, I believe, is defensible. However, under the same lack of restrictions on group definition, attempting to kill all origami enthusiasts would also qualify as genocide. This warrants skepticism, not because the lives of origami enthusiasts are not to be valued, but because they do not form a collectivity beyond their shared interest in the art of folding paper.[15] Similar to Jonassohn and Chalk, Helen Fein includes victims "selected because they were members of the collectivity."[16] However, she limits collectivities to "real collectivities," from which she excludes "pseudogroups" and "nongroups."[17] Meanwhile, John Cox includes "any *recognized, stable, and permanent group* [emphasis in original] as defined by the perpetrator."[18] I believe Fein and Cox push too far in the other direction. Pseudo-groups, non-groups, and groups that are unrecognizable, unstable, and/or nonpermanent *might* include, for example, vegans. Yet, for many of its members, veganism is a philosophy and a way of life. As long as there are vegans, veganism represents a category of permanent group, even if individual membership is fluid. Importantly, the same can be said of other groups, such as political and religious groups.

In my group definition, I meet halfway proponents of an inclusive, but rigid definition, and proponents of a fully exhaustive one. By including national, political, social, ethnic, racial, cultural, and socioeconomic groups, I impose some moderating limitations without excluding groups of people who do not fit neatly into categories of peoples listed on a government census. Similar to my definition, Adam Jones, following Steven Katz, includes "national, ethnic, racial, religious, political, social, gender or economic" groups.[19] The primary difference between my group definition and Jones' is that I treat religious groups as a form of cultural group and gender groups as a form of social group. Thus, my inclusion of national, political, social, ethnic, racial, cultural, and socioeconomic groups is consistent with trends in genocide studies, even if it differs from other scholars in the finer details.

Because of its particular significance to the study of genocide, the omission of political groups from the Genocide Convention requires special attention. The process by which political groups were omitted was itself political. Protection for political groups was included in the General Assembly resolution that initiated the process of prohibiting genocide under international law.[20] Political groups were also included in the Secretariat and Ad Hoc Committee drafts of the Genocide Convention.[21] Thanks in large part to the efforts of the Soviet Union and its voting bloc, political groups were ultimately removed prior to the Genocide Convention's adoption by the General Assembly in 1948.

The Soviet representatives argued that political groups lacked the stability of the other groups protected, and their inclusion could dissuade some states from ratifying the treaty out of fear that efforts to combat domestic subversives would be labeled genocide.[22] Ecuador challenged the Soviet argument, noting that police powers necessary to respond to domestic insurrection were distinct from acts of genocide.[23] Thus, according to Ecuador, the inclusion of political groups would not interfere with a state's right to protect itself against internal subversion. Bolivia noted that political groups, like the other groups protected, "were united by a common ideal."[24] The Netherlands added that "while the Nazis had destroyed millions of human beings...on account of their race or their nationality, they had also destroyed a great many others for their political opinions."[25] Failing to convince enough negotiating parties to support the elimination of protection for political groups, the Soviet Union continued to stress that the Genocide Convention could fail to receive the requisite number of votes to pass if it included protection for political groups. Thus, according to Egypt, political groups were omitted "primarily for practical reasons."[26]

Beyond the coercive process by which political groups were omitted, there are other more substantial justifications for including political groups when redefining genocide. First, political groups have historically been targets of state violence, and there is no reason to think this will change. As Leo Kuper notes, "political differences are at the very least as significant a basis for massacre and annihilation as racial, national, ethnic or religious differences."[27] Thus, Beth Van Schaack argues that the exclusion of political groups from the Genocide Convention equates to the removal from the scope of the Convention the "very crime they [political leaders] may be most likely to commit: the extermination of politically threatening groups."[28]

Omission of political groups also creates a blind spot to which other groups can be consigned. Perpetrators of genocide, as well as their supporters and benefactors, can take advantage of this blind spot by creating misleading narratives, framing the deaths resulting from a policy of genocide as unfortunate collateral damage caused by politically motivated violence. Similarly, Pieter Drost argues that the omission of political groups

> left a wide and dangerous loophole for any Government to escape the human duties under the Convention by putting genocide into practice under the cover of executive measures against political or other groups for security, public order or any other reason of state.[29]

The justifications for including political groups in the definition of genocide are clear. Their members share a common political identity and are susceptible to attack due to their political beliefs.[30] Their inclusion in the definition of genocide, therefore, recognizes that the risk members of political groups face extend well beyond persecution. It also contributes to the elimination of genocide's blind spot.

24   *Redefining genocide*

Inclusion of political groups in my definition of genocide has significant implications for the study of genocide and the US relationship with it. The inclusion of political groups rightly eliminates the uncertainty surrounding whether a number of high profile cases constitute genocide. In addition to the obvious case of Soviet political purges, it also brings clarity to Pakistan's actions in Bangladesh in 1971 and the Khmer Rouge's atrocities in Cambodia from 1975 to 1979. Even though there is already a broad consensus that the slaughter of Tutsi in Rwanda in 1994 constitutes genocide, the inclusion of political groups erases any doubts based on the political nature of the ethnic killings. The inclusion of political groups also brings within the definition of genocide perhaps the most clear-cut case of genocide against a political group since the Genocide Convention entered into force—Indonesia's genocide of communists in 1965–1966. Interestingly, although the Soviet Union had the most to gain from the exclusion of political groups at the time of the Genocide Convention's negotiations, the US has also greatly benefited from their omission, especially throughout the Cold War. The US maintained close ties with a number of anti-communist governments, including Indonesia, while they were committing genocide, and conducted its own anti-communist efforts. Thus, the inclusion of political groups raises questions regarding US responsibility for the commission of genocide and its ancillary acts.

Victims

In my definition, victims of genocide include both unarmed and armed members of the targeted group. Daniel Chirot and Clark McCauley appear to be the only other genocide scholars to include, as I do, "combatants and noncombatants alike."[31] There is what I believe to be an unfounded insistence among the vast majority of genocide scholars that victims of genocide must be unarmed civilians. For example, Jacques Sémelin defines genocide as a particular process that involves "civilian destruction."[32] This is true even among the small contingent of scholars who recognize a shared relationship between war and genocide.[33] Martin Shaw, perhaps the most significant contributor to the comparative study of war and genocide, states,

> Indeed the civilian category is, in the end, crucial to genocide studies: what all the historical and possible targets of genocide have in common is not the particular types of identity (ethnic, national, class, gender, etc.) for which they are targeted, but the fact that the individuals and groups targeted are predominantly civilians.[34]

There is a direct correlation between assertions that only civilians can be victims of genocide and claims that genocide must be one-sided. Jonassohn and Chalk argue that genocide involves a decisive and measurable imbalance of power between the perpetrators and the victims.[35] Similarly, according to Fein, genocide "is usually conceived of as the asymmetrical slaughter of an unorganized group by an organized force."[36] In other words, genocide "presumes a powerful perpetrator and relatively powerless victim."[37] Put more unambiguously, Manus Midlarsky states that genocide involves the "mass murder of innocent and helpless men, women, and children."[38]

In excluding armed members of a targeted group from victims of genocide, scholars draw a hard line where such distinctions are in fact blurred. If victims of genocide take up arms in defense of themselves and fellow members of the group after the onset of genocide, is it no longer genocide? At what point do victims of genocide become "combatants," who are no longer counted as victims of genocide? Once members of a targeted group take up arms, are the unarmed victims also no longer victims of genocide, but rather victims of war crimes? Does it become a civil war even when the intent of the perpetrator remains the destruction of the targeted group, and when resistance is solely in self-defense? What these questions illustrate is that categorically rejecting the idea that armed members of a group can be victims of genocide denies them membership in the group, dismisses the intent of the perpetrator, and negates the right of a targeted group to resist its own destruction.

Limiting victims of genocide to unarmed members of a group who are in an asymmetrical relationship with the perpetrator requires the rejection of two essential truths. First, armed members of a group killed by a perpetrator who is seeking to destroy the group are victims just as much as the unarmed victims. Armed members of the group are involuntary participants. To deny them their victimhood is to deny that they were attacked without justification with the same intent as the unarmed members of the group. It legitimates illegitimate killings so long as the victims are armed. Second, rejecting that armed individuals can be victims of genocide denies members of a targeted group the right to resist. Relatedly, it dismisses the context in which the violence originates. It essentially places the armed members of the targeted group who are killed by the perpetrator on the same footing as the perpetrators who are killed by members of the victimized group during the act of resistance. In other words, it portrays the perpetrators of genocide and the armed resistance as being involved in a mutual struggle, fighting with the same intent to kill members of the opposing group. However, this is a distortion of reality. The perpetrator's intent is to kill members of the targeted group. The same cannot be said of the use of force by the victimized group. In using force only in response to the perpetrator's attacks, the intent behind the use of force by the victimized group is to prevent its own destruction. Therefore, the fact that members of a targeted group take up arms to resist their own destruction neither changes their status as victims nor the intent of the perpetrator.

Including armed members of a targeted group as victims of genocide has significant implications for the study of genocide. Members of a targeted

26 *Redefining genocide*

group do not lose their membership due to engaging in their right to resist genocide. Therefore, the inclusion of armed members of a group as victims of genocide could require that genocide scholars revisit particular cases of genocide that have involved armed resistance to reconsider who among the dead were victims of genocide. It also, therefore, contributes to the blurring of lines between civil war and genocide. For a special issue of *Human Rights Review,* under the theme of "Genocide or Civil War?: Human Rights and the Politics of Conceptualization," Thomas Cushman asked scholars to consider how we distinguish genocide from civil war. Cushman queried, "When we encounter armed forces killing others in the name of some official ideology of inferiority, is this genocide or civil war?"[39] While Cushman asked scholars to contemplate whether participants in war can be victims of genocide, he limited his inquiry to intrastate armed conflict. However, the inclusion of armed members of a targeted group, along with the right of members of a targeted group to resist their own destruction, raises questions regarding whether interstate conflict can also share a relationship between war and genocide, with members of the military as potential victims of genocide. This will be discussed in detail later in this chapter.

Intent

I define genocide as the attempt to eliminate a protected group, in whole or in part, as such or as a means to achieve a particular political, economic, or social objective. My intent requirement differs from the one in the Genocide Convention in that it includes both specific intent and genocide as a means to an end.[40] The Genocide Convention requires that the intent behind an attempt to destroy a group be the elimination of the group as such. Joy Gordon does an excellent job of elucidating the specific intent requirement. Using Jewish people as an example, Gordon explains that the alleged perpetrator of genocide must want to kill Jews "simply because they are Jews and for no other reason."[41] She continues,

> If there is anything about that desire which has any other element to it—such as economic self-interest or political goals—then the intent is not to destroy the group 'as such,' but only because it happens to be there or because it is a means to a further end.[42]

Most scholars and legal theorists agree that specific intent is an indispensable element of the crime of genocide, even though there is also broad recognition that it is particularly challenging to establish specific intent.[43] Arguments in support of a specific intent requirement emphasize a need to distinguish genocide from other mass death-producing events, such as mass murder, crimes against humanity, and war crimes. For example, Josef Kunz states,

Redefining genocide 27

It has been said that this specific criminal intent makes the Convention useless; that governments, less stupid than that of National Socialist Germany, will never admit the intent to destroy a group as such, but will tell the world that they are acting against traitors and so on.[44]

Yet, Kunz maintains that a specific intent requirement is necessary for distinguishing genocide from other international criminal acts. The logical conclusion is that some planners and perpetrators of genocide will go unpunished due to an inability to prove they acted with a specific intent to destroy the targeted group.[45] It also means that some genocide-like violence against members of a group will fall outside the scope of the Genocide Convention.[46]

In their definitions of genocide, Jonassohn and Chalk, along with Fein, maintain the spirit of the specific intent requirement, while offering alternative means to establishing it. Jonassohn and Chalk argue that the requirement can be satisfied without explicit statements or documentation. Jonassohn and Chalk's criteria include "evidence, even if only circumstantial, of the intent of the perpetrator."[47] With their approach, Jonassohn and Chalk believe that the problem of intent resolves itself. They assert that once reliable and accurate information about the killing operations is obtained, it can be treated as circumstantial evidence of genocidal planning and the intent of the perpetrator. Similarly, Fein writes, "I am now convinced one can demonstrate intent by showing a pattern of purposeful action, constructing a plausible prima facie case for genocide in terms of the Convention."[48]

The International Criminal Tribunal for Rwanda (ICTR) gave legal support to a conception of specific intent that allows intent to be inferred. The ICTR ruled that circumstantial evidence could be used to prove specific intent. For example, in 2008, the ICTR's Appeals Chamber stated that the specific intent to commit genocide "may be proven through inference from the facts and circumstances of a case." Pertinent facts and circumstances include, but are not limited to, the general context of other culpable acts directed against the same group; the scale of atrocities committed; the fact that the victims were deliberately and systematically chosen due to their membership in a particular group, with the exclusion of members of other groups; and the repetition of the destructive acts.[49]

Despite the advances made to genocide's specific intent requirement by expanding it to include implied intent, a specific intent requirement remains flawed. This is not simply because a specific intent requirement makes it difficult to prove when genocide is committed, but rather because applying such a pure standard to acts that are rarely, if ever, purely about the destruction of a particular group does not match the realities of group violence. Other purposes for why groups have been the targets of genocide are numerous. Additionally, the intent behind genocidal acts may not be the same between those who plan and incite genocide, and those who carry it out. In other words, the orchestrators of genocide could plan, order, and incite the

28 *Redefining genocide*

commission of genocide with the purpose of achieving a particular political, social, or economic objective, thus treating the genocidal process and its victims as means to an end. Meanwhile, the actual perpetrators of genocide could participate in the process with a specific intent to destroy the targeted group due to the ways in which the planners incite the violence.

If genocide scholars were to eliminate from their lists every suspected case of genocide that involved some purpose other than the specific intent to destroy the group, how many cases of genocide would remain? Modern history is rife with examples of violence committed against groups of peoples for reasons other than the simple destruction of the group. Take Rwanda as a primary example. Schabas employs an incredibly narrow interpretation of the Genocide Convention's legal definition. Based on his interpretation, Schabas identifies the Tutsi genocide in Rwanda as the only post-Jewish Holocaust case of genocide.[50] Yet, it is arguable that the Tutsi genocide was primarily about political control of Rwanda. Members of Hutu Power and the Akuzu movement orchestrated genocide against the Tutsi in the midst of the implementation of a political power sharing agreement. The Hutu government did not want to share political power with Tutsi, deciding it was better to convince members of the Hutu population that they needed to commit genocide or find themselves the victims of genocide at the hands of Tutsi. During the genocide, moderate Hutu, including Rwanda's prime minister, were also targeted for execution. To be clear, this assessment does not involve any confusion between intent and motive. Rather, it recognizes the possibility that the Tutsi genocide might not have occurred had it not been for the political realities of a country previously under colonial rule, with one ethnic group historically afforded political control over the other.

The genocide in Bangladesh occurred after contentious elections that saw candidates based in East Pakistan win the majority of seats in Pakistan's parliament. President Kahn refused to seat the new government, leading to calls for secession from the East. Pakistan responded with genocide. In Cambodia, genocide was perpetrated as part of a political and social reordering under the Khmer Rouge. In Guatemala, the military regime committed genocide against the Mayans in part due to their support of and sympathy for leftist rebels. In Iraq, Saddam Hussein implemented genocidal plans against members of the Kurdish population. The Kurds had long sought either full sovereignty or greater autonomy. Thus, where do genocide scholars draw the line between cases that involve an unequivocally pure specific intent to commit genocide, and those in which the objectives ranged beyond the destruction of the targeted group as such? Is it a sliding scale?

Some scholars propose that an intentionality criterion be removed from the definition of genocide altogether.[51] Charny defines genocide as "mass killing of substantial numbers of human beings."[52] I believe this goes too far by eliminating a core element of the crime of genocide—the shared group identity of the victims. In defining genocide as the attempt to eliminate a protected group as such or as a means to achieve a particular political, economic, or social objective, I maintain the group requirement, while also recognizing that members of groups are victims of direct and indirect violence for purposes not limited to their destruction as such. I also include in my conception of genocidal intent the perpetrator's knowledge of the real or likely consequences of particular acts and the use of victims as means to an end. Taking into consideration an actor's knowledge of the real or likely consequences of its actions treats such knowledge as evidence of implied intent. Considering whether an actor uses the members of a group as a means to achieve a particular end accounts for the dehumanization of the members of the group when inflicted for such purposes. My definition of genocidal intent, therefore, recognizes that intent can be explicit or implicit, and that prohibited acts may be committed as part of a systematic plan to achieve a particular objective.

Defining genocide as the attempt to eliminate a protected group, in whole or in part, as such or as a means to achieve a particular political, economic, or social objective has significant implications for the study of genocide. It brings within the scope of genocide policies that are genocidal in nature, but are implemented without the sole purpose being the destruction of a targeted or affected group. It also has significant implications for the study of the US' relationship with genocide. The US is responsible for a substantial amount of direct and indirect violence around the world. Its violence is commonly justified as being committed with honorable intentions. Even if such a dubious justification is accepted, the result of US violence, nonetheless, is the same. With genocidal intent defined as the attempt to eliminate, in whole or in part, a protected group as such or as a means to achieve a particular political, economic, or social objective, alleged good intentions no longer immunize the US to allegations of genocide. It also raises additional questions regarding whether a nexus exists between aggressive war and genocide, because wars of aggression are used as means to achieve political objectives. This will be discussed in greater detail later in the chapter.

Methods of genocide

My definition of genocide includes three methods of genocide: killing members of a group; deliberately imposing conditions that are likely to cause the deaths of members of the group; and enacting policies that seek to erase the group's cultural identity, also known as cultural genocide. Genocide scholars universally recognize killing members of the group as a method of genocide. Some scholars believe that only killing members of a protected group through direct means can constitute genocide. Thus, not only do they reject other methods of genocide, they also reject the idea that killing members of a group through "indirect" means can amount to genocide.

30 *Redefining genocide*

Killing members of a group

As noted above, the act of killing members of a group remains central to many definitions of genocide. For many genocide scholars, killing members of a group is also synonymous with murdering them, meaning the result of a direct action committed by the perpetrator against the victim. For example, Charny, Jonassohn, and Chalk define genocide as a form of "mass killing."[53] Midlarsky, Chirot, and McCauley define genocide as a form of "mass murder."[54] These scholars tend to reject the idea that genocide can be inflicted via "indirect" means.[55] Even scholars who view genocide as a process more complex than directly killing members of a group emphasize the importance of physical violence. Shaw asserts, "Certainly violence and killing mark all genocidal processes. The intention to destroy a social group is always pregnant with violence, threatening the grossest violation of individual and collective lives."[56] However, Shaw continues, "Defining genocide by killing misses the social aims that lie behind it. *Genocide involves mass killing but it is much more than mass killing* [emphasis in original]."[57] Thus, my inclusion of killing members of the group is consistent with the broader field of genocide studies.

Deliberately imposing conditions likely to kill members of the group

The inclusion of "indirect" genocide in my definition, however, remains somewhat controversial.[58] Conceptually, it is not clear why killing members of a group would be considered genocide, but deliberately causing the deaths of members of a group would not. Whether a perpetrator murders members of a protected group or deliberately creates and/or maintains conditions that will kill them, members of the group die. Thus, including the former while excluding the latter cannot be justified. Consider the argument that global poverty is a crime against humanity. The Rome Statute of the International Criminal Court defines 'crime against humanity' as a prohibited act "committed as part of a widespread or systematic attack directed against any civilian population."[59] Prohibited acts include, among others, murder; extermination; enslavement; rape; torture; and other "inhumane acts of a similar character intentionally causing great suffering, or serious injury to body or to mental or physical health."

That the above acts are crimes is obvious; what makes them 'crimes against humanity' is the nature of the acts and their widespread or systematic character. Jones describes 'crimes against humanity' as "in essence crimes against one's fellows, viewed in a universal context."[60] In other words, systematic or widespread torture is an egregious violation of the human rights of the victims *and* all humans. Therefore, it ought to be viewed as an assault on all of humanity regardless of whether one is a victim of the assault or a witness to it; whether it is occurring in one's own country or a country halfway around the world.

Redefining genocide 31

It is arguable that global poverty exists as an accumulation of inhumane intentional acts that cause death and widespread human suffering. According to Thomas Pogge, structural violence in the international system "kills more efficiently than the Nazi extermination camps."[61] In his assessment of Pogge's claim, Gwilym David Blunt concludes that global poverty satisfies both the actus reus ("guilty act") and the mens rea ("guilty mind") of crimes against humanity. According to Blunt, "The causes of world poverty...cannot be described as isolated, but rather form part of a widespread and systemic policy pursued by states and international organizations."[62] Further, "despite the apparent lack of malicious intent, the policies that cause global poverty cause grievous harm in foreseeable and avoidable ways."[63]

Pogge's comparison of structural violence to concentration camps raises an important issue—what distinguishes genocide from crimes against humanity? The answer is a relatively simple one. Whereas all genocides are crimes against humanity, not all crimes against humanity are also genocide. Genocide differs from crimes against humanity in two important ways. First, genocide is a crime perpetrated against individuals who are members of a specific human group, while crimes against humanity can be committed indiscriminately. Second, when compared to definitions of genocide that include a specific intent requirement, crimes against humanity differ in that they are not necessarily committed with the intent to destroy a particular human group. Therefore, a state might implement policies in pursuit of, among other objectives, economic gain, access to natural resources, and military power, with knowledge that these policies, together, cause widespread human suffering. Implementation of such policies with knowledge of the suffering they cause could constitute a crime against humanity. Similarly, states can also seek to achieve political, social, and economic objectives while knowingly causing death and human suffering among members of a particular group. Therefore, an intent to kill members of the affected group can be inferred from the continuation of such policies despite the foreseeable consequences. Thus, whereas global poverty can be considered a crime against humanity, deliberately targeting members of a specific group with policies that will kill them can be considered genocide.

The reluctance to include indirect genocide could stem in part from the way people view murder as compared to deaths caused by indirect means, such as structural violence. John Quigley points out that deaths connected to the destruction of infrastructure and other means "do not occur as directly as deaths from, say, military massacres."[64] The intimate nature and the immediacy of murdering members of a group makes such acts more visible. Yet, deliberately starving or denying access to potable water to members of a group will kill them just the same as shooting them; it just takes longer.

Scholars who exclude indirect genocide wrongly treat policies that deliberately kill members of a group as less severe than murdering members of a group. There is a difference between treating such acts as distinct, and

32 *Redefining genocide*

treating one as a method of genocide while excluding the other. The inclusion of policies that deliberately cause the deaths of members of a group in my definition of genocide has further implications for the study of genocide and the US relationship with it. Indirect genocide brings within the scope of genocide forms of collective punishment, such as economic sanctions, directed at a particular group that cause death and human suffering among group members. This is especially true when taken in combination with my intent requirement. This raises significant questions regarding the utility of economic sanctions as an "alternative" to military force. It also raises questions regarding whether the US, as the principal actor that employs the use of economic sanctions, has committed genocide through its collective punishment of various national groups, most notably the people of Iraq.

Cultural genocide

I include in my definition of genocide the attempt to destroy a group as such by erasing a group's cultural identity, also known as cultural genocide. Because methods of destroying a group's culture can come in many forms, I adopt Short's broad definition of cultural genocide as "a method of genocide which destroys a social group through the destruction of their culture."[65] Policies that contribute to cultural genocide include, but are not limited to, criminalization or de facto prohibition of a group's language, religious practices, customs, and traditions; destruction or appropriation of cultural heritage sites, artifacts, artwork, historical records, and books; and indoctrination of the group's children.

Like protection for political groups, cultural genocide was included in the Secretariat and Ad Hoc Committee drafts of the Genocide Convention before it was removed from the text that was adopted in 1948. In the Secretariat Draft, cultural genocide was included in Article II, alongside physical and biological genocide. However, the Ad Hoc Committee Draft segregated cultural genocide from physical and biological genocide, placing the former in Article III and the latter two in Article II. During negotiations, two competing arguments were made. The negotiating parties that supported the inclusion of cultural genocide asserted that a group could be destroyed as such either through its physical destruction or through the destruction of the group's culture. Negotiating parties that opposed the inclusion of cultural genocide argued that a treaty prohibiting genocide should be restricted to the most severe acts, i.e. physical genocide. Due to pressure from the US, the negotiating parties struck a compromise, which resulted in the separation of cultural genocide from physical and biological genocide in the Ad Hoc Committee Draft. The US recommended the separation to "enable Governments to make reservations on a particular point of the Convention."[66] Following the compromise, the Ad Hoc Committee voted six to one in favor of retaining the prohibition of cultural genocide.[67] Despite the compromise, which would have allowed the US to support the treaty, while also submitting a reservation stating it does not recognize the crime of cultural genocide, the US cast the lone dissenting vote.

Following its failed attempt to exclude cultural genocide in the deliberations of the Ad Hoc Committee, the US employed a strategy similar to the one used by the Soviet Union to ensure the omission of political groups. The US proclaimed,

> Were the Committee to attempt to cover too wide a field in the preparation of a draft convention for example, in attempting to define cultural genocide—however reprehensible that crime might be—it might well run the risk to find some States would refuse to ratify the convention.[68]

At the Sixth Committee, the US and its supporters succeeded in excluding cultural genocide by a vote of twenty-five to sixteen, with four abstentions.[69] The Soviet Union made one last effort to reinsert cultural genocide at the General Assembly prior to the official vote on the Genocide Convention. The Soviet proposal was soundly defeated, with fourteen votes in favor of inclusion, thirty-one against, and ten abstentions.[70]

There has been considerable debate among genocide scholars regarding whether cultural destruction is a form of genocide. While certainly still a minority, there is a growing tendency for genocide scholars to include cultural genocide in their definitions. As Jones notes, "Unsurprisingly, it is aboriginal and indigenous peoples, and their supporters in activist circles and academia, who have placed the greatest emphasis on cultural genocide in issuing appeals for recognition and restitution."[71] Inclusion of cultural genocide grows out of a recognition of the lived and ongoing experiences of indigenous communities. For example, Robert van Krieken points to the "heartfelt and persistent sense of inflicted violence, pain and suffering at the heart of the settler-colonial project" and argues that "it may be ill-advised to stand too stubbornly on the conceptual purity of a 'correct' definition of genocide."[72]

Yet, there seems to be general agreement among the majority of genocide scholars that the crime of genocide is limited only to those acts that threaten the physical survival of the targeted group.[73] Therefore, cultural genocide does not qualify as genocide, even if its perpetrators seek to destroy a group as such by eliminating the foundation of the targeted group's identity—its culture. Some scholars who reject cultural destruction as a form of genocide employ arguments similar to those made by the Genocide Convention's negotiating parties. For example, Irving Horowitz dismisses outright the concept of cultural genocide, proclaiming "a need to avoid degrading this whole tragic theme by spreading its meaning to include cultural deprivation or the punishment of select individuals, even if they symbolically represent whole populations."[74] According to Horowitz, "actual genocides involve real deaths" as opposed to "symbolic" death.[75] Others argue cultural violence alone cannot constitute genocide, but may act rather as an accompaniment

34 *Redefining genocide*

to physical genocide, as well as evidence of intent to commit genocide. According to Shaw,

> Just as we should reject a view of genocide as only mass killing and physical harm, we should resist defining the suppression of a group's culture as genocide when it is done without physically harming the members of the group.[76]

In other words, mass killings and physical harm "mark all genocidal processes," while cultural destruction does not. However, as Quigley notes, when it accompanies killing members of a group, the "destruction of cultural objects may provide evidence that such acts were done with intent to destroy the group."[77]

Still other scholars argue that cultural genocide warrants its own term that distinguishes it from physical genocide. For example, according to Yehuda Bauer, "When no murder is involved, but oppression, political, cultural or other, accompanied by physical persecutions but not by mass murder, one cannot talk about genocide but one has to use other terms."[78] Jonassohn and Chalk go so far as to recognize the "many cases in history in which the collective memory, identity, or culture of a group was destroyed without the killing of its members," while labeling such cases "ethnocide" rather than cultural genocide.[79] Similarly, Charny divides different elements of cultural genocide into "ethnocide" and "linguicide."[80] He does so to avoid situations in which "destruction of a culture's continuity is labeled as committing genocide while others in which millions of people are actually murdered are not."[81]

Opposition to the inclusion of cultural genocide in the definition of genocide involves a lack of imagination. The destructive potential of any one element of cultural genocide might appear limited. Recognizing the genocidal potential of cultural destruction requires a holistic approach. Rather than focus on whether particular elements of cultural genocide are capable of achieving cultural destruction, the appropriate question is whether a combination of acts when committed systematically has the potential to eliminate a group as such without widespread or sustained physical violence. Insisting on the centrality of physical destruction to the concept of genocide dismisses the very real destructive potential of cultural violence. As Elazar Barkan notes, "the disappearance of peoples and cultures is a reality, not a theoretical construct or a paradigm."[82]

Indigenous communities have been and continue to be especially susceptible to cultural genocide. According to Julian Burger, "Where indigenous peoples do not face physical destruction, they may nevertheless face disintegration as a distinct ethnic group through the destruction of their specific cultural characteristics."[83] Establishing control over a population often involves the forced assimilation of indigenous populations into the colonizer's culture. Cultural genocide, then, acts as a means to expedite indigenous integration without committing genocide in the physical sense.[84] Short states that social figurations are composed of "a fluid network of consensual practical social relations which form a comprehensive culture."[85] To recognize the indispensable role that culturally rooted social practices and relations play in group cohesion is also to recognize the damage that can be inflicted upon individuals and collectives by the deliberate disruption of these practices and relations. Therefore, Short argues,

> If the *genos* in genocide is a social figuration...*then genocide is the forcible breaking down of such relationships*—the destruction of the social configuration, which can be achieved in a variety of ways *not restricted to physical killing* [emphasis in original].[86]

Group survival as such is predicated on the continued existence of the group's culture. Destruction of all remnants of a culture and the coerced assimilation of the members of one culture into another could effectively destroy the group without employing means for its immediate physical destruction. Including cultural genocide in one's concept of genocide recognizes the importance of cultural history, heritage, contributions, practices, and language to a group's collective identity. A group's cultural identity is inseparable from the unique historical and customary foundations from which the culture derives. The suppression, prohibition, and destruction of a group's culture are means to eliminating the group as such through the erasure of their group's shared cultural identity. Destroy a group's culture and you destroy the group, even while permitting survival of the group's members. As David Nersessian states,

> By limiting genocide to its physical and biological manifestations, a group can be kept physically and biologically intact even as its collective identity suffers in a fundamental and irremediable manner. Put another way, the present understanding of genocide preserves the body of the group but allows its very soul to be destroyed.[87]

Put still another way, cultural genocide allows its perpetrators to "kill the Indian, save the man."[88]

By contrast with killing members of a group, cultural genocide seeks to destroy the foundations of the group's identity. Cultural genocide has been described as a 'subtle' genocide, referring to a long-term process which, in spite of its lack of direct physical violence, engenders the same result as genocide: the destruction of a human group, mainly policies of assimilation and dispersal.[89] The effects are also intergenerational, because this 'destruction' precludes the transmission of group culture to subsequent generations. Thus, its effects can be considered as ongoing even long after the process appears to have ended. The harm is therefore multiple: to the individuals, their communities, and humanity as a whole.[90] The inclusion of cultural genocide in

36 *Redefining genocide*

the definition of genocide has implications for the broader historical study of genocide. Genocide scholars who include cultural genocide in their definitions have incorporated cases that include settler colonialism and colonization. Thus, there are obvious implications for the study of the US relationship with genocide as well, due to its treatment of indigenous peoples.

The nexus between aggressive war and genocide

Based on my definition of genocide, a nexus exists between aggressive war and genocide. The combination of political groups, armed members of a group as victims of genocide, and a moderated intent requirement constitute this nexus. Central is including in "political groups" those members of formal institutions who are explicitly or implicitly members of a political group or affiliation, among whom I include members of the military; including members of the military as armed members of a group who can be victims of genocide; and including aggressive war as a means of achieving a particular political, social, or economic objective.

Barbara Harff and Ted Gurr have written extensively about political groups in their research on "politicide." They view this as an act committed by "a state or its agents" against groups that "are defined primarily in terms of their hierarchical position or political opposition to the regime and dominant groups."[91] They stress that victims of politicide "are defined primarily in terms of their political position—their class, political beliefs, or organized opposition to the state and the dominant group….In politicides victims are always engaged in some oppositional activity deemed undesirable by those in power."[92] Harff and Gurr are wrong to treat genocide against political groups as something that can only be perpetrated by a state against non-state actors, for two reasons. First, it denies those in power membership in a political group simply because they are in power. Second, it rejects the possibility that a non-state actor or another state can attack the political group in power with genocidal intent.

Depending on the governmental system of which it is a part, a state's military acts as a political institution or as an institution affiliated with the state's explicitly political institutions. Max Weber defines the state as a "political organization with continuous operations…insofar as its administrative staff successfully upholds the claim to the monopoly of the legitimate use of force in the enforcement of its orders."[93] According to Michael Mann, a state is a "differentiated set of institutions and personnel" from which "political relations radiate to and from a center."[94] As members of a political or pseudo-political institution, members of the military are members of a political group. Military personnel serve the political interests of the state. Therefore, members of the military are either members of a political group or involuntary representatives of a political group—meaning that, in the eyes of an aggressor, members of the military act as representatives of the political group in power regardless of their personal political identification.

Redefining genocide 37

Aggressive war committed by one state against another contains the intent to destroy the members of the political group in power, in whole or in part, for the purpose of achieving a political or economic objective. Therefore, it involves the attempt to kill as many members of a protected group as is necessary to achieve its objective. As Carl von Clausewitz famously wrote, "War is not a mere act of policy but a true political instrument, a continuation of political activity by other means."[95] In war, killing the opposition's forces is a means to an end. They must be destroyed to such an extent that they can no longer resist.[96] Additionally, according to Shaw, in waging war, the intention is to *"destroy the real or imputed power of the enemy group* [emphasis in original], including its economic, political, cultural and ideological power, together with its ability to resist this destruction."[97]

The nexus between aggressive war and genocide is readily apparent in Zygmunt Bauman's description of the genocidal process:

> Among the resources of resistance that must be destroyed to make the violence effective (resources whose destruction, arguably, is the central point of the genocide and ultimately the measure of its effectiveness), by far the most crucial is occupied by the traditional elites of the doomed community. The most seminal effect of the genocide is the 'beheading' of the enemy. It is hoped that the marked group, once deprived of leadership and centers of authority, will lose its cohesiveness and the ability to sustain its own identity, and consequently its defensive potential. The inner structure of the group will collapse, thereby dissipating it into a collection of individuals who may be then picked one by one and incorporated within the new structure administered by the victors, or forcibly reassembled into a subjugated, segregated category, ruled and policed directly by the managers of the new order.[98]

Like Bauman's description of genocide, aggressive war seeks to "behead" a political group in order to deprive it of its leadership and/or its followers. A political group without its members cannot sustain its own identity. Similarly, a political group without its leadership "will lose its cohesiveness and the ability to sustain its own identity, and consequently its defensive potential."[99] In order to remove the group's ability to resist, perpetrators must kill the armed members of the group, i.e. members of the military.

I limit the nexus between war and genocide to aggressive war, because wars of aggression, by definition, constitute an illegitimate use of force. The Charter of the International Military Tribunal defined aggression as the "planning, preparation, initiation or waging of a war of aggression, or a war in violation of international treaties, agreements or assurances, or participation in a common plan or conspiracy for the accomplishment of any of the foregoing."[100] Additionally, the Tribunal described the crime of aggression as "the supreme international crime, differing only from other war crimes in that it contains within itself the accumulated evil of the whole."[101] Wars of

38 *Redefining genocide*

aggression cannot be justified. Therefore, not a single death resulting from the actions of the aggressor is justifiable. This means that all the aggressor's victims, whether unarmed or armed, noncombatant or combatant, are illegitimate victims of an attempt to destroy the political group and its means of resistance to the degree necessary to achieve the aggressor's objective.

This is not to suggest that only aggressive war can involve genocide. Defensive engagement in war, too, can take on a genocidal character. However, defensive participation in war is not by its very nature genocidal. After all, victims of aggression must have a right to defend themselves. Thus, the means used in response to an aggressor determine whether the victim of aggression is also responsible for genocide. Means of genocidal warfare that could implicate the victim of aggression, as well as the aggressor, in the commission of genocide include "strategic bombing" and nuclear warfare. According to Eric Markusen and David Kopf,

> specific instances of modern, total war may be appropriately regarded *genocidal*, if not actual cases of *genocide* [emphasis in original]. Both total war and genocide, in both preparation and implementation, may reflect a collective mindset that deserves to be labeled a 'genocidal mentality'.[102]

Relatedly, Shaw describes war as being fundamentally compromised by a tendency to devolve into "degenerate war," which has the potential to produce "what has come to be known as genocide."[103] Allied bombings during World War II, such as the firebombing of Hamburg and Dresden and the use of the atomic bombs against the populations of Hiroshima and Nagasaki, are commonly cited as examples of genocidal war.[104] Shaw describes the Allies' bombing campaigns during the second half of the war as "a new climax in aerial destruction" that "constituted something more than degenerate war, which we call 'genocide.'"[105]

Most genocide scholars insist on a clear delineation between war and genocide. For example, Paul Bartrop argues that genocide should not be equated with war and, therefore, they should not be considered synonymous.[106] Similarly, Matthew Krain claims that there are fine lines that separate war from genocide.[107] Horowitz argues that it is "operationally imperative to distinguish warfare from genocide" and defends his position by citing "the weight of current empirical research that indicates that domestic destruction and international warring are separate dimensions of struggle."[108] Fein views attempts to connect mass killings in war to genocide as an unnecessary conflation of war crimes with genocide.[109] Jonassohn and Chalk assert that

> nobody has yet shown that our understanding is enriched by comparing such unlike phenomena as wartime casualties and genocides. The fact that both war and genocide produce massive casualties is a terrible

Redefining genocide 39

commentary on man's inhumanity to man, but it does not help to understand either phenomenon.[110]

The most obvious reason why my view of the relationship between war and genocide differs so substantially from other genocide scholars is my inclusion of elements in my definition that are absent from others'. Without the inclusion of members of political groups who are in power and members of the military, scholars would not recognize them as potential victims of genocide. Similarly, scholars who maintain a specific intent requirement in their definitions of genocide would reject the idea that war, even wars of aggression, share a nexus with genocide, because the intent in war is not solely the destruction of the victimized group; the intent is to "win" the war. Thus, in addition to the armed members of the group killed in war, civilian victims, also, would not qualify as victims of genocide; they would be victims of war crimes. Yet, there might be additional factors behind the rejection of a nexus between aggressive war and genocide. War is treated as a normalized and legitimized act of state violence—an "instrument of foreign policy," as Horowitz puts it.[111] War has its own set of rules, codified in international humanitarian law. An act that has rules is a legitimate act, with the stipulation that those who participate in the act follow the rules. Horowitz's strategy for distinguishing war from genocide exemplifies this. For him, "democratic and libertarian states" can be differentiated from "repressive or totalitarian states" by the types of state violence they engage in.[112] According to Horowitz,

> wars have been fought between democratic and authoritarian states throughout the twentieth century. And while this is by no means a simple struggle between good and evil, the fact does remain that wars are common to all sort of social systems. Genocide, on the other hand, is the operational handmaiden of a particular social system, the totalitarian system.[113]

Horowitz's treatment of war is telling for two reasons. First, he treats war as normal state behavior because democracies participate in such behavior. Democracies fight wars for good and just reasons. Therefore, war has utility, and this utility distinguishes war from genocide. Second, Horowitz fails to consider war with the nuance it requires. He portrays war as though democratic and authoritarian states were equally responsible for the onset of wars between them, rather than providing some context regarding aggressor states and victimized states, meaning those who engage in true self-defense. This latter point is directly relevant to the former. If totalitarian states were regularly the aggressors in wars between themselves and democratic states, war would not be treated with the same deference. Aggressive war would be a tool of violence and oppression found only in the totalitarian belt. It would

40 *Redefining genocide*

be treated with the unequivocal contempt it deserves. Perhaps more scholars would even consider aggressive war a form of genocide.

The implications of a nexus between aggressive war and genocide are substantial for the study of genocide and war. It appropriately redefines wars of aggression as a crime that involves not only the commission of a war crime, but also potentially the crime of genocide. This makes identifying which wars are wars of aggression that much more important. Historically, members of the military have been excluded from consideration when it comes to potential victims of genocide. The distinction between "combatants" and "civilians" is part of a long-standing campaign to socialize warfare—to make it acceptable, even if only for use in extraordinary circumstances. Because the US has been involved in more acts of aggression than any other state since the end of World War II, the nexus between aggressive war and genocide also has significant implications for the study of the US' relationship with genocide.

State responsibility for genocide

State responsibility for internationally wrongful acts is an underexplored mechanism of accountability for genocide. It offers a measure of responsibility that addresses the role of the state in the commission of genocide while avoiding the entanglements of state bureaucracies. In other words, it shifts the focus of accountability from the institutional complexities surrounding internal decision-making to the role of the state as an international actor. Therefore, it separates the acts of a state from the interactions of individual government institutions and actors. It recognizes that objections to a particular policy may be raised within the state. There may even be attempts to impede the policy. Nonetheless, if the policy persists, the prohibited act can be attributed to the state, regardless of whether the policy lacked the support of some state organs or actors.

Though the Nuremberg trials recognized the role of the state in the commission of aggressive war and crimes against peace, the Nuremberg Principles focused primarily on individual criminal responsibility. By the end of the trials, as Nina Jørgensen notes, "state responsibility, although a key issue, was increasingly viewed as an unworkable concept, and consequently took a back seat."[114] However, in 1976, the International Law Commission (ILC) recognized the relationship between individuals and the state apparatus through which international criminal acts are committed.[115] Antonio Cassese describes this relationship:

> Strikingly, most of the offenses that international criminal law proscribes and for the perpetration of which it endeavours to punish the individuals that allegedly committed them, also are regarded by international law as particularly serious violations *by states* [emphasis in original] to the extent that they are large-scale and systematic: they are

international delinquencies entailing the 'aggravated responsibility' of the state on whose behalf the perpetrators have acted.[116]

Twenty-five years later, the ILC adopted the Articles on the Responsibility of States for Internationally Wrongful Acts. The ILC concluded that the commission of an "internationally wrongful act" by a state "entails the international responsibility" of that state. The ILC defined such acts as "conduct consisting of an action or omission" that is "attributable to the State under international law" and "constitutes a breach of an international obligation of the State."[117] While individual criminal responsibility and state responsibility for a crime committed by the same individual can run concurrently, the form of accountability is very different. The ILC rejected the concept of state criminal responsibility, deciding instead that states responsible for internationally wrongful acts are "under an obligation to make full reparation for the injury caused by the internationally wrongful act."[118] This is because individual criminal responsibility is part of a system of punitive justice, whereas state responsibility for an internationally wrongful act would contribute to remediation and reparatory justice. Thus, if a state were found to have committed an internationally wrongful act, it would owe to the victimized state and its people appropriate restitution. Additionally, such a finding should also contribute to an initiation of criminal investigations. A state is not capable of committing internationally wrongful acts without individuals steering the state to commit such acts.

Ronald Kramer, Raymond Michalowski, and Dawn Rothe developed a definition of state crime that is applicable to the analysis of suspected state violations of international criminal law. State crime

> is any action that violates public international law, international criminal law, or domestic law when these actions are committed by individuals acting in official or covert capacity as agents of the state pursuant to expressed or implied orders of the state, or resulting from state failure to exercise due diligence over the actions of its agents.[119]

Importantly, Kramer, Michalowski, and Rothe include overt state acts, meaning those conducted as part of official state policy, and covert acts, meaning those conducted through unofficial channels, with limited oversight. Further, as the authors rightly contend, their definition of state crime "recognizes that potential offenders under international law or domestic law can be states *qua* states and/or officials using state power in pursuit of state goals."[120]

Specific to the crime of genocide, mechanisms for adjudicating state responsibility are already in place. Under Article IX of the Genocide Convention, state disputes related to

42 *Redefining genocide*

the interpretation, application or fulfilment of the present Convention, including those relating to the responsibility of a State for genocide or for any of the other acts enumerated in article III, shall be submitted to the International Court of Justice at the request of any of the parties to the dispute.[121]

Article III of the Genocide Convention enumerates genocide's ancillary crimes, including conspiracy to commit genocide and complicity in genocide. Furthermore, in 2007, the International Court of Justice (ICJ) issued its first ruling in a state responsibility case, establishing significant legal precedent.

The Bosnia v. Serbia Precedent

On March 20, 1993, Bosnia filed the first application for institutional proceedings at the ICJ regarding the interpretation and application of the Genocide Convention.[122] In its application, Bosnia claimed that "Yugoslavia (Serbia and Montenegro) has breached its solemn obligations under Article I. The Respondent has planned, prepared, conspired, promoted, encouraged, aided and abetted and committed genocide against the People and State of Bosnia and Herzegovina."[123] Specifically, Bosnia alleged,

> The People and State of Bosnia and Herzegovina have suffered and are now suffering from the effects of genocide imposed upon them by Yugoslavia (Serbia and Montenegro) and its agents and surrogates in Bosnia and elsewhere, whose ultimate goal is no less than the destruction of both the State of Bosnia and its People.[124]

After rejecting a number of procedural challenges submitted by Serbia, the ICJ addressed the substantive issues of the case, including states' obligations under the Genocide Convention and whether Serbia had breached such obligations in committing genocide at Srebrenica in 1995. Serbia argued that its obligations under the Genocide Convention were limited to the adoption and enforcement of domestic legislation outlawing genocide, along with the accompanying obligation to prosecute or extradite those suspected of planning and committing genocide. Bosnia, however, argued that because genocide is a crime under international law, the obligation to prevent genocide extends to an obligation to refrain from genocide, and from the other acts enumerated in Article III of the Genocide Convention.

Citing Article 31 of the Vienna Convention on the Law of Treaties, the ICJ observed that obligations imposed under the Genocide Convention depended on the "ordinary meaning of the terms of the Convention read in their context and in the light of its object and purpose."[125] The ICJ began its consideration of the obligations imposed by the Genocide Convention with Article I. Article I states that "Contracting Parties confirm that genocide, whether committed in time of peace or in time of war, is a crime under international law which they undertake to prevent and to punish."[126] The ICJ found that "Article I, in particular its undertaking to prevent, creates obligations distinct from those which appear in the subsequent Articles. That conclusion is also supported by the purely humanitarian and civilizing purpose of the Convention."[127]

The ICJ then moved to the specific question of what obligations the Genocide Convention imposed. While it may seem obvious that the legal prohibition of genocide requires that genocide not be committed by states, "such an obligation is not expressly imposed by the actual terms of the Convention."[128] However, the ICJ determined that the Genocide Convention's object and purpose is the prevention of genocide and, therefore, it prohibits states from committing genocide. This is also clear in genocide's categorization as a crime under international law. Thus, the ICJ concluded,

> It would be paradoxical, if States were thus under an obligation to prevent, but were not forbidden to commit such acts through their own organs, or persons over whom they have such firm control that their conduct is attributable to the State concerned under international law. In short, the obligation to prevent genocide necessarily implies the prohibition of commission of genocide.[129]

To summarize, the ICJ ruled that parties to the Genocide Convention are obligated not only to prevent genocide within their own territories, but to refrain from committing genocide in the territories of other states, both directly and through "persons over whom they have such firm control that their conduct is attributable to the State concerned under international law."[130] The ICJ also found that obligations under the Genocide Convention extend beyond a state's territory:

> The substantive obligations arising from Articles I and III are not on their face limited by territory. They apply to a State wherever it may be acting or may be able to act in ways appropriate to meeting the obligations in question.[131]

The ICJ's determination of states' obligations as parties to the Genocide Convention was consistent with established human rights law. As the primary actors in the international system and the only actors capable of being parties to human rights treaties, states have responsibilities that extend not only to their populations, but also extraterritorially to the international community. As Anja Seibert-Fohr notes, human rights law

> also obliges states to refrain from any conduct contributing even remotely to a human rights abuse. Therefore human rights law does not only become relevant if state officials are the immediate perpetrators or

44 *Redefining genocide*

if the abuser can be attributed to the state. The obligations under the human rights conventions are broader than the actual crimes.[132]

In its adjudication of Bosnia v. Serbia, the ICJ sought to determine whether Serbia was a direct participant in, or oversaw the commission of, genocide at Srebrenica; was responsible for the other punishable acts under Article III of the Genocide Convention; or had failed to use its influence over the Bosnian Serbs to uphold its obligation to prevent genocide. In its ruling, the ICJ found only that Serbia failed to uphold its obligation to prevent genocide. How the ICJ came to its findings is important to determining US responsibility for genocide.

The ICJ dismissed the charge that Serbia was responsible for the commission of genocide because it found that Serbian agents did not directly participate in the massacres at Srebrenica. The ICJ also found that Bosnia failed to establish

> that those massacres were committed on the instructions, or under the direction of organs of the Respondent State, nor that the Respondent exercised effective control over the operations in the course of which those massacres, which constituted the crime of genocide, were perpetrated.[133]

In other words, Bosnia was unable to prove that anyone who could be deemed a representative of Serbia had directly participated in the planning and/or commission of the crime; that the crimes were committed at Serbia's behest; or that Serbia controlled those who committed the genocide.

The finding that Serbia did not exercise effective control over the Bosnian Serbs who committed genocide at Srebrenica also contributed to the ICJ's finding regarding the charge of conspiracy to commit genocide. The ICJ rejected the conspiracy charge because it found that Bosnia had failed to prove that Serbia had instructed the Bosnian Serbs to commit genocide at Srebrenica. Specifically, the ICJ found that the "decision to kill the adult male population of the Muslim community in Srebrenica was taken by some members of the VRS Main Staff, but without instructions from or effective control by the FRY."[134] Importantly, the ICJ also determined that Serbia did not demonstrate specific genocidal intent along with the Bosnian Serbs. Thus, conspiracy to commit genocide involves the participation of a state conspirator that shares the genocidal intent of the direct perpetrator.

In determining whether Serbia was complicit in genocide, the ICJ explained that

> the conduct of an organ or a person furnishing aid or assistance to a perpetrator of the crime of genocide cannot be treated as complicity in genocide unless at the least that organ or person acted knowingly, that

is to say, in particular, was aware of the specific intent *(dolus specialis)* of the principal perpetrator.[135]

Whereas state responsibility for conspiracy requires that the assisting state shares the genocidal intent of the perpetrator of the crime, complicity only requires that the assisting state be fully aware that its assistance will facilitate the crime. The determining factor is whether the state in question had or should have had knowledge of the perpetrator's intentions. As Paolo Palchetti summarizes, "In the first place, a state must supply aid and assistance to the perpetrators of the genocide; the second requirement is that the assisting state must have acted in full knowledge of the facts."[136] In its decision, the ICJ found that the available evidence failed to establish beyond doubt that Serbia supplied and continued to supply the Bosnian Serbs with aid and assistance with the knowledge that genocide was about to be committed or was already underway.

The ICJ's final question concerned whether Serbia fulfilled its obligation to prevent genocide. Prior to addressing the facts of the case, the ICJ delivered some preliminary remarks concerning state responsibility in this regard. According to the ICJ, states are not obligated to succeed in preventing genocide, but "rather to employ all means reasonably available to them, so as to prevent genocide so far as possible."[137] State responsibility for a failure to prevent genocide is incurred when the state in question

> manifestly failed to take all measures to prevent genocide which were within its power, and which might have contributed to preventing the genocide. In this area the notion of 'due diligence', which calls for an assessment *in concreto*, is of critical importance.[138]

It is clear that establishing a failure to prevent genocide involves a lesser standard of proof than that of the punishable acts under Article III of the Genocide Convention. The standard of proof incorporates a mix of the concept of the "reasonable person" and the notion of "due diligence" in cases of negligence under common law. Determining whether Serbia failed to fulfill its obligation to prevent genocide, therefore, involved a three-part exercise. First, Bosnia needed to establish that Serbia was aware or should have been aware that something like what happened at Srebrenica was possible. Second, Bosnia needed to establish that Serbia wielded the requisite influence necessary to have a direct obligation to prevent genocide. Finally, Bosnia needed to establish that Serbia failed to fulfill its obligation. Regarding the first element, the ICJ determined that Serbian leadership was "fully aware of the climate of deep-seated hatred which reigned between the Bosnian Serbs and the Muslims in the Srebrenica region."[139] The ICJ also found that Serbia wielded the requisite influence needed to incur an obligation to prevent genocide due to "the strength of the political, military and financial

46 *Redefining genocide*

links" it shared with Bosnian Serbs.[140] Finally, the ICJ concluded that Serbia failed to demonstrate that it took

> any initiative to prevent what happened, or any action on its part to avert the atrocities which were committed. It must therefore be concluded that the organs of the Respondent did nothing to prevent the Srebrenica massacres, claiming that they were powerless to do so, which hardly tallies with their known influence over the VRS.[141]

The ICJ ruling in Bosnia v. Serbia set an historic precedent regarding state responsibility for genocide. It provides scholars with means to assess the acts of states, both as the direct perpetrator of genocide and as states responsible for genocide's ancillary crimes. Therefore, it has significant implications for the study of genocide in that it resituates the acts of external states within a responsibility paradigm, rather than a "humanitarian" one. In other words, rather than assessing the acts of commission and omission of a third-party state to determine whether they could have done more to prevent genocide, it assesses such acts to determine whether they contributed in any way to the commission of genocide. This has particular relevance to the study of the US relationship with genocide. The US has maintained close relations with numerous states while they were committing genocide, which raises the question of whether the US has conspired to commit genocide or has been complicit in the crimes of others.

Notes

1 Convention on the Prevention and Punishment of the Crime of Genocide, http://www.ohchr.org/EN/ProfessionalInterest/Pages/CrimeOfGenocide.aspx (accessed May 1, 2015).
2 Ibid.
3 For analysis of the significance of the omission of political groups from the Genocide Convention's protection see, among others Matthew Lippman, "The 1948 Convention on the Prevention and Punishment of the Crime of Genocide: Forty-Five Years Later," *Temple International and Comparative Law Journal* 8, no. 1 (1994); Matthew Lippman, "The Drafting of the 1948 Convention on the Prevention and Punishment of the Crime of Genocide," *Boston University International Law Journal* 3 (1984); John Quigley, *The Genocide Convention: An International Law Analysis* (Burlington, VT: Ashgate, 2006); William Schabas, *Genocide in International Law: The Crime of Crimes* (Cambridge: Cambridge University Press, 2000); and Beth Van Schaack, "The Crime of Political Genocide: Repairing the Genocide Convention's Blind Spot," *The Yale Law Journal* 106, no. 7 (1997). For the most detailed accounts of the decision to exclude cultural genocide from the Genocide Convention, see Lippman, "The Drafting of the 1948 Convention"; Schabas, *Genocide in International Law.*
4 There is a large body of literature concerning the pros and cons of the specific intent requirement. See, among others, Lawrence LeBlanc, "The Intent to Destroy Groups in the Genocide Convention: The Proposed U.S. Understanding," *The American Journal of International Law* 78, no. 2 (1984); Lippman, "The

Drafting of the 1948 Convention"; Lippman, "The 1948 Convention on the Prevention and Punishment of the Crime of Genocide"; Quigley, *The Genocide Convention*; Schabas, *Genocide in International Law*.

5 Lassa Oppenheim, *International Law: A Treatise Vol. 1* (Philadelphia, PA: David McKay Company, 1955), 751.

6 William Schabas, Interview, 17 September 2011.

7 David Moshman, "Conceptual Constraints on Thinking about Genocide," *Journal of Genocide Research* 3, no. 3 (2001): 433.

8 Levon Chorbajian, "Introduction," in *Studies in Comparative Genocide*, eds. Levon Chorbajian and George Shirinian (London: Palgrave Macmillan, 1999), xxi.

9 Ibid.

10 Israel W. Charny, "Toward a Generic Definition of Genocide," in *Genocide: Conceptual and Historical Dimensions*, ed. George J. Andreopoulos (Philadelphia, PA: University of Pennsylvania Press, 1997), 64.

11 Damien Short, *Redefining Genocide: Settler Colonialism, Social Death and Ecocide* (London: Zed Books, 2016), 14. Other scholars who subscribe to an all-inclusive definition of genocide include, among others, Pieter N. Drost, *The Crime of State: Genocide* (Leyden: A.W. Sythoff, 1959); Jacques Sémelin, *Purify and Destroy: The Political Uses of Massacre and Genocide* (New York: Columbia University Press, 2009); Frank Chalk, "Redefining Genocide," in *Genocide: Conceptual and Historical Dimensions*, ed. George J. Andreopoulos (Philadelphia, PA: University of Pennsylvania Press, 1997); Kurt Jonassohn, "What Is Genocide?" in *Genocide Watch*, ed. Helen Fein (New Haven, CT: Yale University Press, 1992); and Charny, "Toward a Generic Definition of Genocide."

12 Jonassohn, "What Is Genocide?", 19.

13 Ibid., 18.

14 Ibid.

15 Of course, this would be a different scenario if all of the victims were Japanese.

16 Helen Fein, "Genocide, Terror, Life Integrity, and War Crimes: The Case for Discrimination," in *Genocide: Conceptual and Historical Dimensions*, ed. George J. Andreopoulos (Philadelphia, PA: University of Pennsylvania Press, 1997), 95.

17 Helen Fein, "Introduction," in *Genocide Watch*, ed. Helen Fein (New Haven, CT: Yale University Press, 1992), 4.

18 John Cox, *To Kill a People: Genocide in the Twentieth Century* (Oxford: Oxford University Press, 2016), 11.

19 Adam Jones, "Gendercide and Genocide," *Journal of Genocide Research* 2, no. 2 (2000): 199.

20 Resolution 96(I), passed by the General Assembly on December 11, 1946, states, "Many instances of such crimes of genocide have occurred when racial, religious, political, and other groups have been destroyed, entirely or in part."

21 The Secretariat Draft includes protection for political groups alongside racial, national, linguistic, and religious groups. Similarly, the Ad Hoc Committee Draft includes national, racial, religious, and political groups within the scope of its protection.

22 Matthew Lippman, "The Drafting of the 1948 Convention," 30.

23 Ibid., 42.

24 Ibid.

25 Van Schaack, "The Crime of Political Genocide," 2265.

26 Schabas, *Genocide in International Law*, 139.

27 Leo Kuper, *Genocide: Its Political Use in the Twentieth Century* (New Haven, CT: Yale University Press, 1982), 39.

28 Van Schaack, "The Crime of Political Genocide," 2268.

48 *Redefining genocide*

29 Drost, *The Crime of State,* 123.
30 Barbara Harff, "Recognizing Genocide and Politicide," in *Genocide Watch*, ed. Helen Fein (New Haven, CT: Yale University Press, 1992), 29.
31 Daniel Chirot and Clark McCauley, *Why Not Kill Them All?: The Logic and Prevention of Mass Political Murder* (Princeton, NJ: Princeton University Press, 2010), 17.
32 Sémelin, *Purify and Destroy*, 340.
33 Some scholars recognize the strong correlation between when genocides have been committed and when wars have been fought. In other words, they recognize that genocide and war often share a common space and time. For example, Jones states that war and genocide share an "intimate bond between the two." Cited in Adam Jones, *Genocide: A Comprehensive Introduction*, 2nd ed. (London: Routledge, 2011), 81. Martin Shaw argues that the problems genocide and war pose are linked to such an extent that they need to be viewed within a common frame. See Martin Shaw, *War & Genocide* (Malden, MA: Polity Press, 2003), 34–53.
34 Martin Shaw, "The General Hybridity of War and Genocide," *Journal of Genocide Research* 9, no. 3 (2007): 465.
35 Jonassohn, "What Is Genocide?", 22.
36 Helen Fein, "Discriminating Genocide from War Crimes: Vietnam and Afghanistan Reexamined," *Denver Journal of International Law and Policy* 22, no. 1 (1993): 31.
37 Jonassohn, "What Is Genocide?", 18.
38 Manus L. Midlarsky, *The Killing Trap: Genocide in the Twentieth Century* (Cambridge: Cambridge University Press, 2005), 10.
39 Thomas Cushman, "Genocide or Civil War?: Human Rights and the Politics of Conceptualization," *Human Rights Review* 1, no. 3 (2000): 13.
40 All three of the formal drafts of the Genocide Convention include a specific intent requirement. The Secretariat Draft defines genocide as any of the prohibited acts committed against a protected group "with the purpose of destroying it in whole or in part or of preventing its preservation or development." Both the Ad Hoc Committee Draft and the adopted text define genocide as any of the prohibited acts committed against a protected group with the intent to destroy it. The Ad Hoc Committee Draft defines genocide as "any of the following deliberate acts committed with the intent to destroy a national, racial, religious or political group, on grounds of the national or racial origin, religious belief, or political opinion of its members." The adopted text defines genocide as "any of the following acts committed *with intent to* destroy, in whole or in part, a national, ethnical, racial or religious group, as such."
41 Joy Gordon, "When Intent Makes All the Difference in the World: Economic Sanctions on Iraq and the Accusation of Genocide," *Yale Human Rights and Development Journal* 5, no. 2 (2014): 63.
42 Ibid.
43 Jones, *Genocide*, 2nd ed. 37–38.
44 Josef Kunz, "The United Nations Convention on Genocide," *The American Journal of International Law* 43, no. 4 (1949): 743.
45 Lippman, "The 1948 Convention on the Prevention and Punishment of the Crime of Genocide," 77.
46 Matthew Lippman, "The Convention on the Prevention and Punishment of the Crime of Genocide: Fifty Years Later," *Arizona Journal of International and Comparative Law* 15 (1998): 507.
47 Jonassohn, "What Is Genocide?", 19.
48 Fein, "Genocide, Terror, Life Integrity, and War Crimes," 97.

Redefining genocide   49

49 Summary of the Judgment of the Appeals Chamber, *The Prosecutor v. Athanase Seromba*. Available at www.unictr.org/Cases/tabid/127/PID/42/default.aspx?id=5& mnid=4.
50 William Schabas, Interview, 17 September 2011.
51 George J. Andreopoulos, "Introduction: The Calculus of Genocide," in *Genocide: Conceptual and Historical Dimensions*, ed. George J. Andreopoulos (Philadelphia, PA: University of Pennsylvania Press, 1997), 7.
52 Charny, "Toward a Generic Definition of Genocide," 75.
53 Ibid.; Chalk, "Redefining Genocide," 52.
54 Midlarsky, *The Killing Trap*, 10; Chirot and McCauley, *Why Not Kill Them All*, 17.
55 Jones, *Genocide*, 2nd ed., 45.
56 Martin Shaw, *What Is Genocide?* (Malden, MA: Polity Press, 2007), 34.
57 Ibid.
58 It is important to note that the exclusion of indirect means of genocide is far from unanimous. For example, Jack Porter includes starvation and, along with Isidor Walliman and Michael Dobkowski, economic subjugation. Fein includes the imposition of conditions that cause increasing infant mortality. All cited in Jones, *Genocide*, 2nd ed., 17–18.
59 Rome Statute of the International Criminal Court, July 1, 2002, www.icc-cpi. int/nr/rdonlyres/ea9aeff7-5752-4f84-be94-0a655eb30e16/0/rome_statute_ english.pdf (accessed July 1, 2016).
60 Adam Jones, *Crimes against Humanity: A Beginner's Guide* (Oxford: Oneworld Publications, 2008), 6.
61 Thomas Pogge, *Politics as Usual: What Lies Behind the Pro-Poor Rhetoric?* (Cambridge: Polity Press, 2010), 2.
62 Gwilym David Blunt, "Is Global Poverty a Crime against Humanity?" *International Theory* 7, no. 3 (2015): 559.
63 Ibid.
64 Quigley, *The Genocide Convention*, 204.
65 Short, *Redefining Genocide*, 3.
66 Schabas, *Genocide in International Law*, 181.
67 Hirad Abtahi and Philippa Webb, *The Genocide Convention: The Travaux Préparatoires* (Leiden: Martinus Nijhoff Publishers, 2008), 731.
68 Ibid., 727.
69 Ibid.
70 Ibid.
71 Jones, *Genocide*, 2nd ed., 30.
72 Robert van Krieken, "Cultural Genocide Reconsidered," *Australian Indigenous Law Review* 12 (2008): 77.
73 See, among others, Andreopoulos, "Introduction"; Jones, *Genocide*, 2nd ed.; Harff, "Recognizing Genocide and Politicide"; Barbara Harff and Ted Gurr, "Toward Empirical Theory of Genocides and Politicides: Identification and Measurement of Cases Since 1945," *International Studies Quarterly* 32, no. 4 (1988); Drost, *The Crime of State*; Irving L. Horowitz, "Science, Modernity and Authorized Terror," in *Studies in Comparative Genocide*, eds. Levon Chorbajian and George Shirinian (London: Palgrave Macmillan, 1999); Sémelin, *Purify and Destroy*; Steve T. Katz, *The Holocaust in Historical Context: Volume 1: The Holocaust and Mass Death before the Modern Age* (Oxford: Oxford University Press, 1994); Chirot and McCauley, *Why Not Kill Them All*.
74 Horowitz, "Science, Modernity and Authorized Terror," 25.
75 Ibid.
76 Shaw, *What Is Genocide?*, 106.

50 *Redefining genocide*

77 Quigley, *The Genocide Convention*, 105.
78 Yehuda Bauer, "Comparison of Genocides," in *Studies in Comparative Genocide*, eds. Levon Chorbajian and George Shirinian (London: Palgrave Macmillan, 1999), 35.
79 Jonassohn, "What Is Genocide?", 21.
80 Charny, "Toward a Generic Definition of Genocide," 84.
81 Ibid.
82 Elazar Barkan, "Genocides of Indigenous Peoples: Rhetoric of Human Rights," in *The Specter of Genocide: Mass Murder in Historical Perspective*, eds. Robert Gellately and Ben Kiernan (Cambridge: Cambridge University Press, 2003), 120.
83 Julian Burger, *Report from the Frontier: The State of the World's Indigenous Peoples* (New York: Zed Books, 1987), 31.
84 Shamiran Makos, "Cultural Genocide and Key International Instruments: Framing the Indigenous Experience," *International Journal on Minority and Group Rights* 19 (2012): 177.
85 Damien Short, "Cultural Genocide and Indigenous Peoples: A Sociological Approach," *The International Journal of Human Rights* 14, no. 6 (2010): 842.
86 Ibid.
87 David Nersessian, "Cultural Genocide," in *Genocide: A Reader*, ed. Jens Meierhenrich (Oxford: Oxford University Press, 2014), 81.
88 Stated by Captain Richard Henry Pratt, founder of the United States Indian Industrial School in Carlisle, Pennsylvania, when describing the objective of Indian residential schools. Quoted in Ward Churchill, *Kill the Indian, Save the Man: The Genocidal Impact of American Indian Residential Schools* (San Francisco, CA: City Light Books, 2004), 14.
89 Elisa Novic, *The Concept of Cultural Genocide: An International Law Perspective* (Oxford: Oxford University Press, 2016), 5.
90 Ibid.
91 Harff and Gurr, "Toward Empirical Theory of Genocides and Politicides," 360.
92 Harff, "Recognizing Genocide and Politicide," 29.
93 Max Weber, *Economy and Society: An Outline and Interpretive Sociology* (Oakland, CA: University of California Press, 1978), 54.
94 Michael Mann, *The Source of Social Power: The Rise of Classes and Nation-States* (Cambridge: Cambridge University Press, 1993), 55.
95 Carl Clausewitz, *On War* (Oxford: Oxford University Press, 2007), 87.
96 Ibid; Similarly, Martin Shaw states that war is an act of force that seeks to "destroy the power of an enemy and its will to resist." Quoted in Shaw, *War & Genocide*, 18.
97 Shaw, *What Is Genocide?*, 35.
98 Zygmunt Bauman, *Modernity and the Holocaust* (Ithaca, NY: Cornell University Press, 1989), 139.
99 Ibid.
100 Quoted in Steven R. Ratner and Jason S. Abrams, *Accountability for Human Rights Atrocities in International Law: Beyond the Nuremberg Legacy* (Oxford: Oxford University Press, 2001), 124.
101 Ibid.
102 Eric Markusen and David Kopf, *The Holocaust and Strategic Bombing: Genocide and Total War in the Twentieth Century* (Boulder, CO: Westview Press, 1995), 62.
103 Shaw, *War & Genocide*, 26.
104 See, among others, Leo Kuper, *Genocide: Its Political Use in the Twentieth Century* (New Haven, CT: Yale University Press, 1982), 46; Eric Markusen and David Kopf, *The Holocaust and Strategic Bombing: Genocide and Total War in the Twentieth Century* (Boulder, CO: Westview Press, 1995), 181.

Redefining genocide 51

105 Shaw, *The New Western Way of War*, 44.
106 Paul Bartrop, "The Relationship between War and Genocide in the Twentieth Century: A Consideration," *Journal of Genocide Research* 4, no. 4 (2002): 529.
107 Matthew Krain, "State-Sponsored Mass Murder: The Onset and Severity of Genocides and Politicides," *The Journal of Conflict Resolution* 41, no. 3 (1997): 356.
108 Irving L. Horowitz, *Taking Lives: Genocide and State Power* (New Brunswick: Transaction Books, 1982), 32.
109 Fein, "Discriminating Genocide from War Crimes," 31.
110 Jonassohn, "What Is Genocide?", 22.
111 Horowitz, "Science, Modernity and Authorized Terror," 22.
112 Ibid.
113 Ibid.
114 Nina H. B. Jørgensen, *The Responsibility of States for International Crimes* (Oxford: Oxford University Press, 2001), 27.
115 Ibid.
116 Antonio Cassese, *International Criminal Law* (Oxford: Oxford University Press, 2008), 11.
117 International Law Commission, Articles on the Responsibility of States for Internationally Wrongful Acts, 2001.
118 Ibid.
119 Ronald Kramer, Raymond Michalowski, and Dawn Rothe, "'The Supreme International Crime': How the U.S. War in Iraq Threatens the Rule of Law," *Social Justice* 32, no. 2 (2005): 56.
120 Ibid.
121 Convention on the Prevention and Punishment of the Crime of Genocide.
122 The case is formally known as the Application of the Convention on the Prevention and Punishment of the Crime of Genocide (Bosnia and Herzegovina v. Serbia and Montenegro). The full judgment of February 26, 2007 is available at www.icj-cij.org/docket/files/91/13685.pdf.
123 International Court of Justice, Application Instituting Proceedings filed in the Registry of the Court on 20 March 1993, 52.
124 Ibid., 2.
125 International Court of Justice, Summary of the Judgment of 26 February 2007, 6.
126 Convention on the Prevention and Punishment of the Crime of Genocide.
127 International Court of Justice, Reports of Judgments, Advisory Opinions and Orders: Case Concerning Application of the Convention on the Prevention and Punishment of the Crime of Genocide (Bosnia and Herzegovina v. Serbia and Montenegro) Judgment of 26 February 2007, 111. www.icj-cij.org/docket/files/91/13685.pdf.
128 Ibid., 113.
129 Ibid.
130 Ibid.
131 Ibid., 120.
132 Anja Seibert-Fohr, "State Responsibility for Genocide under the Genocide Convention," in *The UN Genocide Convention: A Commentary*, ed. Paola Gaeta (Oxford: Oxford University Press, 2009), 363.
133 International Court of Justice, Judgment of 26 February 2007, 214.
134 Ibid., 215.
135 Ibid., 218.
136 Paolo Palchetti, "State Responsibility for Complicity in Genocide," in *The UN Genocide Convention: A Commentary*, ed. Paola Gaeta (Oxford: Oxford University Press, 2009), 391.
137 International Court of Justice, Judgment of 26 February 2007, 221.

52 *Redefining genocide*

138 Ibid.
139 Ibid., 225.
140 Ibid., 223.
141 Ibid., 225.

Bibliography

Abtahi, Hirad, and Philippa Webb. *The Genocide Convention: The Travaux Prépara-toires*. Leiden: Martinus Nijhoff Publishers, 2008.

Ad Hoc Committee Draft of the Convention on the Prevention and Punishment of the Crime of Genocide. Accessed May 1, 2015. www.preventgenocide.org/law/convention/drafts/.

Andreopoulos, George J. "Introduction: The Calculus of Genocide." In *Genocide: Conceptual and Historical Dimensions*, edited by George J. Andreopoulos, 1–28. Philadelphia, PA: University of Pennsylvania Press, 1997.

Barkan, Elazar. "Genocides of Indigenous Peoples: Rhetoric of Human Rights." In *The Specter of Genocide: Mass Murder in Historical Perspective*, edited by Robert Gellately and Ben Kiernan, 117–140. Cambridge: Cambridge University Press, 2003.

Bartrop, Paul. "The Relationship between War and Genocide in the Twentieth Century: A Consideration." *Journal of Genocide Research* 4, no. 4 (2002): 519–532.

Bauer, Yehuda. "Comparison of Genocides." In *Studies in Comparative Genocide*, edited by Levon Chorbajian and George Shirinian, 31–45. London: Palgrave Macmillan, 1999.

Bauman, Zygmunt. *Modernity and the Holocaust*. Ithaca, NY: Cornell University Press, 1989.

Blunt, Gwilym David. "Is Global Poverty a Crime against Humanity?" *International Theory* 7, no. 3 (2015): 539–571.

Burger, Julian. *Report from the Frontier: The State of the World's Indigenous Peoples*. London: Zed Books, 1987.

Cassese, Antonio. *International Criminal Law*. Oxford: Oxford University Press, 2008.

Chalk, Frank. "Redefining Genocide." In *Genocide: Conceptual and Historical Dimensions*, edited by George J. Andreopoulos, 47–63. Philadelphia, PA: University of Pennsylvania Press, 1997.

Charny, Israel. "Toward a Generic Definition of Genocide." In *Genocide: Conceptual and Historical Dimensions*, edited by George J. Andreopoulos, 64–94. Philadelphia, PA: University of Pennsylvania Press, 1997.

Chirot, Daniel, and Clark McCauley. *Why Not Kill Them All? The Logic and Prevention of Mass Political Murder*. Princeton, NJ: Princeton University Press, 2010.

Chorbajian, Levon. "Introduction." In *Studies in Comparative Genocide*, edited by Levon Chorbajian and George Shirinian, xv–xxxv. London: Palgrave Macmillan, 1999.

Churchill, Ward. *Kill the Indian, Save the Man: The Genocidal Impact of American Indian Residential Schools*. San Francisco, CA: City Light Books, 2004.

Clausewitz, Carl. *On War*. Oxford: Oxford University Press, 2007.

Convention on the Prevention and Punishment of the Crime of Genocide. Accessed May 1, 2015. www.ohchr.org/EN/ProfessionalInterest/Pages/CrimeOfGenocide.aspx.

Cox, John. *To Kill a People: Genocide in the Twentieth Century*. Oxford: Oxford University Press, 2016.

Cushman, Thomas. "Genocide or Civil War?: Human Rights and the Politics of Conceptualization." *Human Rights Review* 1, no. 3 (2000): 12–14.

Drost, Pieter N. *The Crime of State: Genocide*. Leyden: A.W. Sythoff, 1959.

Fein, Helen. "Discriminating Genocide from War Crimes: Vietnam and Afghanistan Reexamined." *Denver Journal of International Law and Policy* 22, no. 1 (1993): 29–62.

Fein, Helen. "Genocide, Terror, Life Integrity, and War Crimes: The Case for Discrimination." In *Genocide: Conceptual and Historical Dimensions*, edited by George J. Andreopoulos, 95–107. Philadelphia, PA: University of Pennsylvania Press, 1997.

Fein, Helen. "Introduction." In *Genocide Watch*, edited by Helen Fein, 1–14. New Haven, CT: Yale University Press, 1992.

Gordon, Joy. "When Intent Makes All the Difference in the World: Economic Sanctions on Iraq and the Accusation of Genocide." *Yale Human Rights and Development Journal* 5, no. 2 (2014): 57–84.

Harff, Barbara. "Recognizing Genocide and Politicide." In *Genocide Watch*, edited by Helen Fein, 27–41. New Haven, CT: Yale University Press, 1992.

Harff, Barbara, and Ted Gurr. "Toward Empirical Theory of Genocides and Politicides: Identification and Measurement of Cases since 1945." *International Studies Quarterly* 32, no. 4 (1988): 359–371.

Horowitz, Irving L. "Science, Modernity and Authorized Terror." In *Studies in Comparative Genocide*, edited by Levon Chorbajian and George Shirinian, 15–30. London: Palgrave Macmillan, 1999.

Horowitz, Irving L. *Taking Lives: Genocide and State Power*. New Brunswick: Transaction Books, 1982.

International Court of Justice. Application Instituting Proceedings filed in the Registry of the Court on 20 March 1993.

International Court of Justice. Reports of Judgments, Advisory Opinions and Orders: Case Concerning Application of the Convention on the Prevention and Punishment of the Crime of Genocide (Bosnia and Herzegovina v. Serbia and Montenegro) Judgment of 26 February 2007.

International Court of Justice. Summary of the Judgment of 26 February 2007.

International Law Commission. Articles on the Responsibility of States for Internationally Wrongful Acts, 2001.

Jonassohn, Kurt. "What Is Genocide?" In *Genocide Watch*, edited by Helen Fein, 17–26. New Haven, CT: Yale University Press, 1992.

Jones, Adam. *Crimes against Humanity: A Beginner's Guide*. Oxford: Oneworld Publications, 2008.

Jones, Adam. "Gendercide and Genocide." *Journal of Genocide Research* 2, no. 2 (2000): 185–211.

Jones, Adam. *Genocide: A Comprehensive Introduction*, 2nd ed. London: Routledge, 2011.

Jørgensen, Nina H. B. *The Responsibility of States for International Crimes*. Oxford: Oxford University Press, 2001.

Katz, Steven T. *The Holocaust in Historical Context: Volume 1: The Holocaust and Mass Death before the Modern Age*. Oxford: Oxford University Press, 1994.

54 Redefining genocide

Krain, Matthew. "State-Sponsored Mass Murder: The Onset and Severity of Genocides and Politicides." *The Journal of Conflict Resolution* 41, no. 3 (1997): 331–360.

Kramer, Ronald, Raymond Michalowski, and Dawn Rothe. "'The Supreme International Crime': How the U.S. War in Iraq Threatens the Rule of Law." *Social Justice* 32, no. 2 (2005): 52–81.

Kunz, Josef. "The United Nations Convention on Genocide." *The American Journal of International Law* 43, no. 4 (1949): 738–746.

Kuper, Leo. *Genocide: Its Political Use in the Twentieth Century.* New Haven, CT: Yale University Press, 1982.

LeBlanc, Lawrence. "The Intent to Destroy Groups in the Genocide Convention: The Proposed U.S. Understanding." *The American Journal of International Law* 78, no. 2 (1984): 369–385.

Lippman, Matthew. "The 1948 Convention on the Prevention and Punishment of the Crime of Genocide: Forty-Five Years Later." *Temple International and Comparative Law Journal* 8, no. 1 (1994): 1–84.

Lippman, Matthew. "The Convention on the Prevention and Punishment of the Crime of Genocide: Fifty Years Later." *Arizona Journal of International and Comparative Law* 15 (1998): 415–514.

Lippman, Matthew. "The Drafting of the 1948 Convention on the Prevention and Punishment of the Crime of Genocide." *Boston University International Law Journal* 3 (1984): 1–65.

Makos, Shamiran. "Cultural Genocide and Key International Instruments: Framing the Indigenous Experience." *International Journal on Minority and Group Rights* 19 (2012): 175–194.

Mann, Michael. *The Source of Social Power: The Rise of Classes and Nation-States.* Cambridge: Cambridge University Press, 1993.

Markusen, Eric. "Genocide and Warfare." In *Genocide, War, and Human Survival*, edited by Charles B. Strozier and Michael Flynn, 75–86. Lanham, MD: Rowman & Littlefield, 1996.

Markusen, Eric, and David Kopf. *The Holocaust and Strategic Bombing: Genocide and Total War in the Twentieth Century.* Boulder, CO: Westview Press, 1995.

Midlarsky, Manus L. *The Killing Trap: Genocide in the Twentieth Century.* Cambridge: Cambridge University Press, 2005.

Moshman, David. "Conceptual Constrains on Thinking about Genocide." *Journal of Genocide Research* 3, no. 3 (2001): 431–450.

Nersessian, David. "Cultural Genocide." In *Genocide: A Reader*, edited by Jens Meierhenrich, 80–81. Oxford: Oxford University Press, 2014.

Novic, Elisa. *The Concept of Cultural Genocide: An International Law Perspective.* Oxford: Oxford University Press, 2016.

Oppenheim, Lassa. *International Law: A Treatise Vol. 1.* Philadelphia, PA: David McKay Company, 1955.

Palchetti, Paolo. "State Responsibility for Complicity in Genocide." In *The UN Genocide Convention: A Commentary*, edited by Paola Gaeta, 381–395. Oxford: Oxford University Press, 2009.

Pogge, Thomas. *Politics as Usual: What Lies Behind the Pro-Poor Rhetoric?* Cambridge: Polity Press, 2010.

Quigley, John. *The Genocide Convention: An International Law Analysis.* Burlington, VT: Ashgate, 2006.

Ratner, Steven R., and Jason S. Abrams. *Accountability for Human Rights Atrocities in International Law: Beyond the Nuremberg Legacy*. Oxford: Oxford University Press, 2001.

Rome Statute of the International Criminal Court. Accessed July 6, 2016. www.icc-cpi.int/nr/rdonlyres/ea9aeff7-5752-4f84-be94-0a655eb30e16/0/rome_statute_english.pdf.

Schabas, William. *Genocide in International Law: The Crime of Crimes*. Cambridge: Cambridge University Press, 2000.

Secretariat Draft of the Convention on the Prevention and Punishment of the Crime of Genocide. Accessed May 1, 2016. www.preventgenocide.org/law/convention/drafts/.

Seibert-Fohr, Anja. "State Responsibility for Genocide under the Genocide Convention." In *The UN Genocide Convention: A Commentary*, edited by Paola Gaeta, 349–373. Oxford: Oxford University Press, 2009.

Sémelin, Jacques. *Purify and Destroy: The Political Uses of Massacre and Genocide*. New York: Columbia University Press, 2009.

Shaw, Martin. "The General Hybridity of War and Genocide." *Journal of Genocide Research* 9, no. 3 (2007): 461–473.

Shaw, Martin. *The New Western Way of War*. Malden, MA: Polity Press, 2005.

Shaw, Martin. *War & Genocide*. Malden, MA: Polity Press, 2003.

Shaw, Martin. *What Is Genocide?* Malden, MA: Polity Press, 2007.

Short, Damien. "Cultural Genocide and Indigenous Peoples: A Sociological Approach." *The International Journal of Human Rights* 14, no. 6 (2010): 833–848.

Short, Damien. *Redefining Genocide: Settler Colonialism, Social Death and Ecocide*. London: Zed Books, 2016.

Summary of the Judgment of the Appeals Chamber. *The Prosecutor v. Athanase Seromba*. Accessed May 11, 2017. www.unictr.org/Cases/tabid/127/PID/42/default.aspx?id=5&mnid=4.

United Nations General Assembly. Resolution 96(I) of 11 December 1946. Retrieved May 1, 2016. http://daccess-dds-ny.un.org/doc/RESOLUTION/GEN/NR0/033/47/IMG/NR003347.pdf?OpenElement.

Van Krieken, Robert. "Cultural Genocide Reconsidered." *Australian Indigenous Law Review* 12 (2008): 76–81.

Van Schaack, Beth. "The Crime of Political Genocide: Repairing the Genocide Convention's Blind Spot." *The Yale Law Journal* 106, no. 7 (1997): 2259–2291.

Weber, Max. *Economy and Society: An Outline and Interpretive Sociology*. Oakland, CA: University of California Press, 1978.

3 Cultural genocide

Nullum crimen sine lege

Borrowing from Damien Short, I define cultural genocide as any attempt to destroy a group as such by eliminating the group's culture.[1] Acts that constitute cultural genocide include criminalization or de facto prohibition of a group's language, religious practices, customs, and traditions; destruction of cultural heritage sites, artifacts, artwork, historical records, and books; and indoctrination and forced assimilation of a group's children into another group. I include cultural genocide in my definition of genocide because, like physical violence, destruction of a group's culture has the potential to eliminate the group's existence as such, even while the individual members of the group survive. A cultural group's survival as a unique entity is predicated on the continued existence of its culture. Cultural groups have unique histories, heritages, historical contributions, practices, languages, and values. Destruction of a culture and the coerced assimilation of the members of one culture into another could effectively destroy the group without employing means for its immediate physical destruction. As David Nersessian puts it, prohibiting only a group's physical destruction "preserves the body of the group but allows its very soul to be destroyed."[2]

Cultural genocide is a multidimensional crime. To succeed, perpetrators of cultural genocide must attack the very foundation of the targeted group's shared identity—its culture. Thus, as noted above, cultural genocide includes acts that range from the destruction of books to the forced assimilation of a group's children into another group. Any one act is not likely to achieve the purpose of eliminating a group as such by erasing the group's unique cultural existence. However, perpetrators do not need to engage simultaneously in all the acts that constitute cultural genocide in order for the state to be responsible for its commission. Rather, what matters is that any of the prohibited acts are carried out as part of a plan to destroy a group as such through the elimination of its shared cultural identity.

Cultural genocide was a key element of Raphael Lemkin's conception of the crime of genocide. Thanks, in large part, to Lemkin's role in drafting the Secretariat Draft and his subsequent advocacy, the crime of cultural genocide was included in the first two formal drafts of the Genocide Convention. However, during the treaty's negotiations, states that opposed the inclusion of cultural genocide, the US chief among them, won a vote that resulted in its removal. Significantly, prior to, during, and subsequent to the treaty's adoption and entry into force, the US enforced policies that contained elements of cultural genocide.

The title of this chapter reflects my belief that the US was purposeful in its effort to remove cultural genocide from the Genocide Convention—after all, there is "no crime without law." Relatedly, as Beth Van Schaack points out, it was in the interests of the Genocide Convention's negotiating parties to ensure that the treaty "could not implicate member nations on the drafting committee."[3] With this in mind, this chapter is divided into three parts. In the first part, I provide a broad overview of Lemkin's conception of cultural genocide. Next, I explain the role the US played in eliminating cultural genocide from the adopted text of the Genocide Convention. In the final section, I situate US treatment of its indigenous population within the definition of cultural genocide, concluding that the US is responsible for this form of the crime.

Raphael Lemkin and cultural genocide

In his early thinking, Lemkin was especially concerned by systematic acts of what he called "vandalism," specifically the destruction of cultural symbols, such as artistic works and religious artifacts. In 1933, while speaking at the International Conference for Unification of Criminal Law, Lemkin depicted Acts of Vandalism as "offenses against the law of nations."[4] He argued that vandalism, like "barbarity," [5] could be systematic in nature, and target "the unique genius and achievement of a collectivity."[6] Further, in systematically targeting a group's collective contributions, the perpetrator

> causes not only the immediate irrevocable losses of the destroyed work as property and as the culture of the collectivity directly concerned (whose unique genius contributed to the creation of this work); it is also all humanity which experiences a loss by this act of vandalism.[7]

By presenting acts of vandalism and acts of barbarity as two means by which the existence of groups of peoples can be threatened, Lemkin provided initial insight into his developing concepts of cultural and physical genocide.

Over the next ten years, in the shadows of World War II and the Jewish Holocaust, Lemkin continued to develop his concept of crimes against human collectivities. In 1944, he first introduced the term "genocide" in his seminal work, *Axis Rule in Occupied Europe*. In it, he wrote:

> Generally speaking, genocide does not necessarily mean the immediate destruction of a nation, except when accomplished by mass killing…It is intended rather to signify a coordinated plan of different actions aiming at the destruction of the essential foundations of the life of national

58 *Cultural genocide*

groups, with the aim of annihilating the groups themselves. The objectives of such a plan would be disintegration of the political and social institutions, of culture, language, national feelings, religion, and the economic existence of national groups, and the destruction of personal security, liberty, health, dignity, and even the lives of the individuals belonging to such groups.[8]

As he did at the International Conference for Unification of Criminal Law, Lemkin portrayed destruction of a group by mass killing and by a coordinated effort to destroy a group's unique and essential foundation as distinct acts. He made this clear in stressing that genocide can be accomplished by a mass killing campaign against members of a group, as well as by a slower systematic attack against the life of the group through means other than mass killing. The former involves the elimination of members of a targeted group; the latter the elimination of the group's existence through the erasure of its culture and, hence, its identity.

This is an important distinction, one that unfortunately has often been lost in the study of genocide. While the outright physical extermination of a group was certainly a part of Lemkin's conceptualization of genocide, it was neither a necessary feature, nor even a predominant one. Instead, what was essential to Lemkin's conception of genocide was that the attempt to remove from existence a targeted group as such be conducted as a matter of policy.[9] For Lemkin, means of committing genocide without perpetrating physical violence against members of a group include "desecration and destruction of cultural symbols (books, objects of art, loot, religious relics, etc.), destruction of cultural leadership, destruction of cultural centers (cities, churches, monasteries, schools, libraries), prohibition of cultural activities or codes of behavior, forceful conversion, [and] demoralization."[10] Lemkin argued that coercively undermining a group's culture could result in the group's disintegration, forcing its members to "either become absorbed in other cultures...or succumb to personal disorganization and, perhaps, physical destruction"; he concluded that "the destruction of cultural symbols is genocide."[11]

In Lemkin's conception, the physical survival of the group was the norm rather than the exception.[12] This is firmly established in Lemkin's two phases of genocide. The first phase involves the "destruction of the national pattern of the oppressed group."[13] The second phase involves the "imposition of the national pattern of the oppressor."[14] According to Lemkin, "This imposition, in turn, may be made on the oppressed population which is allowed to remain, or upon their territory alone, after the removal of the population and colonization of the area by the oppressor's own nationals."[15]

In 1945, Lemkin described physical genocide as derived from an unsuccessful attempt at cultural genocide. Lemkin wrote that genocide "refers to a coordinated plan aimed at destruction of the essential foundations of the

Cultural genocide 59

life of national groups so that these groups wither and die like plants that have suffered a blight."[16] However, Lemkin continued,

> When these means fail the machine gun can always be utilized as a last resort. Genocide is directed against a national group as an entity and the attack on individuals is only secondary to the annihilation of the national group to which they belong.[17]

Again, Lemkin emphasized that genocide was not limited to the physical destruction of a group. Rather, Lemkin saw physical genocide as a corollary to the failure to achieve the goal of a group's destruction through cultural genocide. In other words, what cannot be accomplished through forced assimilation and cultural erasure can be accomplished through brutal force.

In 1946, a year before he took on a primary role in developing the United Nations Secretariat Draft (the first formal draft of the Genocide Convention), Lemkin highlighted the irreparable harm that genocide inflicts not only on the group, but on the world. He wrote, "Our whole heritage is a product of the contributions of all nations."[18] This is best understood, Lemkin asserted, if we consider the loss the world would have suffered if Jews

> had not been permitted to create the Bible, or to give birth to an Einstein, a Spinoza; if the Poles had not had the opportunity to give to the world a Copernicus, a Chopin, a Curie; the Czechs, a Huss, a Dvorak; the Greeks, a Plato and a Socrates; the Russians, a Tolstoy and a Shostakovich.[19]

On December 11, 1946, the United Nations General Assembly unanimously adopted Resolution 96(I), affirming that genocide is a crime under international law and paving the way for the development of a treaty that would codify it as such. Retaining the spirit of Lemkin's conception of genocide, Resolution 96(I) stated that genocide "results in great losses to humanity in the form of cultural and other contributions represented by these human groups."[20] A little more than three months later, the Economic and Social Council passed a resolution instructing Secretary-General Trygve Halvdan Lie to undertake the study of genocide and preparation of a draft of the treaty. Halvdan Lie delegated this duty to the Division of Human Rights and solicited the aid of Lemkin, himself a lawyer, in this task, along with the help of Henri Donnedieu de Vabres, Professor at the Paris Faculty of Law, and Professor Vespasian Pella, President of the International Association for Penal Law.

While completing the Secretariat Draft, Lemkin disagreed with Donnedieu and Pella over whether protection of cultures ought to be included in a treaty prohibiting genocide. Lemkin insisted on the need for the protection against cultural genocide, arguing that the existence of a group required the preservation of "its spirit and moral unity."[21] Pella and

60 *Cultural genocide*

Donnedieu disagreed not necessarily with Lemkin's concern, but rather with whether a treaty prohibiting genocide was an appropriate way to confront the issue of cultural destruction. They saw the prohibition of cultural genocide as "an undue extension of the notion of genocide" to the protection of minorities "under cover of the term genocide."[22] In other words, Donnedieu and Pella did not believe that crimes against cultures, even those carried out with the intent to eliminate the culture's existence, ought to be placed alongside physical attacks against members of a group conducted with the intent to destroy the group.

With Lemkin's insistence and Resolution 96(I)'s recognition that genocide results in the loss of cultural contributions to humanity as a whole, cultural genocide was included alongside physical and biological genocide in the Secretariat Draft submitted to the Economic and Social Council in May 1947. Even though they involve different means, physical, biological, and cultural genocide were granted equal status in Article II of the Secretariat Draft. As Ward Churchill notes, "Significantly, no hierarchy is attached to these classifications. The perpetration of cultural genocide is presented as an offense every bit as serious—and subject to exactly the same penalties—as perpetration of physical or biological genocide."[23]

The US and the exclusion of cultural genocide

After receiving the Secretariat Draft in May 1947, the Economic and Social Council appointed an Ad Hoc Committee on Genocide to continue drafting the treaty. The US chaired the committee, which also included China, France, Lebanon, Poland, the Soviet Union, and Venezuela. Using its position as chair, the US exerted significant influence to exclude cultural genocide from the committee's draft of the treaty. For example, in a formal declaration, the US asserted:

> The prohibition of the use of language, systematic destruction of books, and destruction and dispersion of documents and objects of historical or artistic value, commonly known in this Convention to those who wish to include it, as 'cultural genocide' is a matter which certainly should not be included in this Convention. The act of creating the new international crime of genocide is one of extreme gravity and the United States feels that it should be confined to those barbarous acts directed against individuals which form the basic concept of public opinion on this subject. The acts provided for in these paragraphs are acts which should appropriately be dealt with in connection with the protection of minorities.[24]

Whereas the Secretariat Draft included cultural genocide as one of three forms of genocide, all of which were equally prohibited, the US dismissed cultural genocide as an act that did not warrant the same concern as the

Cultural genocide 61

other two forms of genocide. The US rejected the idea that prohibiting a group from using its language and systematically destroying the group's books, documents, and historical artifacts constituted "barbarous acts."

The US launched a sustained campaign to exclude cultural genocide from the Genocide Convention. Its opposition was so strong that it threatened the entire treaty process. The US warned,

> Were the Committee to attempt to cover too wide a field in the preparation of a draft convention for example, in attempting to define cultural genocide—however reprehensible that crime might be—it might well run the risk to find some States would refuse to ratify the convention.[25]

Despite this aggressive effort to pressure fellow members, retaining a prohibition against cultural genocide commanded majority support among members of the Ad Hoc Committee. However, with US opposition now evident, and with subsequent rounds of negotiations still to come, the Ad Hoc Committee backed away in an attempt to garner unanimous support for its draft of the treaty.

At the behest of the US, with France's support, the Ad Hoc Committee separated cultural genocide from physical and biological genocide, retaining physical and biological genocide in Article II of the Ad Hoc Committee Draft and moving cultural genocide to Article III. The US recommended the separation in order to "enable Governments to make reservations on a particular point of the Convention."[26] In other words, by splitting cultural genocide from physical and biological genocide, the US could freely support the treaty, recognizing the crimes of physical and biological genocide, while also submitting a reservation stating it did not recognize the crime of cultural genocide. With this compromise in place, the Ad Hoc Committee voted six to one in favor of including cultural genocide in Article III of the Ad Hoc Committee Draft of the treaty.

Though it was primarily responsible for the compromise, the US cast the lone dissenting vote. Even with the freedom to submit a reservation, something that assuaged France's concerns, the US voted against the inclusion of cultural genocide. Nonetheless, with six votes in favor of retaining cultural genocide, it was included in the Ad Hoc Committee Draft as sent to the Sixth Committee for further deliberation. The Sixth Committee acted as the General Assembly's standing committee and primary forum for the consideration of legal questions. Unlike the Ad Hoc Committee, which was limited to seven members, the Sixth Committee included representatives from every UN member state at the time. Thus, the US had another opportunity to exert its influence over the negotiations and the newly involved parties in an effort to remove cultural genocide from the scope of the Genocide Convention's protection.

At the Sixth Committee, the US found new partners in its quest who were equally dismissive. Unsurprisingly, it was European settler-colonial regimes

62 *Cultural genocide*

who joined the US. For example, Denmark argued that equating mass murder and the closing of libraries demonstrated a clear lack of logic and proportionality.[27] Similarly, the US once again argued that the treaty should be limited to those acts that "shocked the conscience of mankind."[28] Of course, Lemkin and the proponents of retaining cultural genocide were not equating the two acts, but rather equating the intent behind both acts, as well as the possible consequences—the destruction of a group as such.

The Netherlands went so far as to question whether "all cultures, even the most barbarous, deserved protection, and whether the assimilation resulting from the civilizing action of a State also constituted genocide."[29] Further, according to the Netherlands, when such acts have a "civilizing" effect, meaning the "betterment" of the members of the group, they should not be denigrated by the label "genocide."[30] In other words, the Netherlands believed states ought to have the right to commit acts of cultural genocide as long as they were for the "betterment" of the affected group of people. Such arguments did not sit well with some of the negotiating parties. For example, having only recently emerged from British colonial rule in August 1947 with the partition of India, Pakistan pushed back, arguing that the motive for genocide was the destruction of the ideas and values of the targeted group's culture. Therefore, physical destruction was just one means to achieve that end. According to Pakistan, "Thus, the end and the means were closely linked together; cultural genocide and physical genocide were indivisible. It would be against all reason to treat physical genocide as a crime and not to do the same for cultural genocide."[31] Pakistan also noted that "assimilation" could be used as a "euphemism concealing measures of coercion designed to eliminate certain forms of culture."[32]

Despite its centrality to Lemkin's conception of genocide, and the support it received from some of the negotiating parties, the US and other opponents of including cultural genocide succeeded in expunging it from the Genocide Convention. The vote at the Sixth Committee was twenty-five to sixteen, with four abstentions.[33] In its campaign, the US likely benefitted from the colonial context in which the Genocide Convention was negotiated. Had the Genocide Convention been drafted and negotiated after wider decolonization, Leo Kuper argues that the "representatives of the colonial powers would have been somewhat on the defensive, sensitive to criticism of their policies in non-self-governing territories."[34] Robert Davis and Mark Zannis state that the intent to commit cultural genocide is inherent in colonization:

> The intention to replace independence with dependence, an integral factor for all colonial systems, is proof of intent to destroy. Colonialism controls through the deliberate and systematic destruction of racial, political and cultural groups. Genocide is the means by which colonialism creates, sustains and extends its control to enrich itself.[35]

In a postcolonial world, there would have been significantly more former colonies shaping the drafts of the Genocide Convention.

Cultural genocide 63

Following the successful removal of cultural genocide from the Convention at the Sixth Committee, the US defended its vote, asking "whether it was more important to protect the right of a group to express its opinions in the language of its choice...or to protect its right to free expression of thought, whatever the language."[36] According to the US, "If the object were to protect the culture of a group, then it was primarily freedom of thought and expression for the members of the group which needed protection."[37] Even with this success, the US felt bound to take a parting shot at the concept of cultural genocide. In so doing, it erased the various means through which a culture can be eliminated, paring them down to prohibiting a group from using its language. The US then dismissed the importance of a group's language to its existence as such. Protecting the rights of the members of a group to speak their ancestral language, it argued, was not as important as protecting the rights of the individuals to freely express themselves. Essentially, the US claimed that without freedom of expression, a group would be voiceless regardless of which language the group speaks. Yet, the US painted the situation as one of either freedom of expression or freedom to communicate in one's cultural language. In other words, for the US, social and cultural rights were secondary to civil and political rights, rather than complementary.

According to Nersessian, "Collective identity is not self-evident but derives from the numerous, inter-dependent aspects of a group's existence." [38] This the US rejected in aggressively opposing the inclusion of cultural genocide, even threatening to undermine the treaty's viability if it were included. In doing so, the US not only failed to recognize the essential role culture plays in group identity; it openly dismissed it.

Kristina Hon challenges the US argument that cultural genocide lacks the severity of the crime of physical genocide. According to Hon, "The underpinnings of society, culture, and communities ... *are* ... threatened by prohibitions on books and languages, thereby lowering quality of life and weakening identity."[39] Davis and Zannis carry Hon's argument to its logical conclusion; when systematic and long-term, the impacts Hon described often result in more profound consequences. They assert,

> A culture's destruction is not a trifling matter. A healthy culture is all-encompassing of human lives, even to the point of determining time and space orientation. If a people suddenly lose their 'prime symbol,' the basis of culture, their lives lose meaning. They become disoriented, with no hope. As social disorganization often follows such loss, they are often unable to ensure their own survival.[40]

Davis and Zannis describe exactly what the Genocide Convention was supposedly created to prevent. Genocide represents a refusal by its perpetrator to recognize the rights of members of a group to express their cultural identity.[41] Thus, according to Matthew Lippman, "The central purpose of the Genocide Convention is to preserve and promote pluralism in order to perpetuate the progress which historically has resulted from the clash of cultures."[42]

64 *Cultural genocide*

Cultural genocide, then, is far more destructive than the US allowed. The US treated prohibition of a group's language, the systematic destruction of a group's books, and the destruction of a group's artifacts as minor human rights violations. Essentially, the US equated a form of vandalism—burning books—with the kind of vandalism Lemkin viewed as a central element of his conception of genocide. Nersessian emphasizes this point, noting that, thanks to the exclusion of cultural genocide, human rights law "redresses the intentional and systematic eradication of a group's cultural existence (for example, destroying original historical texts or prohibiting all use of a language) with the same mechanisms as it would consider the redaction of an art textbook."[43]

While threatening to undermine adoption of the Genocide Convention if cultural genocide was included, the US was also engaged in long-standing practices that violated the draft provisions in this regard. At one point during debate at the Sixth Committee, the Belarusian representative essentially questioned whether the US was negotiating in good faith, considering its treatment of indigenous peoples, stating that the "North American Indian had almost ceased to exist in the United States."[44] In successfully excluding cultural genocide from the Genocide Convention, Churchill asserts that the US accomplished "a maneuver serving to exempt a range of its own dirty linen from scrutiny."[45] He argues that, along with the Soviet Union, the US was one of two countries with "sufficient clout to effect the sort of mutual exoneration from culpability through *a priori* alteration of law which ultimately prevailed."[46] The US had two choices. It could support a definition of genocide that recognized the different means by which a group of people could be destroyed as such, which would have required that the US change the way it was treating its indigenous peoples; or it could fight aggressively to ensure that cultural genocide was excluded from the Genocide Convention. It chose the latter course.

US responsibility for cultural genocide

Historically, the US assault on its indigenous populations was not limited to practices that constitute cultural genocide. In the initial stages of the genocide, the US employed a combination of physical and cultural genocide. As Makos notes,

> Within North America, the American-Indian experience is one rooted in both physical and cultural dissipation. This becomes evident upon a closer examination of the way in which law and colonialism were instruments of genocide, both in the physical and cultural forms....Beyond physical extermination, the State implemented policies of acculturalization by enacting laws that restricted land entitlements to Indians who had renounced tribal citizenship.[47]

Examples of physical genocide can be found in the well-known case of the Cherokee and the relatively lesser known case of the Yuki. In 1832, the US Supreme Court ruled in *Worcester v. Georgia* that Georgia law did not apply on Native American lands. Chief Justice John Marshall concluded,

> The Cherokee nation is…a distinct community, occupying its own territory, with boundaries accurately described, in which the laws of Georgia can have no force, and which the citizens of Georgia have no right to enter, but with the assent of the Cherokees themselves, or in conformity with treaties, and with the acts of congress.[48]

This decision was important because it supported Cherokee claims under the Indian Removal Act, which was signed into law by President Andrew Jackson in 1830, that the US had no right to forcibly remove them from their land. Unfortunately for the Cherokee, President Jackson decided his administration was not bound by such decisions, allegedly declaring: "Marshall has made his law, now let him enforce it."[49] Regardless of whether Jackson derided Marshall in this manner, the result was the same. In total disregard of the law, the US military forced all members of the Cherokee tribe to leave their homes and travel west along what would become known as the Trail of Tears. Members of the tribe were forced to walk around fifteen to twenty miles each day in sub-zero temperatures without proper clothing. An estimated 4,000 Cherokees out of a total population of about 8,000 died during their forced removal.[50]

Clearly, the Cherokee were victimized by a deliberate policy that inflicted on the group conditions of life calculated to bring about its physical destruction in whole or in part—an act subsequently prohibited under Article II of the Genocide Convention. California's Yuki Indians were victims of a more direct physical assault—a "deadly combination of settler-colonial brutality and government complicity."[51] With the commencement of the "Gold Rush" in 1847, "settlers robbed and murdered Yuki men and enslaved the women, crimes that were condoned and even encouraged by the state government, which helped organize militias that indulged in genocidal slaughter."[52] In the 1840s, the Yuki maintained a population of around 20,000. Within six years of the settlers' arrival, the Yuki population was reduced by 85–90 percent. By 1880, only 168 Yuki remained; as John Cox notes, the mass murder of the Yuki represents "one of history's few near-total genocides."[53] Direct physical violence of this sort was part and parcel of settler-state colonialism. To enable an ever-increasing occupation of the land by white settlers, the US had to reduce the indigenous population both in size and in terms of its ability to resist.[54]

In the late 19th century, with the end of the "Indian Wars" and the aggregate North American indigenous population reduced by approximately 98 percent (from an estimated fifteen million in 1500 to 250,000 in 1890), the means of destroying the indigenous groups as such evolved.[55] The new policy was, as Captain Richard Henry Pratt, founder of the United States

66 *Cultural genocide*

Indian Industrial School in Carlisle, Pennsylvania put it, to "kill the Indian, save the man."[56] In this context, "saving" has multiple meanings. Not only would the lives of Native Americans be saved from death, but Native Americans would also be saved from themselves. This was the source of the US cultural genocide against its indigenous populations: the view that the white man was civilized and Native Americans were savages.

As early as the 1870s, there were those in the US who used their influence to lobby for a more cost-effective alternative to physical attacks for dealing with the Native "problem"—the complete elimination of indigenous cultures through the assimilation of the remaining Native American population.[57] "Since then," writes James Waller, "the ongoing destruction of American Indians is best characterized as 'ethnocide'—that is, the destruction of a culture rather than a people per se."[58] Of course, as Churchill points out, Lemkin coined the term "ethnocide" at the same time that he coined the term "genocide," not (as it is used today) to describe actions different from genocide, but as a synonym for it.[59]

In 1883, the Court of Indian Offenses was created to monitor the behavior of Native Americans and punish those who committed so-called "Indian offenses." These included performing the "sun-dance," the "scalp-dance," and the "war-dance." The "usual practices" of medicine men were also designated as offenses.[60] The practice of important cultural traditions was met by withheld rations, heavy fines, forced labor, and jail time.[61] Laws were also passed that forced Native Americans to abandon their customary means of governance and adopt systems of government, police forces, and judicial systems that emulated American institutions.[62] Communal land dislocation was another key to assimilation policy. The US sought to abolish the indigenous practice of holding land in common, replacing it with the Anglicized system of individual property ownership with the goal of undermining the cohesiveness of Native American societies.[63]

All these strategies played significant roles in the effort to eradicate indigenous cultures. However, education was the "linchpin of assimilationist aspirations" by which Native Americans were to be "civilized."[64] The "compulsory transfer of native children into boarding schools designed to assimilate them into white society" was the primary method of erasing indigenous cultural identity while sparing the physical lives of the members of the group.[65] Sending Native American children to boarding schools was clearly part of a long-term strategy aimed at the complete eradication of Native American cultures, one that formally began in 1879 when the US Congress began appropriating money to build off-reservation boarding schools.[66] That same year, the previously mentioned United States Indian Industrial School opened, the first of its kind. The boarding school program, which lasted nearly a century, was intended to remove all aboriginal children from their homes, communities, and cultures from the earliest possible age. An indigenous person would be held for years in state-sponsored 'educational' facilities, systematically deculturated, and simultaneously indoctrinated to see her/his own heritage—and him/herself as well—in terms deemed appropriate by a society that despised both to the point of seeking as a matter of policy their utter eradication.[67]

Eliminating Native American languages was considered central to deculturalization. Thus, when the US insisted on excluding cultural genocide from the Genocide Convention, arguing that it was not as important to protect the right of a group to use its language as it was to protect the right of the group to freely express itself "whatever the language," the US position was consistent with regulations first issued by the Bureau of Indian Affairs in 1885. In its regulations for boarding schools, the Bureau of Indian Affairs decreed that all schools would maintain an English-only policy. In support of the language restriction, J.D.C. Atkins, Commissioner of Indian Affairs, proclaimed,

> This language, which is good enough for a white man and a black man, ought to be good enough for the red man. It is also believed that teaching an Indian youth in his own barbarous dialect is a positive detriment to him. The first step to be taken toward civilization, toward teaching the Indians the mischief and folly of continuing in their barbarous practices, is to teach them the English language.[68]

Supporters of US education policy for Native American youth made their case on a number of different levels. They argued that the older generations of Native Americans could not be "civilized," as they were too old and set in their ways and, therefore, beyond redemption. An agent to the Lakota people stated, "It is a mere waste of time to attempt to teach the average adult Indian the ways of the white man. He can be tamed, and that is about all."[69] The process of "taming" the average adult Native American included prohibiting participation in spiritual ceremonies, often referred to as "heathen ceremonies." Education advocates believed that by educating Native American children, the US could expedite the process of "cultural evolution."[70] Thus, not only did the US prey on the most malleable members of the indigenous groups, but it also targeted the most vulnerable—children.

To these advocates, the goal of "educating" Native American youth was an unadulterated good. As George Tinker asks, "Who can quarrel with education?"[71] After all, writes Tinker, the "Indian residential schools... were the best attempt of the liberal colonizer to advance the state of Indian peoples in North America. Such is the colonizer's apologetic for colonization and rationalization of conquest."[72] The great "benefits" the Native Americans would receive were widely discussed during a series of annual meetings held at Lake Mohonk, New York. US Commissioner of Education William Torey Harris explained that the attributes of civilization included

68 *Cultural genocide*

individualism; ownership of private property; acceptance of Christian doctrine; abandonment of the tribal community; production and consumption of material goods; and belief in the noble accomplishment of man's conquest of nature.[73] While it was believed that all societies could be marked on a continuum denoting their evolution from savagism to civilization, it was also held that the US had attained the zenith of cultural development. Thus, as David Wallace Adams writes,

> Under the proper conditions, that is to say under white tutelage, Indians too might one day become as civilized as their white brothers…From all of this it followed that just as savagism must give way to civilization, so Indian ways must give way to white ways.[74]

Francis Leupp, Commissioner of the Bureau of Indian Affairs from 1904 to 1909, was another believer in the "civilizing" effects of education.[75] As a central element of assimilation policy, Leupp saw education as part of "a mighty pulverizing engine for breaking up the tribal mass."[76]

By the 1920s, there were 77 schools "whose express purpose was the complete assimilation of Native American children, remolding their conception of life and their attitudes toward the land."[77] Charles Burke, one of Leupp's successors at the Bureau of Indian Affairs (1921–1929), stated, "It is not consistent with the general welfare to promote [American Indian national or cultural] characteristics and organization."[78] At boarding schools, tribal religions were suppressed, use of the native tongue was physically punished, and students were taught to read and write English, as well as act and dress like white children.[79] Upon arriving at a boarding school, indigenous children were typically "cleansed" of all Native cultural characteristics that could be removed. They were forced to relinquish their given names, and to answer only to their newly given English names. Long hair was cut and traditional dress was banned.[80] Boarding schools also included Christian indoctrination in the curriculum.[81]

One rationale behind the use of boarding schools was the need to "free" Native American children "from the language and habits of their untutored and often savage parents."[82] Tonya Gonnella Frichner, a former lawyer for the American Indian Law Alliance, aptly summarizes the methods by which boarding schools were used to displace Native American children from their homes, as well as their cultures. Frichner notes,

> The schools were usually located far from tribal communities, so children spent either minimal or no time living at home. The children were in many cases forcefully removed from their homes as early as three years of age and sent to these schools.[83]

Native American children were prohibited from maintaining their customs—compliance being compelled by the threat of corporal punishment. The

Cultural genocide 69

faith-based groups that often administered the schools also sought to "indoctrinate the children with non-native religious views."[84] "In sum," writes Frichner, "these schools were hostile to native ways of life, and the children who attended them were unable to maintain close cultural ties with their native community, causing harm to the children and the communities."[85]

The forced removal of Native American children from their families and their ways of life did not end with boarding school education. Some of the schools employed an "outing system" in which Native American children were transferred from the boarding school to the homes of white families, where they were subjected to further indoctrination in the American way of life. According to an Association on American Indian Affairs study, 25–35 percent of Native American children were transferred to foster care or placed with adoptive families. The number of indigenous children living outside their homes and away from their families was staggering in and of itself, but its extraordinary nature becomes clearer when it is compared to figures for non-indigenous children. On average, indigenous children were placed in foster care or adoptive housing at a rate five to seven times that of non-indigenous children—25–35 percent for indigenous children compared to 5 percent for non-indigenous. In areas where indigenous populations were higher, so too was the comparative rate of transfer into foster and adoptive services. In South Dakota, for example, placement of indigenous children was sixteen times more frequent than for non-indigenous children.[86]

The history of cultural genocide in the US provides an important context, because it was during the late 19th and early 20th centuries that US policy of forcibly transferring Native American children to boarding schools and white families originated. Although the policies were initiated prior to the Genocide Convention's creation, adoption, and entry into force, they continued throughout the drafting of the Genocide Convention and beyond, until the Indian Child Welfare Act was passed in 1978. In 1971, twenty years after the Genocide Convention entered into force, 34,000 indigenous children, representing 17 percent of the total, were still attended boarding schools. "The effect of the situation to indigenous nations, who were losing children by the thousands," writes Frichner, "was essentially cultural genocide."[87] The defunct policy of forcibly relocating Native Americans from their land was also reestablished during a new period of assimilationist policies in the late 1940s, and would continue for decades.[88] For example, in 1956, as part of a series of "Termination Acts," Congress passed Public Law 959, the Relocation Act, to "help adult Indians who reside on or near Indian reservations to obtain reasonable and satisfactory employment" through "vocational training that provides for vocational counseling or guidance, institutional training in any recognized vocation or trade, apprenticeship, and on the job training."[89]

Despite the allegedly noble intentions of Public Law 959, Churchill argues that the real goal was to bring about the permanent alienation of Native Americans from their land. More than "half the entire native population

70 *Cultural genocide*

was dispersed from its own landbase into urban localities where it was mostly subsumed within 'mainstream' society by the 1980s."[90] Churchill also argues that there was a connection between land dislocation and the ways Native American religious lands and shrines have been appropriated:

> As to the disposition of American Indian religious shrines, one need only consider the creation of Mt. Rushmore National Monument and a correspondingly vast tourist industry in the Black Hills—the most sacred geography of the Lakotas, Cheyennes, and other peoples—to get the idea.[91]

State responsibility for violations of international law entails "conduct consisting of an action or omission" that is "attributable to the State under international law" and "constitutes a breach of an international obligation of the State."[92] When responsible for such a violation, states are "under an obligation to make full reparation for the injury caused by the internationally wrongful act."[93] There is no question that indigenous peoples in the US have been victims of cultural genocide. Indigenous youth were forced to attend boarding schools where they were prohibited from practicing their religion and speaking their language, and were required to learn English and dress like white children. Upon their arrival at their boarding school, indigenous children were given new names to which they had to answer. Native American children were also transferred from boarding schools into the homes of white families where the children could be further assimilated into the "American way of life." All these strategies are central to the concept of cultural genocide, whether one uses my definition, Lemkin's, or those included in the Secretariat and Ad Hoc Committee drafts of the Genocide Convention. It is also undeniable that the US is responsible for the Native American cultural genocide. In large part, the acts of cultural genocide originated in US Congressional legislation and were overseen by representatives of the state and those acting on its behalf. This is true of both boarding school administrators and staff, and white families that participated in the outing system.

Conclusion

In June 2015, the Truth and Reconciliation Commission of Canada released the summary of its six-volume report—*Honoring the Truth, Reconciling for the Future.* From its first words, the summary provides a brutally honest assessment of Canada's mistreatment of the land's aboriginal population and its responsibility for it:

> For over a century, the central goals of Canada's Aboriginal policy were to eliminate Aboriginal governments; ignore Aboriginal rights; terminate the Treaties; and, through a process of assimilation, cause

Cultural genocide 71

Aboriginal peoples to cease to exist as distinct legal, social, cultural, religious, and racial entities in Canada. The establishment and operation of residential schools were a central element of this policy, which can best be described as 'cultural genocide.'[94]

The Commission went on to detail specific acts of cultural genocide, including destruction of political and social institutions; land seizure and forcible transfer of populations; restriction of movement; prohibition of the use of their languages and spiritual practices; persecution of spiritual leaders; and disruption and prevention of transmission of cultural values and identity between generations.[95]

The US is similarly responsible for all the described acts. Yet, to this day, the US government has failed to accept state responsibility for the acts committed by the state and on its behalf. According to Lindsay Glauner,

> As parties to the Convention on the Prevention and Punishment of the Crime of Genocide and according to customary international law, the United States is bound by international law to prosecute and extradite the perpetrators of these crimes. Once this task is accomplished, a public apology and reparations must be made to every victim of the genocide in order to facilitate the healing process.[96]

The genocide of Native Americans and Native cultures was ultimately incomplete, not owing to a lack of effort, but due to the perseverance of Native communities. The US ensured the omission of cultural genocide from the Genocide Convention at the same time that it was committing cultural genocide. Yet, genocide scholars often exclude this reality from their studies. Churchill argues that this is no accident. According to Churchill, such constraints allow "virtually every perpetrator regime or society other than the Germans under Hitler to dodge not only the stigma of their history but other potential consequences of their crime(s)."[97] Small wonder, Churchill continues, "that such a truncation and deformation of the definition of genocide has long been a practice embraced enthusiastically and all but universally by the world's ruling elites and the 'responsible' intellectual establishments they sponsor."[98] In-depth analysis of how cultural genocide was excluded from the Genocide Convention, who was primarily responsible, and the context in which it occurred (with the US role preeminent) is largely missing from genocide studies. This is true even in Samantha Power's treatise on the US and genocide, though she dedicates the first four chapters of her book to Raphael Lemkin.

Notes

1 Short defines cultural genocide as "a method of genocide which destroys a social group through the destruction of their culture." Quoted in Damien Short, *Redefining Genocide: Settler Colonialism, Social Death and Ecocide* (London: Zed Books, 2016), 3.

72 Cultural genocide

2 David Nersessian, "Cultural Genocide," *Genocide: A Reader*, ed. Jens Meier-henrich (Oxford: Oxford University Press, 2014), 81.

3 Beth Van Schaack, "The Crime of Political Genocide: Repairing the Genocide Convention's Blind Spot," *The Yale Law Journal* 106, no. 7 (1997): 2268.

4 Raphael Lemkin, "Acts Constituting a General (Transnational) Danger Considered as Offences against the Law of Nations," 1933. Available at www.preventgenocide.org/lemkin/madrid1933-english.htm (last accessed June 22, 2015).

5 Whereas Lemkin associated "acts of vandalism" with cultural genocide, "acts of barbarity" were closely associated with physical genocide. For Lemkin, "barbarity" included "acts of extermination directed against the ethnic, religious or social collectivities whatever the motive (political, religious, etc.)," as well as "all sorts of brutalities which attack the dignity of the individual in cases where these acts of humiliation have their source in a campaign of extermination directed against the collectivity in which the victim is a member." Quoted in Lemkin, "Acts Constituting a General (Transnational) Danger."

6 Ibid.

7 Ibid.

8 Raphael Lemkin, *Axis Rule in Occupied Europe: Laws of Occupation, Analysis of Government, Proposals for Redress* (Washington, DC: Carnegie Endowment for International Peace, 1944), 79.

9 Ward Churchill, "Genocide by Any Other Name: North American Indian Residential Schools in Context," in *Genocide, War Crimes & the West*, ed. Adam Jones (New York: Zed Books, 2004), 80.

10 Quoted in Michael McDonnell and A. Dirk Moses, "Raphael Lemkin as Historian of Genocide in the Americas," *Journal of Genocide Research* 7, no. 4 (2005): 504–505.

11 Quoted in A. Dirk Moses, "Raphael Lemkin, Culture, and the Concept of Genocide," in *The Oxford Handbook of Genocide Studies*, eds. Donald Bloxham and A. Dirk Moses (Oxford: Oxford University Press, 2010), 25.

12 Churchill, "Genocide by Any Other Name," 81.

13 Lemkin, *Axis Rule in Occupied Europe*, 79.

14 Ibid.

15 Ibid.

16 Raphael Lemkin, "Genocide: A Modern Crime," *Free World* (1945): 39.

17 Ibid.

18 Raphael Lemkin, "Genocide," *American Scholar* 15, no. 2 (1946): 228.

19 Ibid.

20 United Nations General Assembly, "The Crime of Genocide," Resolution 96(I), 11 December 1946, http://daccess-dds-ny.un.org/doc/RESOLUTION/GEN/NR0/033/47/IMG/NR003347.pdf?OpenElement (accessed May 1, 2016).

21 Hirad Abtahi and Philippa Webb, *The Genocide Convention: The Travaux Préparatoires* (Leiden: Martinus Nijhoff Publishers, 2008), 11.

22 Matthew Lippman, "The Drafting of the 1948 Convention on the Prevention and Punishment of the Crime of Genocide," *Boston University International Law Journal 3* (1984): 11.

23 Churchill, "Genocide by Any Other Name," 82. Churchill cites R. J. Lifton and Eric Markusen as the source of the phrase "genocidal mentality." See R. J. Lifton and Eric Markusen, *The Genocidal Mentality: Nazi Holocaust and Nuclear Threat* (New York: Basic Books, 1990).

24 Abtahi and Webb, *The Genocide Convention*, 1061.

25 Ibid.

26 William Schabas, *Genocide and International Law: The Crime of Crimes* (Cambridge: Cambridge University Press, 2000), 181.

27 Abtahi and Webb, *The Genocide Convention*, 1504.

Cultural genocide 73

28 Ibid., 727.
29 Ibid., 1514.
30 Ibid.
31 Lippman, "The Drafting of the 1948 Convention," 44.
32 Ibid.
33 Vote cited in Schabas, *Genocide and International Law*, 213.
34 Leo Kuper, *Genocide: Its Political Use in the Twentieth Century* (New Haven: Yale University Press, 1982), 31.
35 Robert Davis and Mark Zannis, *The Genocide Machine in Canada: The Pacification of the North* (Montreal: Black Rose Books, 1983), 30. Jean-Paul Sartre similarly argues that colonization "cannot take place without systematically liquidating all the characteristics of the native society" in *On Genocide* (Boston, MA: Beacon Press, 1968), 63.
36 Johannes Morsink, "Cultural Genocide, the Universal Declaration, and Minority Rights," *Human Rights Quarterly* 21, no. 4 (1999): 1039.
37 Ibid.
38 Nersessian, "Cultural Genocide," 81.
39 Kristina Hon, "Bringing Cultural Genocide in by the Backdoor: Victim Participation at the ICC," *Seton Hall Law Review* 43, no. 1 (2013): 368.
40 Davis and Zannis, *The Genocide Machine*, 20.
41 Matthew Lippman, "The 1948 Convention on the Prevention and Punishment of the Crime of Genocide: Forty-Five Years Later," *Temple International and Comparative Law Journal* 8, no. 1 (1994): 74.
42 Ibid.
43 Nersessian, "Cultural Genocide," 81.
44 Morsink, "Cultural Genocide, the Universal Declaration, and Minority Rights," 1048.
45 Ward Churchill, *A Little Matter of Genocide: Holocaust and Denial in the Americas 1492 to the Present* (San Francisco, CA: City Lights, 1997), 365.
46 Ibid.
47 Shamiran Makos, "Cultural Genocide and Key International Instruments: Framing the Indigenous Experience," *International Journal on Minority and Group Rights* 19 (2012), 177.
48 Richard Peters, *Reports of Cases Argued and Adjudged in The Supreme Court of the United States, January Term 1832* (Philadelphia, PA: James Kay, Jun, & Co., 1832), 520.
49 Rennard Strickland, "The Eagle's Empire: Sovereignty, Survival, and Self-Governance in Native American Law and Constitutionalism," in *Studying Native America: Problems and Prospects*, ed. Russell Thornton (Madison, WI: University of Wisconsin Press, 1998), 258.
50 Grant Foreman, *The Five Civilized Tribes* (Norman, OK: University of Oklahoma Press, 1934), 282.
51 John Cox, *To Kill a People: Genocide in the Twentieth Century* (Oxford: Oxford University Press, 2016), 17.
52 Ibid.
53 Ibid.
54 George E. Tinker, "Tracing a Contour of Colonialism: American Indians and the Trajectory of Educational Imperialism," in *Kill the Indian, Save the Man: The Genocidal Impact of American Indian Residential Schools* (San Francisco, CA: City Light Books, 2004), xiv.
55 Churchill, *A Little Matter of Genocide*, 245.
56 Quoted in Ward Churchill, *Kill the Indian, Save the Man: The Genocidal Impact of American Indian Residential Schools* (San Francisco, CA: City Light Books, 2004), 14.
57 Ibid.

74 *Cultural genocide*

58 James Waller, *Becoming Evil: How Ordinary People Commit Genocide and Mass Killing* (Oxford: Oxford University Press, 2007), 28.
59 Churchill, *Kill the Indian, Save the Man*, 7.
60 United States Department of the Interior, Indian Affairs, "Rule Governing the Court of Indian Offenses" (March 30, 1883).
61 Ibid.
62 Sharon O'Brien, "Federal Indian Policies and the International Protection of Human Rights," in *American Indian Policy in the Twentieth Century,* ed. Vine Deloria, Jr. (Norman, OK: University of Oklahoma Press, 1985), 43.
63 Churchill, *Kill the Indian, Save the Man*, 12.
64 Ibid., 13.
65 Cox, *To Kill a People*, 28.
66 Lindsay Glauner, "The Need for Accountability and Reparations: 1830–1976 the United States Government's Role in the Promotion, Implementation, and Execution of the Crime of Genocide against Native Americans," *DePaul Law Review* 51, no. 9 (2002): 940–941.
67 Ward Churchill, *Kill the Indian, Save the Man*, 13.
68 J. D. C. Atkins, "Barbarous Dialects Should Be Blotted Out," in *Language Loyalties: A Source Book on the Official English Controversy*, ed. James Crawford (Chicago, IL: University of Chicago Press, 1992), 51.
69 Quoted in David Wallace Adams, *Education for Extinction: American Indians and the Boarding School Experience 1875–1928* (Lawrence, KS: University of Kansas Press, 1995), 18.
70 Adams, *Education for Extinction*, 19.
71 Tinker, "Tracing a Contour of Colonialism," xiii.
72 Ibid.
73 Adams, *Education for Extinction*, 15.
74 Ibid., 13.
75 Ibid., 19.
76 United States Department of the Interior, *Thirty-Second Annual Report of the Board of Indian Commissioners to the Secretary of the Interior 1900* (Washington, DC: Government Printing Office, 1901), 29.
77 Eduardo Hernandez-Chavez, "Language Policy in the United States: A History of Cultural Genocide," in *Linguistic Human Rights: Overcoming Linguistic Discrimination*, ed. Tove Skutnabb-Kangas and Robert Phillipson (The Hague: Mouton de Gruyter, 1995), 145.
78 Quoted in Churchill, *A Little Matter of Genocide*, 245.
79 Hernandez-Chavez, "Language Policy in the United States, 145.
80 Glauner, "The Need for Accountability and Reparations," 941–942; Churchill, *Kill the Indian, Save the Man*, 19.
81 Glauner, "The Need for Accountability and Reparations," 942.
82 *United States Department of Interior, Bureau of Indian Affairs, Annual Report of the Commissioner of Indian Affairs to the Secretary of Interior (Washington, DC: U.S. Government Printing Office, 1886),* xxiii.
83 Tonya Gonnella Frichner, "The Indian Child Welfare Act: A National Law Controlling the Welfare of Indigenous Children," *United Nations Department of Economic and Social Affairs*, www.un.org/esa/socdev/unpfii/documents/The%20 Indian%20Child%20Welfare%20Act.v3.pdf (accessed May 21, 2016), 3–4.
84 Ibid.
85 Ibid.
86 Ibid.
87 Ibid., 2.
88 Churchill, *A Little Matter of Genocide*, 248.

89 United States Congress, "An Act Relative to Employment for Certain Adult Indians on or Near Indian Reservations," Public Laws of the Eighty-Fourth Congress, Second Session, Public Law 959. August 3, 1956, available at http:// digital.library.okstate.edu/kappler/Vol6/html_files/v6p0771.html (last accessed July 14, 2014).
90 Churchill, *A Little Matter of Genocide*, 367.
91 Ibid.
92 International Law Commission, Articles on the Responsibility of States for Internationally Wrongful Acts, 2001.
93 Ibid.
94 Truth and Reconciliation Commission of Canada, *Honouring the Truth, Reconciling for the Future: Summary of the Final Report of the Truth and Reconciliation Commission of Canada*, 31 May 2015, 1.
95 Ibid.
96 Glauner, "The Need for Accountability and Reparations," 961.
97 Churchill, "Genocide by Any Other Name," 79.
98 Ibid.

Bibliography

Abtahi, Hirad, and Philippa Webb. *The Genocide Convention: The Travaux Préparatoires*. Leiden: Martinus Nijhoff Publishers, 2008.

Adams, David Wallace. *Education for Extinction: American Indians and the Boarding School Experience 1875–1928*. Lawrence, KS: University of Kansas Press, 1995.

Atkins, J. D. C. "Barbarous Dialects Should Be Blotted Out." In *Language Loyalties: A Source Book on the Official English Controversy*, edited by James Crawford, 51–52. Chicago, IL: University of Chicago Press, 1992.

Churchill, Ward. *A Little Matter of Genocide: Holocaust and Denial in the Americas 1492 to the Present*. San Francisco, CA: City Lights Books, 1997.

Churchill, Ward. "Genocide by Any Other Name: North American Indian Residential Schools in Context." In *Genocide, War Crimes & the West*, edited by Adam Jones, 78–115. London: Zed Books, 2004.

Churchill, Ward. *Kill the Indian, Save the Man: The Genocidal Impact of American Indian Residential Schools*. San Francisco, CA: City Light Books, 2004.

Cox, John. *To Kill a People: Genocide in the Twentieth Century*. Oxford: Oxford University Press, 2016.

Davis, Robert, and Mark Zannis. *The Genocide Machine in Canada: The Pacification of the North*. Montreal: Black Rose Books, 1983.

Foreman, Grant. *The Five Civilized Tribes*. Norman, OK: University of Oklahoma Press, 1934.

Frichner, Tonya Gonnella. "The Indian Child Welfare Act: A National Law Controlling the Welfare of Indigenous Children." *United Nations Department of Economic and Social Affairs*. Accessed May 21, 2016. www.un.org/esa/socdev/unpfii/documents/The%20Indian%20Child%20Welfare%20Act.v3.pdf.

Glauner, Lindsay. "The Need for Accountability and Reparations: 1830–1976 the United States Government's Role in the Promotion, Implementation, and Execution of the Crime of Genocide against Native Americans." *DePaul Law Review* 51, no. 9 (2002): 911–962.

Hernandez-Chavez, Eduardo. "Language Policy in the United States: A History of Cultural Genocide." In *Linguistic Human Rights: Overcoming Linguistic*

76 *Cultural genocide*

Discrimination, edited by Tove Skutnabb-Kangas and Robert Phillipson, 141–158. The Hague: Mouton de Gruyter, 1995.

Hon, Kristina. "Bringing Cultural Genocide in by the Backdoor: Victim Participation at the ICC." *Seton Hall Law Review* 43, no. 1 (2013): 359–407.

Kuper, Leo. *Genocide: Its Political Use in the Twentieth Century.* New Haven, CT: Yale University Press, 1982.

Lemkin, Raphael. "Acts Constituting a General (Transnational) Danger Considered as Offences against the Law of Nations." *Prevent Genocide International.* Accessed June 22, 2015. www.preventgenocide.org/lemkin/madrid1933-english.htm.

Lemkin, Raphael. *Axis Rule in Occupied Europe: Laws of Occupation, Analysis of Government, Proposals for Redress.* Washington, DC: Carnegie Endowment for International Peace, 1944.

Lemkin, Raphael. "Genocide." *American Scholar* 15, no. 2 (1946): 227–230.

Lemkin, Raphael. "Genocide: A Modern Crime." *Free World* (1945): 39.

Lifton, R. J., and Eric Markusen. *The Genocidal Mentality: Nazi Holocaust and Nuclear Threat.* New York: Basic Books, 1990.

Lippman, Matthew. "The 1948 Convention on the Prevention and Punishment of the Crime of Genocide: Forty-Five Years Later." *Temple International and Comparative Law Journal* 8, no. 1 (1994): 1–84.

Lippman, Matthew. "The Drafting of the 1948 Convention on the Prevention and Punishment of the Crime of Genocide." *Boston University International Law Journal* 3 (1984): 1–65.

Makos, Shamiran. "Cultural Genocide and Key International Instruments: Framing the Indigenous Experience." *International Journal on Minority and Group Rights* 19 (2012): 175–194.

McDonnell, Michael, and A. Dirk Moses. "Raphael Lemkin as Historian of Genocide in the Americas." *Journal of Genocide Research* 7, no. 4 (2005): 501–529.

Morsink, Johannes. "Cultural Genocide, the Universal Declaration, and Minority Rights." *Human Rights Quarterly* 21, no. 4 (1999): 1009–1060.

Moses, Dirk A. "Raphael Lemkin, Culture, and the Concept of Genocide." In *The Oxford Handbook of Genocide Studies*, edited by Donald Bloxham and A. Dirk Moses, 19–41. Oxford: Oxford University Press, 2010.

Nersessian, David. "Cultural Genocide." In *Genocide: A Reader*, edited by Jens Meierhenrich, 80–81. Oxford: Oxford University Press, 2014.

O'Brien, Sharon. "Federal Indian Policies and the International Protection of Human Rights." In *American Indian Policy in the Twentieth Century,* edited by Vine Deloria, Jr., 35–62. Norman, OK: University of Oklahoma Press, 1985.

Peters, Richard. *Reports of Cases Argued and Adjudged in The Supreme Court of the United States, January Term 1832.* Philadelphia, PA: James Kay, Jun, & Co., 1832.

Sartre, Jean-Paul Sartre. *On Genocide.* Boston, MA: Beacon Press, 1968.

Schabas, William. *Genocide in International Law: The Crime of Crimes.* Cambridge: Cambridge University Press, 2000.

Short, Damien. *Redefining Genocide: Settler Colonialism, Social Death and Ecocide.* London: Zed Books, 2016.

Strickland, Rennard. "The Eagle's Empire: Sovereignty, Survival, and Self-Governance in Native American Law and Constitutionalism." In *Studying Native America: Problems and Prospects*, edited by Russell Thornton, 247–270. Madison, WI: University of Wisconsin Press, 1998.

Tinker, George. "Tracing a Contour of Colonialism: American Indians and the Trajectory of Educational Imperialism." In *Kill the Indian, Save the Man: The Genocidal Impact of American Indian Residential Schools*, xiii–xli. San Francisco, CA: City Light Books, 2004.

United Nations General Assembly. Resolution 96(I) of 11 December 1946. Accessed May 1, 2016. http://daccess-dds-ny.un.org/doc/RESOLUTION/GEN/NR0/033/47/IMG/NR003347.pdf?OpenElement.

United States Congress. "An Act Relative to Employment for Certain Adult Indians on or Near Indian Reservations." Public Laws of the Eighty-Fourth Congress, Second Session, Public Law 959, August 3, 1956. Accessed March 20, 2016. http://digital.library.okstate.edu/kappler/Vol6/html_files/v6p0771.html.

United States Department of the Interior. *Annual Report of the Commissioner of Indian Affairs to the Secretary of Interior. Washington, DC: U.S. Government Printing Office, 1886.*

United States Department of the Interior. "Rule Governing the Court of Indian Offenses." March 30, 1883.

United States Department of the Interior. *Thirty-Second Annual Report of the Board of Indian Commissioners to the Secretary of the Interior 1900.* Washington, DC: Government Printing Office, 1901.

Van Schaack, Beth. "The Crime of Political Genocide: Repairing the Genocide Convention's Blind Spot." *The Yale Law Journal* 106, no. 7 (1997): 2259–2291.

Waller, James. *Becoming Evil: How Ordinary People Commit Genocide and Mass Killing.* Oxford: Oxford University Press, 2007.

4 Conspiracy to commit genocide in Indonesia

Between 1965 and 1966, the Indonesian Army and its civilian proxies participated in one of the worst episodes of systematic murder in modern human history. Over a six-month period, hundreds of thousands of people who were either members of Indonesia's Communist Party (Partai Komunis Indonesia, PKI), members of groups affiliated with the party, supporters of the party, or perceived to be any of the above, were targeted for death. Hundreds of thousands more were imprisoned, tortured and starved, and deprived of their property.

Douglas Kammen and Katharine McGregor cite two studies that put the number of people killed at 500,000.[1] Benedict Anderson puts the minimum number of people killed at 600,000, with the possibility of upwards of two million deaths.[2] A never-published Indonesian government study concluded that one million people were killed.[3] Hundreds of thousands more were imprisoned for years without trial, often tortured and starved, and deprived of their property.[4] While Indonesia was killing alleged communist members of its population, the US provided Indonesian officials with material and diplomatic support. Among the different means of support, the US systematically compiled a list of as many as 5,000 names of alleged Indonesian Communist leaders, which it delivered to Indonesian officials.

In this chapter, I seek to answer two primary questions. First, did Indonesia commit genocide against its communist citizens? Second, if so, does the US share responsibility with Indonesia due to its commission of any of genocide's ancillary acts? Whether Indonesia committed genocide against members of Indonesia's Communist Party in 1965–1966 depends on whether the victims can be considered members of a protected group and on the intent behind the killings. Whether the US shares responsibility for genocide in Indonesia, then, depends first on whether Indonesia committed genocide, and second on what role, if any, the US played. The remainder of this chapter is divided into three main sections. In the first section, I summarize the events of 1965 and 1966. In the second section, I answer the question of whether Indonesia committed genocide, based on the events and my definition of genocide. Finally, I assess the US relationship with Indonesia at

Conspiracy to commit genocide in Indonesia 79

the time of the atrocities using the Bosnia v. Serbia Precedent to determine whether the US is responsible for any of genocide's ancillary acts.

Mass murder of communists in Indonesia

Prior to the murderous assault on the PKI and its followers, Indonesia was racked with political tension. Before 1957, the PKI was excluded from government office. This changed when President Sukarno suspended parliamentary rule in 1957 and implemented his Guided Democracy program. Guided Democracy was part of a more authoritarian system in which Sukarno sought to construct a political order combining three competing streams in Indonesian politics. As reflected in Sukarno's NASAKOM, these streams included nationalism (NAS), religion (A, agama, the Sanskrit word for religion), and communism (KOM).[5] Though NASAKOM was part of an effort to appease all parties involved in a virtual political standoff, Sukarno attempted to move Indonesia to the left, a move from which the PKI benefited greatly.[6]

With the implementation of Guided Democracy, PKI members began to hold a range of political positions, especially in Java, from mayors of several cities to provincial governors. Over the next few years, PKI membership increased dramatically. By 1965, the PKI had over three million members, the largest number outside of the "Communist world." Additionally, millions more Indonesians were affiliated with the PKI through labor unions and other politically active organizations.[7] In total, the PKI commanded the loyalty of more than twenty million people in a country with a population of 110 million.[8]

Prior to being targeted, the PKI used its growing numbers and increasing influence to support plantation and industrial workers. The PKI sought to enforce legislation, such as the 1959 Crop Sharing Law and the 1960 Basic Agrarian Law, against landlords who failed to comply.[9] PKI efforts in support of the working class placed it at odds with members of the Indonesian Army, whose upper echelons of command were dominated by "developmentalists" hostile to the PKI and its ideology. This hostility intensified when the PKI-affiliated Plantation Workers' Union attempted to seize rubber plantations held by the US Rubber Company in North Sumatra in February 1965.[10]

The Indonesian Army General Staff was essentially divided into two factions—the center and the right. At the center were the generals who had been appointed at the same time as General Yani, and were loyal to him. Though no friend of the PKI, Yani was reluctant to challenge Sukarno's policies and his alliance with the PKI. On the right were the generals, including Generals Nasution and Suharto, who opposed Yani and his tepid support for Sukarno. While all the generals were anti-PKI, support for or opposition to Sukarno was at the heart of the divide.[11]

80 *Conspiracy to commit genocide in Indonesia*

The Indonesian Army became increasingly concerned by the growing assertiveness of the PKI and its supporters. However, according to Anderson, "With its weapons and a powerful grip on important government posts, including cabinet positions, governorships and directorships of state-owned companies, the army was a formidable opponent for the communists."[12] The events of October 1, 1965 gave the Indonesian Army the excuse it sought to systematically eliminate the PKI and its supporters. During the early hours of October 1, a small group of men who were in the Indonesian Army abducted and murdered six high-ranking generals and a lieutenant. The bodies were dumped in a well outside of Halim Perdanakusuma Air Force Base on the outskirts of Jakarta.[13] At 7:15 a.m., national radio in Indonesia read a prepared announcement stating that a self-proclaimed 30 September Movement had acted under the leadership of Lieutenant Colonel Untung, who was the commander of Sukarno's presidential guard, to safeguard President Sukarno against a coup planned by the CIA-backed Council of Generals.[14]

Later the same day, the 30 September Movement announced that it had formed a Revolutionary Council. However, by this point, Suharto, commander of the Army Strategic Reserve, had begun developing plans to initiate counter operations.[15] By the morning of October 2, Suharto, in collaboration with other army officers, had successfully put down the movement and banned all newspapers except those run by the military.[16] Thus, while confusion still reigned surrounding the events of the previous day, Suharto seized control of the flow of information. The army used the sources it controlled to vilify Indonesia's Communist Party by propagating the false story that the PKI-affiliated Indonesian Women's Movement had gouged out the eyes and mutilated the sex organs of the six murdered members of the military.[17] The army called for the PKI and all its affiliates to be banned.

Though available evidence is inconclusive, the PKI is typically cited as responsible for the 30 September Movement.[18] For example, David Schmitz states decisively that "the communist-led September 30 Movement captured and killed six army generals," while also declaring that the murders were part of a "failed coup attempt," even though Untung proclaimed that the 30 September Movement was meant to head off a planned coup against Sukarno.[19] However, Kai Thaler states that the true role of the PKI in the 30 September Movement might never be known, "but most scholars agree that while the PKI might have been peripherally tied to the plotters and some elements of the party expressed support for the group, the party was not responsible for G-30-S."[20] For his part, Robert Cribb supports the possibility of a conspiracy. While he does not dismiss entirely the possibility that the PKI was involved in the plan to remove members of the army's high command, he notes that there exists "inconclusive but not entirely negligible evidence" that the coup was prompted or planned by Suharto and the CIA in order to put the PKI in a compromised position.[21] Either explanation would be consistent with widespread expectations of a coup in the late summer of 1965, whether one carried out by the military or by the PKI.[22]

Conspiracy to commit genocide in Indonesia 81

Regardless which version of the events is closest to the truth, Suharto successfully propagated the claim of the PKI's direct involvement to amplify existing political tensions.[23] Suharto also used the alleged PKI coup attempt to spread rumors of a broader communist plot to torture and murder their "enemies."[24] On October 8, the Indonesian Army published its official account of what happened on October 1. According to the army, Untung's 30 September Movement, which the army rebranded as GESTAPU, had been masterminded by the PKI. Though the acronym GESTAPU is derived from Gerakan September Tiga Puluh, which means "Movement September 30," it is clear in the rearranging of the name that the purpose of the rebranding was to evoke Nazi Germany's Gestapo. Rumors were circulated that PKI members had prepared mass graves disguised as rubbish pits in which to dump the bodies of their opponents. Graphic accounts proliferated of how PKI supporters had been trained to take simple implements, such as rubber-tapping instruments, and turn them into eye-gouging tools.[25] Additionally, rumors flew that the PKI had been compiling lists of non-communists to be killed, contributing to a climate of hostility and fear.[26] Sukarno attempted to challenge the falsehoods, but Suharto and the army had already ensured the dominance of their message, skillfully exploiting rumor and propaganda to thoroughly demonize the PKI and its supporters. As Thaler writes, "Through the media and official statements, the PKI were not only blamed, but systematically dehumanized."[27] Attesting to the success of this propaganda, Thaler quoted a participant in the mass killings who said, "I did not kill people. I killed wild animals."[28]

By the middle of October, Suharto had seized the momentum and used it to effectively take control of the Indonesian Army.[29] Under pressure from Suharto and his allies, Sukarno named Suharto the army's commander. Having gained full control over the army and succeeded in fueling anti-communist rage, Suharto initiated the first in a series of direct actions aimed at destroying the PKI. He ordered troops from the Army Para-Commando Regiment to launch operations against the PKI and its followers, now collectively labeled the "Gestapu-PKI," in Central Java. "Mass killings of Communist Party members and sympathizers commenced."[30] The first wave of killings occurred in Aceh at the end of the first week in October.[31] In an alliance with anti-communists, the army unleashed an assault on the PKI and its supporters. Party members and their supporters were detained, tortured, and massacred. Later, a regional military commander stated approvingly that "due to the quick and appropriate actions of the people, Aceh was the first region to be cleansed" of PKI elements.[32] Central and East Java were next. Toward the end of 1965, the mass killings spread to West Java, North Sumatra, and Bali. By the end of the year, as many as 100,000 people had been killed in Central Java; 200,000 in East Java; 10,000 in West Java; 15,000 in North Sumatra; and 45,000 in Bali.[33]

In most cases, the killings were triggered by the arrival of anti-communist special forces, such as the Army Para-Commando Regiment, or by local

82 *Conspiracy to commit genocide in Indonesia*

armed forces who made clear that the killing of communists was sanctioned.[34] While military units occasionally took part in the killings, local militias were more commonly used. In Indonesia, political parties often had associated youth organizations. The army took advantage of these organizations, primarily Muslim and Christian, whose activities prior to October 1, 1965 included intimidation, protection, and small-scale violence. The army recruited, trained, and armed tens of thousands of civilians, many from the youth organizations, as paramilitary killing squads.[35] According to Sarwo Edhie, the officer in command of anti-communist operations in Java, "We gave them two or three days' training, then sent them out to kill the Communists."[36]

The youth organizations moved from village to village with lists of "guilty" individuals, meaning those identified as PKI party members and affiliates, who were taken away to be executed.[37] In some cases, entire villages were wiped out. Some victims were killed with knives and swords. Others were beaten to death. Bodies were intentionally desecrated, which, for Muslims, is an act that damages the victim's soul. According to Cribb,

> In some cases, the victims were forced to dig their own shallow, mass graves in secluded places, or the bodies were dumped in rivers, or concealed in caves…. In a few cases, the bodies, or body parts, of victims were put on display, sometimes laid out on rafts, which were floated down rivers.[38]

Did Indonesia commit genocide?

My definition of genocide includes national, political, social, ethnic, racial, cultural, and socioeconomic groups as targets. Members of these groups are victims of genocide when a perpetrator kills them or deliberately imposes conditions that are likely to cause their deaths with the purpose of destroying the group as such, or achieving a particular political, social, or economic objective. Therefore, whether Indonesia committed genocide can be determined by answering three additional questions. First, did Indonesia kill members of its population? Second, were the individuals killed members of a protected group? Third, were they killed because of their membership in the group, with the purpose of destroying the group as such or achieving another objective?

The answer to the first question is obvious. Between 1965 and 1966, Indonesia's army and its civilian proxies murdered between 500,000 and one million communists who were either members of the PKI, members of groups affiliated with the PKI, supporters of the PKI, or perceived to be any of the above. Though Sukarno remained president of Indonesia until 1967, Suharto maintained direct control over Indonesia after he ascended to supreme command of the army. Indonesian officials working under Suharto ordered and sanctioned the murder of communists. Thus, the murders are attributable to the state, because individuals in positions of authority within the state apparatus directed or acquiesced to them.

The answer to the second question is also straightforward. The Indonesians murdered were clearly members of a political group. Communism is based on an economic-political philosophy. Those who subscribe to this philosophy share a common political identity based on a specific set of values and beliefs. Official members of the PKI were members of the communist political group. Those affiliated with or openly supporting the PKI were also members of this group. As noted earlier, by 1965, the PKI had over three million members, with millions more affiliated through labor unions and other politically active organizations, and many millions of other loyalists.

Finally, Indonesian communists were murdered to achieve political and economic objectives, as well as with the intent to destroy the communist political group in Indonesia—goals that were intimately connected. PKI ambitions conflicted with those of Indonesia's army leadership. The PKI sought to enforce legislation that benefited the working class, placing it at odds with members of the Indonesian Army, whose upper echelons of command were dominated by "developmentalists." As noted earlier, the army's hostility towards the PKI greatly intensified when the PKI-affiliated Plantation Workers' Union attempted to seize rubber plantations held by the US Rubber Company in North Sumatra in February 1965, jeopardizing foreign investment.

According to Thaler, the PKI in Indonesia "was destroyed as a political force."[39] The architects and perpetrators of the genocide sought to destroy the PKI's ability to function as a political entity and, therefore, its ability to challenge its political opponents. In the process, the Indonesian Army attempted to eliminate as many communists in Indonesia as possible. This is a clear signifier of genocidal intent when committed against a political group. Jason Campbell identifies the following as indicators of intent to commit political genocide: (1) potential victims are reluctant to accept state-endorsed ideology; (2) the state's ideology seeks to eliminate a part of the population within the state's jurisdiction; and (3) refusal to accept the state's ideology is punishable by death or forced emigration.[40] Barbara Harff similarly describes the intent in "politicide" as the "attempt to destroy the ability of opposition groups to challenge or resist the regime by targeting their potential supporters."[41] All these elements are pertinent in the Indonesian case. Indonesia killed a substantial number of people who were members of a political group with the dual purpose of achieving its political and economic objectives, and destroying the group as such in Indonesia. This is genocide.

Does the US share responsibility for genocide in Indonesia?

Whether the US is responsible for any of genocide's ancillary acts depends on multiple factors. In the case of Bosnia v. Serbia, the ICJ issued a number

84 *Conspiracy to commit genocide in Indonesia*

of important rulings. It thereby established precedents regarding what constitutes state responsibility for failure to prevent genocide, complicity in genocide, and conspiracy to commit genocide. Regarding the obligation to prevent genocide, the ICJ asserted that states are required to "employ all means reasonably available to them, so as to prevent genocide so far as possible."[42] Whether such an obligation has been triggered is determined by "the strength of the political, military and financial links" between a state and the perpetrator of genocide.[43] Complicity in genocide is similar to failure to prevent genocide, except that the state maintaining close relations with the perpetrator of genocide must be aware of the perpetrator's intent to commit genocide when providing it with aid or assistance. Importantly, in the case of complicity, a state provides the aid or assistance without necessarily sharing the perpetrator's genocidal intent. Finally, state responsibility for conspiracy to commit genocide requires the participation of a state conspirator that shares the perpetrator's genocidal intent.

What follows is a detailed analysis of the US' relationship with Indonesia and its role in the genocide. It begins with a summary of the US relationship with Indonesia before and during the genocide. Based on this relationship, it addresses three questions: (1) did the US have a responsibility to prevent genocide in Indonesia and, if so, did the US meet its obligation; (2) was the US complicit in genocide; and (3) did the US conspire with Indonesia to commit genocide?

US–Indonesia relations

By the late 1950s, the CIA and Pentagon had forged extensive connections with the Indonesian military.[44] The Indonesian military's officer corps had been largely trained by the US. As much as one-third of the Indonesian General Staff had received some sort of training, while the same can be said for more than half the officer corps. General Nasution had been especially close to the US military. Sarwo Edhie, who stated explicitly that he trained people in how to kill and then unleashed them on communists, was a CIA "asset."[45]

In 1962, the Kennedy administration aided the Indonesian Army in the development of its Civic Mission or "civic action" programs. The State Department recommended the establishment of a special US Military Training Advisory Group to assist in their implementation. A significant portion of the US training and aid was aimed at bolstering the Indonesian Army's connections to civilian administration, cultural organizations, political parties, and youth groups at regional and local levels.[46] These connections would be central to the organizational structure used for the mass killings of communists in 1965 and 1966. Additionally, as Peter Dale Scott notes, the Army also maintained a US ROTC-like group of students trained in paramilitary operations, commanded by a member of the military who had taken a US army intelligence course in Hawaii.[47]

Conspiracy to commit genocide in Indonesia 85

Following the assassination of Kennedy, the Johnson administration gradually cut off economic aid to Indonesia.[48] At the same time, the US shifted its aid to friendly—meaning anti-communist—elements of the Indonesian Army. From 1962 to 1965, the US provided nearly $40 million in military aid, an increase from a little over $28 million during the previous thirteen years. In March 1964, Sukarno told the US to "go to hell with your aid."[49] This actually worked out quite well for the US and public perceptions of its relationship with Indonesia. Some members of US Congress would not support the provision of arms to Indonesia when the Sukarno government was threatening to nationalize US economic interests and using aid from the Soviet Union to challenge the British in Malaysia. Thus, publicly, it appeared as though all aid to Indonesia had stopped. However, Congress had agreed to treat US military aid to Indonesia as a covert matter. This meant that oversight of such aid originating in the Executive Office was limited to two Senate committees and the Speaker of the House, who were also simultaneously involved in CIA oversight.[50]

The State Department viewed the PKI as a threat to US interests in Southeast Asia and, therefore, had an interest in a Suharto victory over the PKI.[51] In multiple internal communications, US officials expressed their belief that destroying communism in Indonesia might be more important than in Vietnam. Unlike Vietnam, the US had substantial economic and strategic interests in Indonesia. As Jonathan Neale notes,

> It was strategically important—the islands of Indonesia lie across the trade routes from Japan, China, and the Pacific to the Indian Ocean. Indonesia was the fifth most populous country in the world. Vietnam mattered for the example it set. Indonesia mattered for itself. Vietnam had rice. Indonesia had oil.[52]

By March 1965, the State Department had decided it was necessary to create conditions in Indonesia that would provoke a confrontation between the Indonesian Army and the PKI, with the army operating from a position of strength.[53] Meanwhile, the CIA proposed covert operations, including "support for existing anti-Communist groups, black letter operations, media operations, including [the] possibility [of] black radio and political action within existing Indonesian institutions and organizations."[54] Notably, US Ambassador to Indonesia Howard Jones stated at a conference that "an unsuccessful coup attempt by the PKI might be the most effective development to start a reversal of political trends in Indonesia."[55]

By the time of the 30 September Movement, the US believed the PKI and its massive support base had to be eliminated as a prerequisite for Indonesia's reintegration into the international political and economic system. With pro-"development" elements, like Suharto, already powerful in the Indonesian Army, the US viewed support for these elements as a logical means to realize its objectives.[56] Following the events of October 2, internal

86 *Conspiracy to commit genocide in Indonesia*

memos reveal that the US was concerned that the Indonesian Army might not take full advantage of the opportunity it was given to destroy the PKI. The cables make clear that the US did not want to see the Indonesian Army limit its response to taking action against those allegedly responsible for the murder of the six generals. According to a US memo, the complete destruction of the PKI could not be achieved unless the Indonesian Army were to "attack communism as such."[57] Thus, the US supported Indonesia "going after Sukarno and the entire PKI apparatus, including unarmed rank-and-file members and affiliates."[58] As Bradley Simpson points out,

> Since no Western intelligence agencies argued that PKI involvement in the September 30th Movement extended to the rank and file, one can only conclude that their greatest fear was that the Army might *refrain* [emphasis in original] from mass violence against the Party's unarmed members and supporters.[59]

An October 1, 1965 memorandum of a telephone conversation between Acting Secretary of State George Ball and Senator William Fulbright shows that Ball believed that if "Nasution takes over he may keep going and clean up the PKI—this is the most optimistic expectation but it is unclear at the moment."[60] By October 2, the Johnson administration was already planning for the resumption of aid to Indonesia that had been cut off due to contentious relations with Sukarno. The Johnson administration also began planning for the provision of covert assistance to the Indonesian Army.[61]

A telegram from the US Embassy in Indonesia to the State Department, dated October 5, 1965, stated that events in Indonesia had placed the PKI and other communist elements on the defensive. The telegram also provided guidelines for how the US should respond. These included:

1 Avoid overt involvement as power struggle unfolds;
2 Covertly, however, indicate clearly to key people in army such as Nasution and Suharto our desire to be of assistance where we can, while at same time conveying to them our assumption that we should avoid appearance of involvement or interference in any way;
3 Maintain and if possible extend our contact with military; and
4 Spread the story of PKI's guilt, treachery and brutality (this priority effort is perhaps most needed immediate assistance we can give army if we can find way to do it without identifying it as solely or largely US effort).[62]

On October 13, in a telegram from the State Department to the embassy in Indonesia, officials described their position as involving a dilemma. The State Department did not want to give the Indonesian Army the impression that the US was trying to interfere in an internal matter "or that we wish to channel army's actions for our—as opposed to Indo's—benefit, or that we are encouraging action against Sukarno or, in fact, anyone except PKI."[63] However, according to the State Department, if the Indonesian Army's "willingness to follow through against PKI is in any way contingent on or subject to influence by US," it was essential that the US takes the opportunity to act.[64] A day later, a telegram from the embassy in Indonesia to the State Department indicated that the embassy was given approval to covertly provide three Motorola P-31 walkie-talkies via an army attaché, in response to a Nasution aide's request to Ambassador Green that portable communications equipment be made available to the Indonesian Army's high command.[65]

An embassy cable to the State Department dated October 20 shows that the US was fully aware that suspected PKI members were being executed. Signed by Ambassador Green, the telegram states that the Indonesian Army was "working hard at destroying PKI and I, for one, have increasing respect for its determination and organization in carrying out this crucial assignment."[66] Additionally, the telegram referred to a separate telegram reporting no evidence that the PKI was planning an insurgency. By the end of October 1965, the embassy in Indonesia had begun receiving reports of widespread killings of, and atrocities against, PKI members and their supporters. On October 29, upon returning from Bandung in West Java, a military adviser reported that PKI members and affiliates were being rounded up and turned over to the army for detention and execution. According to an embassy cable,

> Moslem fervor in Atjeh [Aceh, Sumatra] apparently put all but few PKI out of action. Atjehnese have decapitated PKI and placed their heads on stakes along the road. Bodies of PKI victims reportedly thrown into rivers or sea as Atjehnese refuse 'contaminate Atjeh soil.'[67]

A November 1 telegram from the embassy in Indonesia to the State Department demonstrates that US knowledge progressed from awareness of the killings to awareness of the intent behind them—one it is clear the US shared. In the telegram, Ambassador Green stated that the actions of Indonesia's army in October "foreshadow further major gains" and that Nasution, in tandem with Suharto and other military leaders, "is moving relentlessly to exterminate PKI as far as that is possible to do."[68] On November 4, the embassy informed the State Department that forces under Colonel Edhie's command were training and arming Muslim youth in Central Java. The same cable informed the State Department that the army was arresting and interrogating PKI party leaders, while "smaller fry" were "being systematically arrested and jailed or executed."[69]

By November 8, the embassy had reported that the Indonesian Army, with the help of IP-KI (Association of Supporters of Indonesian Independence) youth organizations, had "continued systematic drive to destroy PKI in northern Sumatra with wholesale killings."[70] An embassy report from

88 *Conspiracy to commit genocide in Indonesia*

November 13 stated that it was informed by a local police chief that "from 50 to 100 PKI members were being killed every night in East and Central Java by civilian anti-Communist troops with blessing of the Army."[71] Another telegram informed the State Department that a missionary in Surabaya had reported 3,500 PKI members killed between November 4 and 9.[72] During this period, the US "conducted wide-ranging secret operations aimed at supporting and encouraging the Army-led slaughter of alleged PKI supporters."[73] On November 9, the CIA completed a paper that assessed the possibility of providing the Indonesian Army with assistance. As John Prados notes, "Its advice was not to avoid involvement but to assess carefully the political direction and longevity of the military leadership, its legal authority, and its de facto control before any overt or readily visible assistance was provided."[74] However, when it came to covert assistance, the CIA warned that US officials

> should avoid being too cynical about [the Army's] motives and its self-interest, or too hesitant about the propriety of extending such assistance *provided* [emphasis in original] we can do so covertly, in a manner which will not embarrass them or embarrass our government.[75]

Reports of the murder of communists would continue into the first few months of 1966. A February 25, 1966 communication from the US embassy reported that in Bali alone, it was estimated that 80,000 PKI members had been killed with "no end in sight."[76] In an April 15 aerogram, the embassy admitted, "We frankly do not know whether the real figure [Indonesia-wide] is closer to 100,000 or 1,000,000 but believe it wiser to err on the side of the lower estimates, especially when questioned by the press."[77]

After the coup and throughout the duration of the genocide, American officials provided Indonesia with vital political and material support. Rather than give the US pause in its support for the Indonesian Army, reports of mass killings led US officials to determine how it could best support the slaughter of communists in Indonesia without being implicated in doing so. According to Simpson,

> The US response to mass murder in Indonesia was enthusiastic. Washington began giving aid to the Army just as the mass killings started. It continued to do so long after it was clear that atrocities on a truly massive scale were being committed—and in the expectation that US assistance would contribute to this end. Not a single official ever expressed concern in public or private about the slaughter.[78]

Simpson's claim was confirmed by Howard Federspiel, a State Department staffer for the Department of Intelligence and Research, who stated: "No one cared as long as they were Communists, that they were being butchered."[79]

Ambassador Marshall Green claims that the "only material assistance we provided of a so-called 'covert' nature was some walkie-talkie equipment and medicines."[80] However, Gabriel Kolko suggests that small arms were transferred to Indonesia, but were "dubbed 'medicines' to prevent embarrassing revelations."[81] This is consistent with the previously detailed CIA recommendations. Additionally, there is evidence that the CIA contributed to the Indonesian Army's highly effective media campaign that incited genocide, by providing the Indonesian Army with support in creating and distributing propaganda about the "PKI's guilt, treachery and brutality."[82]

Perhaps most damning is evidence that the US provided the Indonesian Army with the names of PKI leaders. Following an investigation, journalist Kathy Kadane confirmed that in 1965, US officials systematically compiled a list of as many as 5,000 Indonesian Communist leaders, from the top echelons to village cadres. The names were provided to the Indonesian Army. According to US officials interviewed by Kadane, the US checked off the names of those who had been killed.[83] Robert J. Martens, a former member of the US Embassy in Indonesia's political section, told Kadane,

> It was a really big help to the army. They probably killed a lot of people, and I probably have a lot of blood on my hands, but that's not all bad. There's a time when you have to strike hard at a decisive moment.[84]

Martens headed a group of State Department and CIA officers that spent two years compiling the list, which Martens then delivered to an army intermediary. Obviously proud of the work he did, Martens told Kadane that the people named on the list were largely "captured." According to Martens, "It's a big part of the reason the PKI has never come back."[85] Thus, Kadane concludes, "The U.S. government played a significant role in one of the worst massacres of the century by supplying the names of thousands of Communist Party leaders to the Indonesian army, which hunted down the leftists and killed them."[86]

Did the US uphold its obligation to prevent genocide?

In Bosnia v. Serbia, the ICJ established a three-part test to determine whether Serbia failed to prevent genocide in Bosnia. To find Serbia responsible for a failure to prevent genocide, Bosnia needed to show that Serbia was aware or should have been aware that something like what happened at Srebrenica was possible. Next, Bosnia needed to establish that Serbia wielded the requisite influence necessary to have a direct obligation to prevent genocide. Finally, Bosnia needed to establish that Serbia failed to fulfill its obligation.

The US was unequivocally aware of Indonesia's intent to destroy Indonesia's Communist Party by murdering its members. This is evident in numerous internal memos that discussed the situation. In fact, these same memos offer evidence that the US may have had such an intent even before

90 *Conspiracy to commit genocide in Indonesia*

Indonesian Army officials did. Based on the US' political, financial, and military relationship with Indonesia's army, the US also incurred a clear obligation to prevent genocide. The US developed and maintained relations with members of the Indonesian Army prior to and during the genocide. The US used these relationships to provide the Indonesian Army with material support. Thus, because the US maintained a sufficiently close relationship with Indonesian Army officials to provide them with support, the US thereby incurred an obligation to prevent genocide.

This obligation required that the US employ all means reasonably available to it to prevent genocide in Indonesia to the extent possible. It is clear in US actions before and during the genocide that it did not seek to use its influence to prevent genocide. Instead, it did exactly the opposite: it encouraged the genocide. Recall that a State Department memo stated that "if army's willingness to follow through against PKI is in any way contingent on or subject to influence by US, we do not wish miss opportunity consider US action."[87] Thus, the US is responsible for failing to prevent genocide in Indonesia.

Was the US complicit in Indonesia's genocide?

The ICJ established a two-part test to determine whether Serbia was complicit in the genocide at Srebrenica. As Paolo Palchetti explains,

> In the first place, a state must supply aid and assistance to the perpetrators of the genocide; the second requirement is that the assisting state must have acted in full knowledge of the facts.... Thus, a state incurs responsibility for complicity in genocide only from the moment it supplies aid to the perpetrators in full knowledge that the aid supplied will be used to commit genocide.[88]

Once the Indonesian slaughter began, the US looked for ways to support the army in its efforts. The US covertly provided the army with material support that was used in the commission of genocide. This included walkie-talkies and small arms. As internal memos demonstrate, the US provided this aid fully aware that the army intended to eliminate the PKI and its supporters, and with the knowledge that the aid provided would be used in this manner. This clearly satisfies the two-part test used to determine complicity in genocide. Thus, the US was complicit in Indonesia's genocide.

Did the US conspire with Indonesia to commit genocide?

There is irrefutable evidence that the US provided Indonesia with material support for its genocide, while sharing the intent to commit genocide. Material support included the walkie-talkies and small arms mentioned above, as well as aid in the development and dissemination of propaganda used to

Conspiracy to commit genocide in Indonesia 91

incite genocide. Further, the US supplied Indonesia with a list of approximately 5,000 PKI leaders and cadres. The list was used by the Indonesian army and its proxies to systematically murder communists in Indonesia. The list was also used by the US to keep track of who had been killed, implying that it was provided with the understanding that it would be used for this purpose.

The US was calculated in its efforts to promote the destruction of communism in Indonesia. Internal communications show that the US was aware of the Indonesian army's intent to destroy the PKI, and that the US believed the destruction of communism in Indonesia required the destruction of the PKI and its followers. The US also expressed concern that the Indonesian army might not follow through on the destruction of Indonesia's Communist Party and sought ways to encourage and facilitate its destruction. As Robert Martens declared, there are times "when you have to strike hard at a decisive moment."[89] The US shared Indonesia's intent to commit genocide and provided Indonesia with varied means of aid to facilitate the crime. Thus, the US is responsible for conspiring to commit genocide in Indonesia.

Conclusion

Even without full access to US documents regarding its role in Indonesia's genocide of communists, it is clear the US shares responsibility with Indonesia for the deaths of as many as one million communists, whether actual or alleged. Rather than use its influence over Suharto and the Indonesian army to prevent genocide, the US sought to promote the commission of genocide. Additionally, the US provided Indonesian officials with material support to aid in the commission of genocide, including a list of names used to hunt down and kill individuals. Thus, the US is guilty of failing to prevent genocide, complicity in genocide, and conspiracy to commit genocide.

This conclusion is, or should be, staggering. It raises significant questions regarding why US responsibility for genocide in Indonesia has not received the widespread attention it merits. Most scholars include political groups in their definitions of genocide. In addition, Indonesia and the US acted with the specific intent to commit genocide, meaning a moderated intent requirement is not necessary to recognize the mass slaughter of communists as genocide. Thus, the failure to discuss the role of the US in Indonesia's genocide of communists cannot be explained via reference to scholarly definitions. I cannot help but conclude that the fact that the victims were communists, and that the US conspired to kill them, explains why the genocide receives little attention. As Howard Federspiel explained, "No one cared as long as they were Communists, that they were being butchered."[90]

The failure to critically assess the US relationship with genocide by including cases such as genocide in Indonesia and the US role contributes to the culture of impunity that governs US operations around the world. The US is not merely a bystander to genocide that needs to find the political will

92 *Conspiracy to commit genocide in Indonesia*

and exert the necessary leadership to take preventive action, as Samantha Power, who notably ignores Indonesia's genocide, and others would have us believe. The active US role in Indonesia's genocide shatters the "bystander" myth. The US should be held responsible for its actions in Indonesia, and be required to pay restitution. Further, US officials responsible for conspiring to commit genocide should be prosecuted for their role. There is no statute of limitations to protect those responsible for genocide.

Notes

1 Douglas Kammen and Katharine McGregor, "Introduction: The Contours of Mass Violence in Indonesia, 1965–68," in *The Contours of Mass Violence in Indonesia, 1965–1968*, eds. Douglas Kammen and Katharine McGregor (Honolulu: University of Hawaii Press, 2012), 10.
2 Benedict Anderson, *Violence and the State in Suharto's Indonesia* (Ithaca, NY: Cornell University Press, 2009), 9.
3 Helen Fein, "Revolutionary and Antirevolutionary Genocides: A Comparison of State Murders in Democratic Kampuchea, 1975 to 1979, and in Indonesia, 1965 to 1966," *Comparative Studies in Society and History* 35, no.4 (1993): 802.
4 Anderson, *Violence and the State in Suharto's Indonesia*, 9.
5 Robert Cribb, "Genocide in Indonesia, 1965–1966," *Journal of Genocide Research* 3, no. 2 (2001): 228–229; Kai Thaler, "Foreshadowing Future Slaughter: From the Indonesian Killings of 1965–1966 to the 1974–1999 Genocide in East Timor," *Genocide Studies and Prevention: An International Journal* 7, no. 2 (2012): 205; Vijay Prashad, *The Darker Nations: A People's History of the Third World* (New York: The New Press, 2007), 152.
6 Thaler, "Foreshadowing Future Slaughter," 205.
7 Anderson, *Violence and the State in Suharto's Indonesia*, 16.
8 Prashad, *The Darker Nations*, 153.
9 Kammen and McGregor, "Introduction," 112.
10 Bradley Simpson, "International Dimensions of the 1965–1968 Violence in Indonesia," in *The Contours of Mass Violence in Indonesia, 1965–1968*, eds. Douglas Kammen and Katharine McGregor (Honolulu: University of Hawaii Press, 2012), 54.
11 Harold Crouch, *The Army and Politics in Indonesia* (Ithaca, NY: Cornell University Press, 1978), 80.
12 Anderson, *Violence and the State in Suharto's Indonesia*, 229.
13 Kammen and McGregor, "Introduction," 35.
14 Ibid., Cribb, "Genocide in Indonesia, 1965–1966," 231; Thaler, "Foreshadowing Future Slaughter," 206; Fein, "Revolutionary and Antirevolutionary Genocides," 801.
15 Thaler, "Foreshadowing Future Slaughter," 206.
16 Kammen and McGregor, "Introduction," 29.
17 Ibid., 30; Thaler, "Foreshadowing Future Slaughter," 206.
18 Fein, "Revolutionary and Antirevolutionary Genocides," 801.
19 David F. Schmitz, *The United States and Right-Wing Dictatorships, 1965–1989* (Cambridge: Cambridge University Press, 2006), 2–3.
20 Thaler, "Foreshadowing Future Slaughter," 206.
21 Cribb, "Genocide in Indonesia, 1965–1966," 232.
22 Fein, "Revolutionary and Antirevolutionary Genocides," 800.
23 Thaler, "Foreshadowing Future Slaughter," 208.
24 Cribb, "Genocide in Indonesia, 1965–1966," 232.

Conspiracy to commit genocide in Indonesia 93

25 Ibid.
26 Thaler, "Foreshadowing Future Slaughter," 207.
27 Ibid., 206.
28 Ibid.
29 Fein, "Revolutionary and Antirevolutionary Genocides," 802.
30 Kammen and McGregor, "Introduction," 2.
31 Ibid.; Cribb, "Genocide in Indonesia, 1965–1966," 233; Thaler, "Foreshadowing Future Slaughter," 207.
32 Crouch, *The Army and Politics in Indonesia*, 143.
33 Kammen and McGregor, "Introduction," 18–19.
34 Cribb, "Genocide in Indonesia, 1965–1966," 233.
35 Ibid.; Thaler, "Foreshadowing Future Slaughter," 207.
36 Quoted in Thaler, "Foreshadowing Future Slaughter," 207.
37 Prashad, *The Darker Nations*, 155.
38 Cribb, "Genocide in Indonesia, 1965–1966," 233.
39 Thaler, "Foreshadowing Future Slaughter," 210.
40 Jason Campbell, *On the Nature of Genocidal Intent* (Lanham, MD: Lexington Books, 2013), 7.
41 Barbara Harff, "No Lessons Learned from the Holocaust? Assessing Risks of Genocide and Political Mass Murder since 1955," *American Political Science Review* 97, no. 1 (2003): 59.
42 International Court of Justice, Summary of the Judgment of 26 February 2007, 221.
43 Ibid., 223.
44 Noam Chomsky, and Edward S. Herman, *The Washington Connection and Third World Fascism: The Political Economy of Human Rights: Volume 1* (Boston, MA: South End Press, 1979), 154.
45 Ibid., 207.
46 Ulf Sundhaussen, *The Road to Power: Indonesian Military Politics, 1945–1967* (Oxford: Oxford University Press, 1982), 141.
47 Peter Dale Scott, "The United States and the Overthrow of Sukarno, 1965–1967," *Pacific Affairs* 58, no. 2 (1985): 249.
48 Ibid., 253.
49 Quoted in Scott, "The United States and the Overthrow of Sukarno," 253.
50 Ibid.
51 Fein, "Revolutionary and Antirevolutionary Genocides," 803.
52 Jonathan Neale, *A People's History of the Vietnam War* (New York: The New Press, 2003), 71.
53 Edward C. Keefer, ed. "Sukarno's Confrontation with the United States: December 1964-September 1965," in *Foreign Relations of the United States, 1964–1968, Volume XXVI, Indonesia; Malaysia-Singapore; Philippines* (Washington, DC: United States Government Printing Office, 2000). Available http://nsarchive. gwu.edu/NSAEBB/NSAEBB52/doc189.pdf (accessed July 1, 2016), 235.
54 Ibid.
55 Quoted in Simpson, "International Dimensions of the 1965–1968 Violence in Indonesia," 56.
56 Ibid.
57 Edward C. Keefer, ed. "Coup and Counter Reaction: October 1965-March 1966," in *Foreign Relations of the United States, 1964–1968, Volume XXVI, Indonesia; Malaysia-Singapore; Philippines* (Washington, DC: United States Government Printing Office, 2000), 330. http://nsarchive.gwu.edu/NSAEBB/NSAEBB52/ doc300.pdf (accessed July 1, 2016).
58 Simpson, "International Dimensions of the 1965–1968 Violence in Indonesia," 57–58.

94 *Conspiracy to commit genocide in Indonesia*

59 Ibid.
60 Keefer, ed. "Coup and Counter Reaction," 302–303.
61 Simpson, "International Dimensions of the 1965–1968 Violence in Indonesia," 60.
62 Keefer, ed. "Coup and Counter Reaction," 307–308.
63 Ibid., 320.
64 Ibid.
65 Ibid.
66 Ibid., 330.
67 Ibid., 338.
68 Ibid., 346.
69 Ibid., 354.
70 Ibid., 338.
71 Ibid., 339.
72 Ibid.
73 Simpson, "International Dimensions of the 1965–1968 Violence in Indonesia," 51.
74 John Prados, *Lost Crusader: The Secret Wars of CIA Director William Colby* (Oxford: Oxford University Press, 2003), 154.
75 Keefer, ed. "Coup and Counter Reaction," 362.
76 Ibid., 339.
77 Ibid.
78 Simpson, "International Dimensions of the 1965–1968 Violence in Indonesia," 62.
79 Quoted in William Blum, *Killing Hope: US Military & CIA Interventions since World War II* (London: Zed Books, 2003), 194.
80 Marshall Green, *Indonesia: Crisis and Transformation, 1965–1968* (Washington, DC: The Compass Press, 1990), 69.
81 Gabriel Kolko, *Confronting the Third World: United States Foreign Policy, 1945–1980* (New York: Pantheon Books, 1988), 181.
82 Keefer, ed. "Coup and Counter Reaction," 308.
83 Kathy Kadane, "Ex-Agents say CIA Compiled Death Lists for Indonesians," *San Francisco Examiner*, May 20, 1990. www.namebase.net/kadane.html (accessed December 2, 2015).
84 Ibid.
85 Ibid.
86 Kathy Kadane, "U.S. Accused of Role in Massacres," *Chicago Tribune*, May 23, 1990. http://articles.chicagotribune.com/1990-05-23/news/9002120274_1_pki-central-intelligence-agency-officials-cia-spokesman-mark-mansfield (accessed July 1, 2016).
87 Ibid.
88 Paolo Palchetti, "State Responsibility for Complicity in Genocide," in *The UN Genocide Convention: A Commentary*, ed. Paola Gaeta (Oxford: Oxford University Press, 2009), 391.
89 Kadane, "Ex-Agents say CIA Compiled Death Lists for Indonesians."
90 Quoted in Blum, *Killing Hope*, 194.

Bibliography

Anderson, Benedict. *Violence and the State in Suharto's Indonesia*. Ithaca, NY: Cornell University Press, 2009.

Blum, William. *Killing Hope: US Military & CIA Interventions since World War II*. London: Zed Books, 2003.

Campbell, Jason. *On the Nature of Genocidal Intent*. Lanham, MD: Lexington Books, 2013.

Chomsky, Noam, and Edward S. Herman. *The Washington Connection and Third World Fascism: The Political Economy of Human Rights: Volume 1.* Boston: South End Press, 1979.

Cribb, Robert. "Genocide in Indonesia, 1965–1966." *Journal of Genocide Research* 3, no. 2 (2001): 219–239.

Crouch, Harold. *The Army and Politics in Indonesia.* Ithaca, NY: Cornell University Press, 1978.

Fein, Helen. "Revolutionary and Antirevolutionary Genocides: A Comparison of State Murders in Democratic Kampuchea, 1975 to 1979, and in Indonesia, 1965 to 1966." *Comparative Studies in Society and History* 35, no.4 (1993): 796–823.

Green, Marshall. *Indonesia: Crisis and Transformation, 1965–1968.* Washington, DC: The Compass Press, 1990.

Harff, Barbara. "No Lessons Learned from the Holocaust? Assessing Risks of Genocide and Political Mass Murder since 1955." *American Political Science Review* 97, no. 1 (2003): 57–73.

International Court of Justice. Summary of the Judgment of 26 February 2007.

Kadane, Kathy. "Ex-Agents Say CIA Compiled Death Lists for Indonesians." *San Francisco Examiner.* Accessed December 2, 2015. www.namebase.net/kadane.html.

Kadane, Kathy. "U.S. Accused of Role in Massacres." *Chicago Tribune*, May 23, 1990.

Kammen, Douglas, and Katharine McGregor. "Introduction: The Contours of Mass Violence in Indonesia, 1965–68." In *The Contours of Mass Violence in Indonesia, 1965–1968*, edited by Douglas Kammen and Katharine McGregor, 1–24. Honolulu: University of Hawaii Press, 2012.

Keefer, Edward C. "Coup and Counter Reaction: October 1965-March 1966." In *Foreign Relations of the United States, 1964–1968, Volume XXVI, Indonesia; Malaysia-Singapore; Philippines.* Washington, DC: United States Government Printing Office, 2000.

Keefer, Edward C. "Sukarno's Confrontation with the United States: December 1964-September 1965." In *Foreign Relations of the United States, 1964–1968, Volume XXVI, Indonesia; Malaysia-Singapore; Philippines.* Washington, DC: United States Government Printing Office, 2000.

Kolko, Gabriel. *Confronting the Third World: United States Foreign Policy, 1945–1980.* New York: Pantheon Books, 1988.

Neale, Jonathan. *A People's History of the Vietnam War.* New York: The New Press, 2003.

Palchetti, Paolo. "State Responsibility for Complicity in Genocide." In *The UN Genocide Convention: A Commentary*, edited by Paola Gaeta, 381–395. Oxford: Oxford University Press, 2009.

Prados, John. *Lost Crusader: The Secret Wars of CIA Director William Colby.* Oxford: Oxford University Press, 2003.

Prashad, Vijay. *The Darker Nations: A People's History of the Third World.* New York: The New Press, 2007.

Schmitz, David F. *The United States and Right-Wing Dictatorships, 1965–1989.* Cambridge: Cambridge University Press, 2006.

Scott, Peter Dale. "The United States and the Overthrow of Sukarno, 1965–1967." *Pacific Affairs* 58, no. 2 (1985): 239–264.

96 *Conspiracy to commit genocide in Indonesia*

Simpson, Bradley. "International Dimensions of the 1965–1968 Violence in Indonesia." In *The Contours of Mass Violence in Indonesia, 1965–1968*, edited by Douglas Kammen and Katharine McGregor, 50–74. Honolulu: University of Hawaii Press, 2012.

Sundhaussen, Ulf. *The Road to Power: Indonesian Military Politics, 1945–1967.* Oxford: Oxford University Press, 1982.

Thaler, Kai. "Foreshadowing Future Slaughter: From the Indonesian Killings of 1965–1966 to the 1974–1999 Genocide in East Timor." *Genocide Studies and Prevention: An International Journal* 7, no. 2 (2012): 204–222.

5   Complicity in genocide in Bangladesh and Guatemala

In 1970, Pakistan held its first-ever general elections. They were contentious, with the Awami League, based in East Pakistan (present-day Bangladesh), campaigning on a Six-Point Program seeking maximum autonomy for the East.[1] The Awami League won 167 of 313 seats in Pakistan's National Assembly, becoming the majority party. Yahya Khan, Pakistan's President and Chief Martial Law Administrator, viewed the Awami League's electoral victory as a threat to Pakistan's territorial integrity, and decided to postpone the seating of the National Assembly indefinitely.[2]

During negotiations, Pakistan mobilized its forces in the East. Meanwhile, East Pakistan's call for regional autonomy evolved into a call for full independence following Pakistan's refusal to seat the National Assembly. On March 23, 1971, Sheik Mujibur Rahman, the leader of the Awami League, issued a "Declaration of Emancipation."[3] On March 25, only two days later, Pakistan launched 'Operation Searchlight,' a massive military assault on the East's capital city of Dacca.[4] Rahman accused President Khan of preplanning the "reign of terror." President Khan used this accusation as grounds for charging Rahman with treason, banning the Awami League, and suspending all talks.[5]

From March 1971 to December 1971, Pakistan conducted military operations in East Pakistan, killing between 250,000 and one million people, raping hundreds of thousands of women and girls, and forcing another ten million people to seek refuge in India.[6] The ten million refugees who were able to escape the violence faced "conditions of extreme hardship...with an appalling death rate."[7] Archer Blood, US Consul General in Dacca, described the violence as "a reign of terror by the Pak military" that involved the systematic elimination of Awami League supporters "by seeking them out in their homes and shooting them down."[8] After nine months of fighting, India's unilateral intervention in East Pakistan ended the military campaign and pushed back Pakistani forces. Pakistan surrendered in less than two weeks, signing the Instrument of Surrender on December 16, 1971, in Dacca.

In its attacks on the people of East Pakistan, Pakistan's military murdered individuals who were members of a political group—Awami League

98 *Genocide in Bangladesh and Guatemala*

supporters—an ethno-linguistic group—Bengalis—and a cultural-religious group—Hindus. Hindus, who made up approximately 23 percent of East Pakistan's population at the time, were targeted in particular.[9] President Khan alleged that the Awami League's success in the 1970 elections was attributable to Hindus and their "sinister purposes," even though the Hindu community alone could not have swung the elections.[10] Hindus were also disproportionately represented in the refugee flow to India—accounting for an estimated 80 percent of the refugees.[11]

All three types of groups are included in my definition of genocide, as well as many other scholarly definitions. It is less clear whether Pakistan committed its atrocities with the specific intent to destroy the Bengali ethnic group and/or the Hindu religious group as such in Pakistan. However, Pakistan did intend to destroy the Awami League and its supporters as a viable political group. Pakistan also sought to achieve a range of political objectives—voiding the 1970 election results, maintaining control of the National Assembly, and denying the people of East Pakistan their right to self-determination. Thus, Pakistan's mass murder of real and perceived Awami League supporters represents an attempt to destroy the ability of a political group to resist its subjugation.[12] Pakistan killed a substantial number of people who were members of a political group, as well as ethnic and religious groups, with the dual purpose of achieving its political objectives. Therefore, I conclude that Pakistan committed genocide.

There is also general agreement among scholars that the crimes committed by Pakistan amounted to genocide.[13] Additionally, in 1972, the International Commission of Jurists, an international nongovernmental organization based in Geneva, released a report concluding that Pakistan committed genocide in East Pakistan. The report was the result of an inquiry into suspected violations of human rights and the rule of law. The International Commission of Jurists described the acts perpetrated by Pakistan's military as

> the indiscriminate killing of civilians, including women and children and the poorest and weakest members of the community; the attempt to exterminate or drive out of the country a large part of the Hindu population; the raping of women; the destruction of villages and towns; and the looting of property. All this was done on a scale which is difficult to comprehend.[14]

The Commission concluded there was "a strong prima facie case that the crime of genocide was committed against the group comprising the Hindu population of East Bengal."[15]

As with Pakistan's genocide in East Pakistan, there is general agreement among scholars that Guatemala committed genocide against members of its Mayan population between 1979 and 1983.[16] Other authorities agree. On June 23, 1994, the Commission for Historical Clarification (CEH) was created through the Accord of Oslo with a mandate to "clarify with objectivity, equity and impartiality, the human rights violations and acts of violence connected with the armed confrontation that caused human suffering among the Guatemalan people."[17] In 1999, the CEH issued its report, "Guatemala Memory of Silence," finding that acts of genocide were committed against Guatemala's indigenous Mayan communities. Though violence against the Mayan population would continue, the genocide ended with the ousting of President Efraín Ríos Montt by General Óscar Humberto Mejía Victores in a coup in August 1983.

During Guatemala's civil war, which began in 1962 and ended in 1996, the Guatemalan army killed or "disappeared" more than 200,000 people, 83 percent of whom were Mayan. The genocide began under Fernando Romeo Lucas García and peaked following Ríos Montt's military coup in March 1982.[18] Of the 200,000 people killed throughout the duration of the civil war, more than 100,000 were killed between 1981 and 1983.[19] Upwards of 80,000 of those were killed during Ríos Montt's eighteen months in office.[20]

According to Jens Meierhenrich, "the escalation of the counterinsurgency campaign was a major impetus behind the coup d'état of March 1982."[21] A few months after the coup, on July 8, Ríos Montt's Army Chief of Staff, Héctor Mario López Fuentes, issued the order to launch Operation Sofía.[22] This was part of a "scorched earth campaign" that sought to eliminate anti-government rebels by physically destroying the civilian areas in which they found refuge. As part of this campaign, dwellings were destroyed, crops burned, livestock slaughtered, water supplies poisoned, and cultural symbols desecrated and destroyed. In this way, the genocide in Guatemala closely resembles Raphael Lemkin's original conception of genocide. The perpetrators attacked not only the physical integrity of Guatemala's Mayan population, but also its cultural existence.

In four specific geographic areas, the CEH confirmed that between 1981 and 1983, the Guatemalan military identified the Mayan population as "enemies of the state" and a support base for the rebels. "In this way," according to the CEH, "the Army, inspired by the National Security Doctrine, defined a concept of internal enemy that went beyond guerilla sympathizers, combatants or militants to include civilians from specific ethnic groups."[23] Relatedly, the CEH found that Guatemala deliberately exaggerated both the threat that the leftist rebel insurgency posed to the state and the relationship that existed between Mayan communities and the rebels. According to the CEH,

> The consequence of this manipulation...was massive and indiscriminate aggression directed against communities independent of their actual involvement in the guerilla movement.... The massacres, scorched earth operations, forced disappearances and executions...were not only an attempt to destroy the social base of the guerillas, but above all, to destroy the cultural values that ensured cohesion and collective action in Mayan communities.[24]

100 *Genocide in Bangladesh and Guatemala*

The intensity of the violence against Mayan communities was in part motivated by racism. The CEH found that this was a source of the indiscriminate and brutal nature of the violence, including that carried out against women and children. Children were tortured, raped, and executed. The CEH found that women accounted for approximately one-quarter of the victims. Like children, women were tortured, raped, and executed, sometimes in massacres.[25] Greg Grandin notes,

> Between 1981 and 1983, the Guatemalan anti-Communist army and its right-wing paramilitary allies executed...Mayan peasants so unlucky as to live in a region identified as the seedbed of a Leftist insurgency. The killing was savage, markedly more brutal than similar repressive campaigns conducted elsewhere in Latin America during the same period.[26]

The CEH documented 626 massacres attributable to government forces. Some of these massacres "resulted in the complete extermination of many Mayan communities."[27] The CEH found that Guatemala was responsible for killing members of the Mayan ethnic group, causing serious bodily and mental harm to group members, and deliberately subjecting them to living conditions calculated to bring about the group's physical destruction in whole or in part. Further, the CEH determined that "all these acts were committed 'with the intent to destroy in whole or in part' groups identified by their common ethnicity, by reason thereof, whatever the cause, motive or final objective of these acts may have been."[28] Thus, according to the CEH, Guatemala, "committed acts of genocide against groups of Mayan people which lived in the four regions analyzed."[29] Adam Jones describes the Guatemalan genocide as "probably the worst holocaust unleashed in the Americas in the twentieth century."[30]

The genocides in East Pakistan and Guatemala were chosen for analysis because the US maintained close relations with the governments of each state at the time genocide was committed. In Bosnia v. Serbia, the ICJ emphasized the role external support can play in facilitating the crime of genocide. The ICJ concluded that Serbia "was making its considerable military and financial support available to the Republika Srpska, and had it withdrawn that support, this would have greatly constrained the options that were available to the Republika Srpska authorities."[31] In other words, genocidal governments would find it far more difficult to commit genocide without some level of support from their more powerful benefactors, whether in the form of political, economic, or military aid.

As in the previous chapter on Indonesia, I seek to determine here whether the US is responsible for any of genocide's ancillary crimes in Pakistan and Guatemala. In both cases, I limit my analysis to state responsibility for the ancillary crimes of failure to prevent genocide and complicity in genocide, because there is a lack of publicly available evidence that would implicate the US in a conspiracy to commit genocide. In order to avoid redundancies

Genocide in Bangladesh and Guatemala 101

later, I will briefly reiterate the Bosnia v. Serbia Precedent regarding failure to prevent genocide and complicity in genocide, which will be applied to both the Pakistan and Guatemala cases. Determining failure to prevent genocide involves a three-part test that includes the following questions. In each case, was the US aware or should it have been aware of the violence being perpetrated? If so, did the US wield the requisite influence necessary to have a direct obligation to prevent genocide? Finally, did the US fail to fulfill its obligation? Meanwhile, complicity in genocide is determined by a two-part test. Did the US provide military, economic, or political support that aided in the commission of genocide? If so, was the US aware of the perpetrator's intent to commit genocide? In the remainder of this chapter, I assess the US relationship with Pakistan and Guatemala while they were committing genocide to determine whether the US shares responsibility.

The US role in Pakistan's genocide

The US maintained close relations with Pakistan prior to and throughout the genocide. Pakistan's "eager military subservience to Washington" made it an appealing client state in the region.[32] Just before the 1970 elections, the US announced its decision to sell to Pakistan $50 million worth of replacement parts for its aircraft and as many as 300 armed personnel carriers.[33] Stephen Cohen refers to the generation of officers entering the middle ranks of the Pakistani military in 1971 as the "American generation," because the US arms relationship with Pakistan allowed the Pakistani military to expand its capabilities while limiting its recruitment of officers to a small section of the Pakistani population.[34]

Nixon's decision to ensure the flow of arms to Pakistan was key to his administration's policy.[35] In addition to military weaponry, equipment, and training, the US also exposed Pakistan to American military doctrines.[36] Kissinger and Nixon were committed to "opening up" the People's Republic of China. The maintenance of US military and diplomatic support for Pakistan had roots in its desire to demonstrate its commitment to the newly blossoming relationship with China.[37] Early maneuvers to pursue a US–China rapprochement were kept secret. G.W. Choudhury, a member of Pakistan's cabinet from 1967 to 1971, wrote that "Nixon gave Yahya the special assignment to act as 'courier' between Washington and Peking—an assignment which the latter carried out with the utmost secrecy and conscientiousness."[38] As a reward for Pakistan's role in opening US–China relations, Kissinger agreed to treat the political turmoil and the atrocities in Pakistan as an "internal affair."[39] At the peak of the atrocities, Kissinger is alleged to have sent President Khan a note thanking him for his "delicacy and tact."[40]

During the genocide, the US provided Pakistan with material support. The US supplied $3.8 million in military equipment after Pakistan began the genocide in March 1971.[41] Pakistan also used American tanks, fighter

102   *Genocide in Bangladesh and Guatemala*

jets, jeeps, and munitions during its assault on East Pakistan.[42] While providing its support, the Nixon administration was fully aware that Pakistan was committing atrocities and that it was using US military equipment to commit them, as well as the intentions behind them.

Under the direction of Archer Blood, US Consul General, the Consulate in Dacca "documented in horrific detail the slaughter of Bengali civilians."[43] On March 28, only three days after the onslaught began, Blood sent a cable to Washington with the subject line: "Selective Genocide." In it he wrote, "Here in Dacca we are mute and horrified witnesses to a reign of terror by the Pak military."[44] Blood warned the US that there was evidence that the Pakistani military was "systematically eliminating" Awami League supporters "by seeking them out in their homes and shooting them down."[45] He added that the murderous rampage could not be justified by claims of military necessity, because there was "no resistance being offered in Dacca to military."[46] Death squads, using prepared lists of targets, killed as many as 7,000 people the first night and 30,000 during the first week.[47]

On April 6, having not yet received a response to his previous cable, Blood sent to Washington what would become known as the "Blood Telegram." In it, he wrote:

> Our government has failed to denounce atrocities. Our government has failed to take forceful measures...while at the same time bending over backwards to placate the West Pak[istan] dominated government...Our government has evidenced what many will consider moral bankruptcy, ironically at a time when the USSR sent President Yahya Khan a message defending democracy, condemning the arrest of a leader of a democratically elected majority party incidentally pro-West, and calling for an end to repressive measures and bloodshed....But we have chosen not to intervene, even morally, on the grounds that the Awami conflict, in which unfortunately the overworked term genocide is applicable, is purely an internal matter of a sovereign state.[48]

By September 22, the CIA reported in a memorandum that

> some 200,000 or more residents of the area [East Pakistan] have been killed, and the area has seen one of the largest and most rapid population transfers in modern times. Since March 1971, over 8 million of the 76 million East Pakistanis have fled to India, and this movement continues.[49]

A little over a month later, on November 4, Senator Muskie pointed out that "American tanks, planes and guns have been used to help level un-protected cities and to kill an estimated 200,000 unarmed civilians."[50] Nonetheless, as Blood had charged, the Nixon administration continued to support Pakistan and treat its genocide as an internal matter.

Genocide in Bangladesh and Guatemala 103

In response to the atrocities, massive flow of refugees into India, and increasing calls for intervention, India unilaterally invaded East Pakistan in December.[51] India's intervention instigated something that eight months of genocide did not—a Security Council meeting to discuss events in East Pakistan. Significantly, the US used its influence as a permanent member of the Security Council to provide Pakistan with diplomatic cover in an attempt to impede India's intervention in the genocide. At the first meeting on December 4, the US put on display its unwavering support for Pakistan. The US called for a political solution without demanding that Pakistan end its genocidal campaign or respect the results of the 1970 elections. Instead, the US called for the "immediate cessation of hostilities and the withdrawal of forces" from foreign territories.[52] These demands were further articulated in a US draft resolution, which failed to pass due to a Soviet veto. The draft called upon India and Pakistan to agree to an immediate ceasefire and to withdraw "armed personnel present on the territory of the other to their own side of the India-Pakistan borders."[53]

The US proposal would have forced India to withdraw, while allowing Pakistan to maintain its presence, as East Pakistan was still a recognized part of Pakistan. India rightfully argued that such a requirement would only aid Pakistan in its violent repression of the population of East Pakistan. India proclaimed, "A cease-fire between whom and whom? Shall we release the Pakistan soldiers by a so-called cease-fire so that they can go on a rampage and kill the civilians in Dacca, in Chittagong, and in other places?"[54] India also questioned where all of the newfound concern for saving lives was nine months previously, when Pakistan launched its operations in East Pakistan. Perhaps most significantly, India argued that the motivation of some parties, including the US and China, was to divert attention from Pakistan's genocide in East Pakistan:

> Then there was a great hue and cry to internationalize the problem: diplomatic moves...designed to make it into an Indo-Pakistan dispute. Once it turned into an Indo-Pakistan dispute, people will forget what the Pakistan army is doing in East Pakistan. They can go on burning their villages and raping their women and so on.[55]

The debate continued on December 6. India asked the members of the Security Council why they were not paying attention to "Pakistan's campaign of genocide."[56] It also accused some members of the Security Council of the selective use of international norms to protect their interests. India stated, "This debate has shown that selectivity is the order of the day. Now, several principles have been quoted by various delegations: sovereignty, territorial integrity, noninterference in other peoples' affairs, and so on...What happened to the Convention on genocide?"[57] In response, the US continued its effort to provide Pakistan with political cover, claiming it was not taking sides in the conflict. The US added, "But

104 *Genocide in Bangladesh and Guatemala*

if they say that we insist that these invading forces go back to their own borders, they are correct."[58] The US sought to support its claim to neutrality by insisting that both India and Pakistan withdraw their forces from foreign territories. Yet, as already noted, the withdrawal of forces only from foreign territories would have meant that Pakistan would have been able to keep its forces—those responsible for the genocide—in East Pakistan free of India's intervention. Therefore, the US claims of neutrality and commitment to a political solution were not consistent with its proposed solution to the conflict.

On December 12, the US finally recognized the violence perpetrated by Pakistan in East Pakistan, but only acknowledged the first week of the violence beginning on March 25. The US stated, "We regretted that action, and we took measures promptly to stop certain military and economic aid that was going to Pakistan."[59] Further, according to the US,

> The fact that the use of force in East Pakistan in March can be characterized as a tragic mistake does not, however, justify the actions of India in intervening militarily and placing in jeopardy the territorial integrity and political independence of its neighbor Pakistan.[60]

As has been shown, the US was fully aware that the violence was not limited to a single week. The US also retained some elements of its military aid to Pakistan thereafter.

At the final Security Council meeting on December 13, the US maintained its position that a political solution was required, along with a ceasefire and the withdrawal of all forces from foreign territories. The US submitted another draft resolution with these demands incorporated. It was once again defeated. Meanwhile, the Soviet Union reiterated its call for a political settlement to the conflict based on the results of the December 1970 elections, which it argued would also end India's need to intervene. Additionally, the Soviet Union condemned the US for

> continuing to grant military aid to Pakistan throughout the many months during which the crisis was becoming more acute, in effect encouraging the Pakistan military authorities to continue their policy of armed repression and violence against the East Pakistan population.[61]

The US maintained its focus on India's actions despite being warned early on about the cause and scope of the human suffering in East Pakistan. The US had ample time to recognize the genocide and to respond accordingly. Instead, when resistance to the refusal to seat the new legislature erupted, the US continued its support for the Yahya government and chose to "conceal the widespread massacres in East Pakistan, which from their start represented a genocidal assault on the mass of the Bengali population."[62]

Did the US uphold its obligation to prevent genocide in Pakistan?

To support a finding that the US failed to uphold an obligation to prevent genocide, the US would have needed to know what was happening or that it was possible; would have needed to wield the requisite influence over Pakistan to incur an obligation to prevent genocide; and would have needed to fail to fulfill this obligation. Based on this three-part test, it is undeniable that the US is responsible for failing to prevent genocide in East Pakistan. As was just shown, the US was fully aware that Pakistan was committing genocide in East Pakistan. Archer Blood informed the Nixon Administration of this fact within two weeks of the outbreak of mass killing. Based on the US' military and diplomatic relationship with Pakistan, the US also wielded the necessary influence to prevent the genocide. The US clearly failed to do so; in fact, it did the opposite. It continued to supply Pakistan with military aid and used its seat on the Security Council to provide Pakistan with diplomatic cover. As Gary Bass summarizes:

> As its most important international backer, the United States had great influence over Pakistan. But at almost every turning point in the crisis, Nixon and Kissinger failed to use that leverage to avert disaster.... They did not threaten the loss of U.S. support or even sanctions if Pakistan took the wrong course.... They did not ask that Pakistan refrain from using U.S. weapons to slaughter civilians, even though that could have impeded the military's rampage, and might have deterred the army.[63]

Thus, the US had the necessary influence, knew that Pakistan was murdering its own citizens, and chose not to use its influence in an effort to deter Pakistan from committing genocide. Therefore, the US is guilty of failing to prevent genocide.

Was the US complicit in Pakistan's genocide?

The same evidence that demonstrated that the US failed to uphold its obligation to prevent genocide renders the US complicit in Pakistan's genocide. To be found complicit in genocide, the US needed to furnish Pakistan with aid that facilitated the commission of genocide, with knowledge of Pakistan's intent to commit genocide. The US was fully aware of mass violence being committed in East Pakistan, and that members of its diplomatic corps believed the violence amounted to genocide. This belief was first transmitted by the Consulate in Dacca within days of the outbreak of violence—violence that would continue for nearly nine months.

Despite this knowledge, the US provided Pakistan with military weaponry and equipment that were used to commit genocide. As previously noted, Pakistan used American tanks, fighter jets, jeeps, and munitions during its assaults on East Pakistan. Some of this was provided prior to

106 *Genocide in Bangladesh and Guatemala*

the start of the genocide; however, the US continued its military aid after the genocide began, including sending $3.8 million in military equipment.[64] This led the Soviet Union to accuse the US of "continuing to grant military aid to Pakistan throughout the many months during which the crisis was becoming more acute," which "in effect encouraged the Pakistan military authorities to continue their policy of armed repression and violence against the East Pakistan population."[65]

US political support is also relevant. According to Mark Milanovic, complicit acts include covering up evidence of the crime.[66] The US provision of diplomatic support to Pakistan at the Security Council is evidence of its intent to cover up Pakistan's genocide. Comparing US knowledge in late March 1971 with the positions it took during Security Council meetings many months later, it is clear the US sought to obstruct any measures that aimed to address the violence and its root causes. It is also clear that the US was much more than a simple bystander to the genocide in East Pakistan. As Bass notes,

> Here the United States was allied with the killers. The White House was actively and knowingly *supporting* [emphasis in original] a murderous regime at many of the most crucial moments. There was no question about whether the United States should intervene; it was already intervening on behalf of a military dictatorship decimating its own people.[67]

The US role in Guatemala's genocide

Prior to and throughout Guatemala's genocide, the US primarily provided Guatemala with military support. Though the Carter administration cut off direct military aid to Guatemala in 1977, the Reagan administration decided to send Guatemala items that the US had promised prior to the cutoff. The administration also found creative ways of circumventing Congressional restrictions on military aid.[68] It was reported in the *New York Times* on December 18, 1982 that the Reagan administration was exploiting a loophole in Congressional restrictions on aid to Guatemala to provide military assistance in the form of spare parts, instruction, and informal advice.[69]

The administration spuriously claimed this materiel was of a "civilian" nature. For example, in 1980 and 1981, the US sold Guatemala 23 Bell Helicopters worth $25 million. The helicopters escaped oversight because they were classified as "civilian" by the US Commerce Department. Despite this classification, the helicopters were used by the Guatemalan military. Twenty military pilots were even trained to fly the helicopters at Bell's headquarters in Fort Worth, Texas. On June 10, 1981, the Reagan administration sold Guatemala $3.1 million worth of military cargo trucks and jeeps. These vehicles had been removed from the Crime Control and Detection List only a week earlier.[70] During a session of the Subcommittee on Human Rights and International Organizations, Don Bonker, former Congressional member and chair of the subcommittee, stated,

> Refugees reported that the Guatemalan soldiers arrived in helicopters, trucks, and jeeps, and tortured and murdered innocent unarmed civilians....By selling or giving the Lucas regime helicopter parts, training packages, or jeeps and trucks; we are literally aiding the indiscriminate attacks on innocent peasant villages and households.[71]

Between 1982 and 1984, the Reagan administration succeeded in transferring a further $15 million worth of spare parts and vehicles to the Guatemalan military.[72] This was not the only form of military aid Guatemala received. According to Kaye Doyle,

> Part of the burden of that historical responsibility was that the United States tried to use Guatemala as a bulwark against Communism. The US played a very powerful and direct role in the life of this institution, the army, that went on to commit genocide.[73]

As just one example of this direct role, during Ríos Montt's trial on genocide charges, it was revealed that the CIA had been paying top Guatemalan military officers throughout the period of the genocide.[74] The US also significantly increased its economic aid to Guatemala in the years of the genocide. In 1980, Guatemala received $11 million in economic aid.[75] In 1982, the Reagan administration requested $13 million in aid, along with $250,000 for military training for the following year.[76] By 1986, economic aid had reached $104 million.[77] What the Reagan administration was unable to provide Guatemala directly, it drafted "key clients—Israel and South Korea—to fill gaps in military and 'security' assistance."[78] As Benjamin Beit-Hallahmi describes it, "In the early 1980s, a whole worldwide rightwing network could be seen in action in Guatemala, offering aid in whatever form was needed."[79] According to the *New York Times*, in addition to arms, South Korea provided the Guatemalan military with uniforms.[80] Meanwhile, writes Stephen Kinzer, "During the height of the Guatemalan civil war, Israeli companies supplied nearly all of the army's weaponry—$20 million worth in 1984 alone."[81]

Soon after Reagan took office, the State Department assured Guatemala that it would not "castigate human rights offenders nor forget its friends."[82] The Reagan administration made this pledge even as the CIA was documenting the Guatemalan army's indiscriminate killings of Mayans in rural areas.[83] A February 1982 secret CIA cable confirms that the US was aware of a "sweep" operation conducted by the Guatemalan army in the department of El Quiché. The secret cable identified the basic protocol employed during such operations. Resistance to army incursions led to a designation

108 *Genocide in Bangladesh and Guatemala*

of the entire village as hostile. If the inhabitants abandoned the village prior to the army's arrival, the village was also considered hostile. In either case, hostile villages were destroyed. Further, resistance did not equate to the presence of guerilla forces. According to the cable, the Guatemalan army had not encountered any major guerilla forces in El Quiché. Nonetheless, the army destroyed entire villages and killed their Mayan populations. The cable noted in conclusion, "The well-documented belief by the army that the entire Ixil Indian population is pro-EGP has created a situation in which the army can be expected to give no quarter to combatants and non-combatants alike."[84]

Following the March 1982 coup that brought Ríos Montt to power, the US displayed a willful ignorance of Guatemala's genocide to provide Guatemala with political cover. The political cover was not as public as it was in the case of Pakistan; it did not need to be. The Security Council did not meet a single time to discuss Guatemala's genocide. Instead, the political cover was predominantly focused on domestic constituencies. As Virginia Garrard-Burnett puts it, the Reagan administration viewed Ríos Montt

> as the kind of leader with whom the United States could potentially do business, that is to say, with whom the United States could justify the restoration of military aid but who was still willing to prosecute a vigorous counterinsurgency campaign.[85]

While Guatemala was committing genocide, the Reagan administration sought to formally resume military and economic aid to Guatemala, supposedly to encourage reforms by the new military government. The resumption of (overt) military and economic aid to Guatemala required that the Reagan convince Congress that Guatemala was making significant improvements in human rights protections. Because it was trying to make its case while the violence was intensifying and genocide was being committed, the State Department attempted to detract attention from Ríos Montt's "scorched earth" campaign. It painted Ríos Montt as a reluctant warrior who sought to restore "free world values to a people long crushed by exploitation and strife at the hands of an unwelcome and unwarranted insurgency."[86] For example, Stephen Bosworth, Deputy Assistant Secretary of State, told the Senate Foreign Relations Committee that the only violence Ríos Montt's forces had engaged in were skirmishes with leftist guerillas.[87]

The US Embassy in Guatemala worked to portray the human rights situation in Guatemala as one in which it was impossible to determine who was responsible for the violations. Embassy officials would visit the scenes of massacres and report back with the Guatemalan army's version of events, which placed the blame for the massacres on the guerillas.[88] For example, an October 1982 cable from the American Embassy in Guatemala to Secretary George Shultz informed him of Amnesty International's findings that there had been massive extrajudicial executions in Guatemala since Ríos Montt took power in March 1982. The embassy dismissed the allegations, arguing that Amnesty International ignored the "fact that a war is going on in which both sides inflict casualties on each other; it ignores the fact that the communist insurgency initiated this war."[89] The embassy concluded that Amnesty International's report was part of a disinformation campaign being waged in the US "against the Guatemalan government by groups supporting the communist insurgency in Guatemala."[90] According to the Embassy,

> This is a campaign in which guerilla mayhem and violations of human rights are ignored; a campaign in which responsibility for atrocities is assigned to the GOG without verifiable evidence; a campaign in which GOG responsibility for atrocities is alleged when evidence shows guerilla responsibility; a campaign in which atrocities are cited that never occurred. The campaign's object is simple: to deny the Guatemalan army the weapons and equipment needed from the U.S. to defeat the guerillas.[91]

Later in the same cable, the Embassy official added,

> Although Embassy believes it likely that the Guatemalan Army has indeed committed some atrocities, the assertion that they committed all the massacres attributed to them is not credible, especially since analysis indicates the guerillas are responsible in many cases. If the GOG were indeed engaged in massive extrajudicial executions—a 'mad genocidal' campaign—in the highlands, one must wonder why Indians are joining civil defense patrols in great numbers....[92]

Apparently, it did not occur to the Embassy that Mayans were doing so out of fear for their lives. Further, as can be concluded from CEH findings, the only disinformation campaign was the one being conducted by the US. According to the CEH, just 3 percent of the human rights violations investigated could be attributed to the leftist rebels.[93]

This trend would continue. A secret US State Department cable from late 1982 noted widespread allegations of massacres committed by members of the Guatemalan army. Nonetheless, according to the cable, "The Embassy does not as yet believe that there is sufficient evidence to link government troops to any of the reported massacres."[94] By December 1982, the façade was crumbling, but the Reagan administration remained steadfast in its support. Ten days before Reagan met with Ríos Montt on December 5, 1982, the American Embassy in Guatemala informed the US State Department of a "well-founded allegation of a large-scale killing of Indian men, women, and children in a remote area by the Guatemalan army."[95] In February 1983, US Ambassador Frederic Chapin informed the Reagan administration that he was "firmly convinced that the violence...is government of Guatemala

110 *Genocide in Bangladesh and Guatemala*

ordered and directed violence and not 'right wing violence' and that these were not 'rightist hit squad executions' but again executions ordered by armed services officers close to president Ríos Montt."[96]

Despite the mounting evidence of government responsibility for the atrocities, the Reagan administration continued to argue that the human rights situation in Guatemala was improving.[97] After his December 1982 meeting with Ríos Montt, Reagan described him as "a man of great integrity."[98] Reagan also justified Ríos Montt's coup d'état, pointing out that "he was elected President in 1974 and was never allowed to take office."[99] The coup, then, merely placed Ríos Montt "into the office he'd been elected to."[100] Thus, Reagan concluded, Ríos Montt was "getting a bum rap."[101] Yet, even as the two heads of state were meeting, an elite unit of Guatemalan troops was deploying to a Mayan community named Las Dos Erres with orders to kill its inhabitants. Years later, a forensic team unearthed the victims of this massacre, concluding that at least 162 people were killed, including 67 children.[102] When Ríos Montt was asked by reporters about Guatemala's "scorched-earth" policy, Montt responded, "We have no scorched-earth policy. We have a policy of scorched Communists."[103]

Did the US uphold its obligation to prevent genocide in Guatemala?

As with the case of Pakistan, to find that the US failed to uphold an obligation to prevent genocide, the US would have had to know what was happening or that it was possible; the US would have needed to wield the requisite influence over Guatemala to incur an obligation to prevent genocide; and the US would have had to fail to fulfill this obligation. Based on this three-part test, it is indisputable that the US is responsible for failing to prevent genocide in Guatemala. Despite efforts to portray the situation as ambiguous, the US was clearly aware that Guatemala was committing atrocities against Mayan communities. The US disregarded reports of atrocities committed by the Guatemalan army as part of an effort to portray the human rights situation as improving. The US insisted that allegations of atrocities were part of a communist conspiracy aimed at denying the Guatemalan army weapons and equipment. Internal communications were not the only source of information regarding the atrocities. By June 1982, around the time Ríos Montt named himself Guatemala's president and commander-in-chief, the *New York Times* reported on the existence of mass graves in Guatemala. Thus, there was not an absence of information; the US simply decided to ignore any evidence "that did not serve to advance the United States' immediate political objectives in Guatemala and in the region at large."[104]

Based on the US' military, economic, and diplomatic relationship with Guatemala, the US also wielded the necessary influence to trigger a responsibility to use that influence in an effort to prevent the genocide. The US clearly failed to do so. Instead of attempting to prevent Guatemala's genocide, which could have involved denying military and economic aid, along with condemning rather than praising Ríos Montt, the US continued and actually increased its support. Alan Nairn argues that the Guatemalan army would not have been able to successfully carry out its atrocities had the US "pulled the plug," demonstrating its opposition to the mass killings by abandoning Guatemala's army.[105] Nairn's argument echoes one made by the ICJ directly related to its finding that Serbia failed to fulfill its obligation to prevent genocide in Bosnia. Recall that the ICJ found that Serbia "was making its considerable military and financial support available to the Republika Srpska, and had it withdrawn that support, this would have greatly constrained the options that were available to the Republika Srpska authorities."[106]

Based on its relationship with Guatemala and its knowledge of Guatemala's attacks on members of its Mayan population, the US had an obligation to employ all means reasonably available to it to prevent genocide in Guatemala to the extent possible. It is clear in its actions before and during the genocide that the US did not seek to use its influence to prevent genocide. Instead, it continued to support Guatemala while disingenuously misrepresenting what was occurring. In Bosnia v. Serbia, the ICJ determined that Serbia was fully aware of the hatred of Muslims that existed among Bosnian Serbs in and around Srebrenica. Similarly, the US was aware that Guatemala's Mayan population was at risk. As Garrard-Burnett writes,

> Despite the steady drumbeat of plausible deniability, it is difficult to believe that, given the United States' long-standing involvement in Guatemala and its state-of-the-art 1980s intelligence, US officials did not have a reasonably clear sense of the extent of the violence in the countryside and did not indeed know 'who was killing whom.'[107]

Thus, the US is guilty of failing in its obligation to prevent genocide in Guatemala.

Was the US complicit in Guatemala's genocide?

Evidence that implicates the US in a failure to uphold its obligation to prevent genocide also renders the US complicit in Guatemala's genocide. The two-part test for complicity requires that the US was aware of Guatemala's intent to commit genocide, while furnishing Guatemala with aid that facilitated the commission of genocide. The ambiguity with which US internal communications described the atrocities in Guatemala was not due to a lack of understanding, but rather part of an effort to intentionally mislead, so the Reagan administration could provide Guatemala with even greater support. As was just noted above, it is highly doubtful that the US was unaware of the extent of the violence being committed against Mayan communities and the responsibility of the government of Guatemala for the atrocities. Juan Méndez accuses the US of using "plausible deniability...to

112 *Genocide in Bangladesh and Guatemala*

disguise and justify covert operations."[108] He asserts that atrocities in Guatemala "were at the time denied by American officials and diplomats who knew better, and at best were tolerated—at worst actively encouraged and supported—by American foreign policy."[109]

The US also provided Guatemala with increasing military and economic aid during the genocide. The US sold Guatemala helicopters and provided pilots with training. The US also sold Guatemala cargo trucks and jeeps. During the genocide, the US transferred millions of dollars' worth of spare parts and military vehicles. Further, the CIA had been paying top Guatemalan military officers throughout the period of the genocide.[110] Economic aid also increased exponentially during and after the genocide. What the US was unable to provide, it enlisted others, such as South Korea and Israel, to do so.

There is also evidence that suggests that the military aid was used directly in the commission of genocide. In September 1982, Allan Nairn interviewed Guatemalan soldiers. During one of the interviews, a soldier talked openly about killing civilians. Nairn asked the soldier, "What is the largest amount of people you have killed at once?" The soldier answered, "Well, really, in Sololá, around 500 people." Nairn was also told that when Mayans would flee from the Guatemalan army, the army would "pursue them using U.S. supplied helicopters, U.S.- and Israeli-supplied planes. They would drop U.S. 50-kilogram bombs on them, and they would machine gun them from U.S. Huey and Bell helicopters, using U.S.-supplied heavy-caliber machine guns."[111] In this regard, recall that Don Bonker, former Congressional member and Chair of the Subcommittee on Human Rights and International Organizations, essentially accused the US of complicity, stating, "By selling or giving the Lucas regime helicopter parts, training packages, or jeeps and trucks[,] we are literally aiding the indiscriminate attacks on innocent peasant villages and households."[112]

Anticipating those who would summarily reject an accusation that the US was complicit in Guatemala's genocide, Lauren Carasik asserts, "Charges of U.S. complicity are not just the rallying cry of anti-imperialist critics—they have been confirmed repeatedly by official U.S. government documents."[113] Ajamu Baraka likewise argues compellingly that the US was complicit in Guatemala's genocide. He states that the Reagan administration was

> fully aware of the pogrom against the Ixil people in the mountains of Guatemala at the very moment that the U.S. government was involved in training and arming the Guatemalan military, passing intelligence to its clandestine services, and providing political and diplomatic support to the government.[114]

The real question, then, is not whether the US was complicit in Guatemala's genocide; it is whether the US conspired with Guatemala to commit genocide. Perhaps someday, additional declassified documents will reveal the truth.

Conclusion

US support for Pakistan's and Guatemala's genocides was not unanimous. Elements of the US government disagreed with the support, whether it was the US Consulate in Dacca regarding the former or the US Congress regarding the latter. However, state responsibility for genocide and its ancillary crimes does not require that there be unanimity among the individuals on whose behalf the state acts. It only requires that the state engage in prohibited acts. In each of the above cases, the US incurred an obligation to prevent genocide based on the influence it held over Pakistan's and Guatemala's governments. The US unequivocally failed to use its influence to prevent genocide. Furthermore, in both cases, the US increased its support in varied ways while Pakistan and Guatemala were committing genocide. The US did so fully aware that they were committing genocide, knowing that the aid provided was facilitating the crime. Thus, the US was also complicit in both genocides. As with the previous finding that the US conspired to commit genocide in Indonesia, this is based only on publicly available information. The possibility remains that the US might be additionally responsible for conspiring to commit genocide in one or both cases.[115]

In aiding governments committing genocide, the US placed its own "strategic interests" over the lives of one to two million people. In the case of Pakistan, it was more important to the US that Pakistani leaders, with whom it had developed close relations, maintained control of Pakistan's central government than it was to protect the people living in East Pakistan. Pakistan was an ally of the US—an anti-communist military dictatorship.[116] Pakistan was also acting as an intermediary between the US and China. The ouster of the Pakistani coalition from power would have created uncertainty and the risk of the rise of "forces less dependent on, thus less supportive of, the United States."[117] Meanwhile, the pending triumph of leftist movements in Central America combined with the election of anti-communist Ronald Reagan placed Central America in the middle of the final showdown of the Cold War.[118] The Reagan Doctrine sought to support anti-communist regimes in order to impede or offset communist advances in the Western Hemisphere.[119] This was considered more important than Mayan lives. Thus, in Guatemala, a shared opposition to communism became a justification for the support of a genocidal military dictator. As Irma Alicia Velasquez Nimatuj bluntly writes, "The anticommunist sentiment shared by the two leaders provided an incentive for the armed forces to continue carrying out a genocide against the 22 Maya groups of the country."[120]

Howard Federspiel's reflections on Indonesia's genocide of communists is again relevant here: "No one cared as long as they were Communists, that they were being butchered."[121] This seems true even of those who have analyzed in-depth the US relationship with genocide. In their respective texts, neither Samantha Power nor Peter Ronayne include Guatemala's genocide, ignoring entirely a case in which the US was irrefutably complicit in

114 *Genocide in Bangladesh and Guatemala*

genocide, as well as potentially a conspirator in it. Ronayne also ignores Pakistan's genocide and, therefore, the US role in it. While Power does recognize Pakistan's genocide, she merely states, "The Nixon administration, which was hostile to India and using Pakistan as an intermediary to China, did not protest."[122] When considering their weak criticism of the US, it would appear that it is not coincidental that they omitted cases of genocide for which the US maintained significant influence over the genocidal governments and provided material support to them before, during, and subsequent to the genocides.

While a finding of complicity in genocide in East Pakistan and Guatemala is not quite as severe as the finding that the US conspired to commit genocide in Indonesia, it similarly raises significant questions regarding why the US relationship with genocide is generally portrayed as that of a bystander. It also raises questions regarding why the US is called upon to take action to prevent genocide when it shares responsibility for the commission of genocide. Should the US not be held accountable first for its own relationship with genocide, before being granted the moral authority to determine when and how to stop others from committing genocide?

The US financially, militarily, and politically supported governments committing genocide, because doing so was consistent with its broader "national interest." If Pakistan wanted to commit genocide in East Pakistan while serving as an intermediary between the US and China, so be it. If Guatemala wanted to conduct a "scorched communist" policy, committing genocide against its indigenous Mayan population during the waning years of the Cold War, the US was happy to support it. US policy was not some accident, an inadvertent miscalculation—it was deliberate. This must be understood, and it must be opposed if American foreign policy is ever going to change.

Notes

1 Anne Noronha Dos Santos, *Military Intervention and Secession in South Asia: The Cases of Bangladesh, Sri Lanka, Kashmir, and Punjab* (Westport, CT: Praeger Security International, 2007), 28.

2 Simon Chesterman, *Just War or Just Peace?: Humanitarian Intervention and International Law* (Oxford: Oxford University Press, 2003), 72; Suhail Islam and Syed Hassan, "The Wretched of the Nations: The West's Role in Human Rights Violations in the Bangladesh War of Independence," in *Genocide, War Crimes and the West: History and Complicity*, ed. Adam Jones (London: Zed Books, 2004), 204.

3 Chesterman, *Just War or Just Peace*, 72.

4 Ben Kiernan, *Blood and Soil: A World History of Genocide and Extermination from Sparta to Darfur* (New Haven, CT: Yale University Press, 2007), 575.

5 Feroz Ahmed, Aijaz Ahmad, and Eqbal Ahmad, "Pakistan, Bangladesh, India: 1970–1973," *MERIP Reports* 16 (1973): 9.

6 Simon Chesterman cites at least one million people killed and up to ten million refugees. Ben Kiernan cites a range of 300,000 to one million people killed. Suhail Islam and Syed Hassan cite an even greater range—hundreds of thousands

to as many as three million dead. Samantha Power cites one to two million people killed and the rape of 200,000 girls and women. See Chesterman, *Just War or Just Peace*, 72; Kiernan, *Blood and Soil*, 572; Islam and Hassan, "The Wretched of the Nations," 205; Samantha Power, *"A Problem from Hell": American and the Age of Genocide* (New York: Harper Perennial, 2002), 82.

7 Leo Kuper, *Genocide: Its Political Use in the Twentieth Century* (New Haven, CT: Yale University Press, 1982), 79.

8 Gary J. Bass, *The Blood Telegram: Nixon, Kissinger, and a Forgotten Genocide* (New York: Vintage Books, 2013), 58.

9 Adam Jones, personal communication, 30 July 2017.

10 Farahnaz Ispahani, *Purifying the Land of the Pure: A History of Pakistan's Religious Minorities* (Oxford: Oxford University Press, 2017), 73.

11 Jones, personal communication, 30 July 2017; Richard Sisson and Leo E. Rose, *War and Secession: Pakistan, India, and the Creation of Bangladesh* (Berkeley, CA: University of California Press, 1990), 148.

12 Barbara Harff describes the intent in genocide against a political group as the "attempt to destroy the ability of opposition groups to challenge or resist the regime by targeting their potential supporters." See Barbara Harff, "No Lessons Learned from the Holocaust? Assessing Risks of Genocide and Political Mass Murder since 1955," *American Political Science Review* 97, no. 1 (2003): 59.

13 William Schabas, Leila Nadya Sadat, Beth Van Schaack, and Samuel Totten were interviewed, and Helen Fein's, Adam Jones', and Ben Kiernan's works were reviewed. Using the legal definition of genocide, Sadat, Totten, Fein, Jones, and Kiernan agreed that genocide was committed by Pakistan. Van Schaack was still determining her position, but was leaning towards recognition. Only Schabas firmly rejected the label of genocide. William Schabas, Interview, 17 September 2011; Leila Nadya Sadat, Interview, 26 September 2011; Beth Van Schaack, Interview, 19 September 2011; Totten, interview, 17 September 2011. See Kiernan, *Blood and Soil*, 574; Helen Fein, *Human Rights and Wrongs: Slavery, Terror, Genocide* (Boulder, CO: Paradigm Publishers, 2007), 230; Adam Jones, *Genocide: A Comprehensive Introduction*, 2nd edition (London: Routledge, 2011), 340.

14 International Commission of Jurists, "The Events in East Pakistan, 1971," A Legal Study by the Secretariat of the International Commission of Jurists, Geneva, 1972, 26–27.

15 Ibid., 57.

16 Schabas, Sadat, Van Schaack, and Totten were interviewed, and Fein's, Jones', and Kiernan's works were reviewed. Using the legal definition of genocide, Sadat, Van Schaack, Totten, Fein, Jones, and Kiernan agreed that genocide was committed by Guatemala. Only Schabas rejected the label of genocide. William Schabas, Interview, 17 September 2011; Leila Nadya Sadat, Interview, 26 September 2011; Beth Van Schaack, Interview, 19 September 2011; Totten, interview, 17 September 2011. See Kiernan, *Blood and Soil*, 582; Fein, *Human Rights and Wrongs*, 132; Jones, *Genocide*, 2nd edition, 142.

17 Commission for Historical Clarification, *Guatemala: Memory of Silence*, www. aaas.org/sites/default/files/migrate/uploads/mos_en.pdf (accessed May 15, 2016), 11.

18 Jens Meierhenrich, "Introduction: The Study and History of Genocide," in *Genocide: A Reader*, ed. Jens Meierhenrich (Oxford: Oxford University Press, 2014), 46.

19 Ibid., 45; Greg Grandin, "Politics by Other Means: Guatemala's Quiet Genocide," in *Quiet Genocide: Guatemala 1981–1983*, ed. Etelle Higonnet (New Brunswick, NJ: Transaction Publishers, 2009), 1.

20 Stephen Rabe, *The Killing Zone: The United States Wages Cold War in Latin America* (Oxford: Oxford University Press, 2016), 177.

116 *Genocide in Bangladesh and Guatemala*

21 Meierhenrich, "Introduction," 46.
22 Kate Doyle, "Operation Sofia: Documenting Genocide in Guatemala," National Security Archive Electronic Briefing Book No. 297, http://nsarchive.gwu.edu/NSAEBB/NSAEBB297/ (accessed May 2016).
23 Commission for Historical Clarification, *Guatemala,* 39.
24 Ibid., 23.
25 Ibid.
26 Grandin, "Politics by Other Means," 1.
27 Commission for Historical Clarification, *Guatemala*, 34.
28 Ibid., 41.
29 Ibid.
30 Jones, *Genocide*, 2nd edition, 142.
31 International Court of Justice, Summary of the Judgment of 26 February 2007.
32 Islam and Hassan, "The Wretched of the Nations," 207.
33 Srinath Raghavan, *1971: A Global History of the Creation of Bangladesh* (Cambridge, MA: Harvard University Press, 2013), 84.
34 Stephen Cohen, *The Pakistan Army* (Oakland, CA: University of California Press, 1984), 70.
35 Raghavan, *1971*, 245.
36 Sanjoy Banerjee, "Explaining the American 'Tilt' in the 1971 Bangladesh Crisis: A Late Dependency Approach," *International Studies Quarterly* 31, no. 2 (1987): 210.
37 Robert McMahon, *The Cold War on the Periphery: The United States, India, and Pakistan* (New York: Columbia University Press, 1996), 346.
38 G.W. Choudhury, *India, Pakistan, Bangladesh and the Major Powers* (New York: Free Press, 1976), 68.
39 Islam and Hassan, "The Wretched of the Nations," 208.
40 Ibid., 207.
41 United States Department of State, "Transcript of Telephone Conversation between President Nixon and His Assistant for National Security Affairs," Foreign Relations, 1969–1976, Volume XI, South Asia Crisis, 1971, https://2001-2009.state.gov/r/pa/ho/frus/nixon/xi/45607.htm (accessed August 14, 2017).
42 Bass, *The Blood Telegram*, 67–68.
43 Ibid., xi.
44 Ibid., 58.
45 Ibid.
46 Ibid.
47 Jones, *Genocide*, 2nd edition, 341–342.
48 Ibid., 77–78.
49 United States Central Intelligence Agency, "The Indo-Pakistani Crisis: Six Months Later," Foreign Relations, 1969–1976, Volume E-7, South Asia, 1969–1972, https://2001–2009.state.gov/r/pa/ho/frus/nixon/e7txt/50136.htm (accessed August 14, 2017).
50 Edmund Muskie, "Pakistan," Congressional Record – Senate, www.gpo.gov/fdsys/pkg/GPO-CRECB-1971-pt30/pdf/GPO-CRECB-1971-pt30-3-1.pdf (accessed August 14, 2017), 39210.
51 Adam Jones describes India's intervention as "one of the rare instances of successful outside intervention in genocide." See Jones, *Genocide*, 2nd edition, 343.
52 United Nations Security Council, Official Record of the 1606th Meeting, 4 December 1971, http://dag.un.org/bitstream/handle/11176/74490/S_PV.1606-EN.pdf?sequence=17&isAllowed=y (accessed May 15, 2016), 32.
53 United Nations Security Council, United States: Draft Resolution, 4 December 1971.
54 United Nations Security Council, Official Record of the 1606th Meeting, 16.
55 Ibid.

Genocide in Bangladesh and Guatemala 117

56 United Nations Security Council, Official Record of the 1608th Meeting, 6 December 1971, http://dag.un.org/bitstream/handle/11176/74492/S_PV.1608-EN.pdf?sequence=13&isAllowed=y (accessed May 15, 2016), 27.
57 Ibid.
58 Ibid, 20.
59 United Nations Security Council, Official Record of the 1611th Meeting, 12 December 1971, http://dag.un.org/bitstream/handle/11176/74495/S_PV.1611-EN.pdf?sequence=13&isAllowed=y (accessed May 15, 2016), 2.
60 Ibid.
61 United Nations Security Council, Official Record of the 1613th Meeting, 13 December 1971, http://dag.un.org/bitstream/handle/11176/74497/S_PV.1613-EN.pdf?sequence=13&isAllowed=y (accessed May 15, 2016), 17.
62 Islam and Hassan, "The Wretched of the Nations," 206.
63 Bass, *The Blood Telegram*, xiv.
64 Ibid.; United States Department of State, "Transcript of Telephone Conversation."
65 United Nations Security Council, Official Record of the 1613th Meeting, 17.
66 Mark Milanovic, "State Responsibility for Genocide," *The European Journal of International Law* 17, no. 3 (2006): 573.
67 Bass, *The Blood Telegram*, xiii.
68 Mike Allison, "The Myth of the Squeaky-Clean US," *Al Jazeera*, www.aljazeera.com/indepth/opinion/2013/10/myth-squeaky-clean-us-2013101393636747448.html (accessed May 2016).
69 Richard J. Meislin, "U.S. Military Aid for Guatemala Continuing despite Official Curbs," *New York Times*, www.nytimes.com/library/world/americas/121982guatemala-us.html (accessed May 2016).
70 Tanya Broder and Bernard D. Lambek, "Military Aid to Guatemala: The Failure of U.S. Human Rights Legislation," *Yale Journal of International Law* 13, no. 111 (1988): 130.
71 Ibid.
72 Elisabeth Malkin, "Trial on Guatemalan Civil War Carnage Leaves Out U.S. Role," *New York Times*, www.nytimes.com/2013/05/17/world/americas/trial-on-guatemalan-civil-war-carnage-leaves-out-us-role.html?_r=0 (accessed May 2016).
73 Ibid.
74 Ibid.
75 Greg Grandin, "Guatemalan Slaughter Was Part of Reagan's Hard Line," *New York Times*, www.nytimes.com/roomfordebate/2013/05/19/what-guilt-does-the-us-bear-in-guatemala/guatemalan-slaughter-was-part-of-reagans-hard-line (accessed May 2016).
76 Susan Garland, "US Seeks New Aid for Guatemala," *The Christian Science Monitor*, www.csmonitor.com/1982/0429/042918.html (accessed May 2016).
77 Grandin, "Guatemalan Slaughter Was Part of Reagan's Hard Line."
78 Adam Jones, *Genocide: A Comprehensive Introduction*, 3rd edition (London: Routledge, 2017), 196.
79 Benjamin Beit-Hallahmi, *The Israeli Connection: Whom Israel Arms and Why* (London: I.B. Tauris & Co, 1988), 82.
80 Warren Hoge, "Repression in Guatemala Increases as U.S. Is Seeking to Improve Ties," *New York Times*, www.nytimes.com/1981/05/03/world/repression-in-guatemala-increases-as-us-is-seeking-to-improve-ties.html?pagewanted=all (accessed August 14, 2017).
81 Stephen Kinzer, *Reset: Iran, Turkey, and America's Future* (New York: St. Martin's Press, 2010), 162.
82 Quoted in Kathryn Sikkink, *Mixed Signals: U.S. Human Rights Policy and Latin America* (Ithaca, NY: Cornell University Press, 2004), 161.

118 *Genocide in Bangladesh and Guatemala*

83 Marc Drouin, "Understanding the 1982 Guatemalan Genocide," in *State Violence and Genocide in Latin America*, eds. Marcia Esparza, Henry H. Huttenbach, and Daniel Feierstein (London: Routledge, 2010), 84.

84 United States Central Intelligence Agency, "Counterinsurgency Operations in El Quiché," Central Intelligence Agency, Secret Cable, http://nsarchive.gwu.edu/NSAEBB/NSAEBB11/docs/doc14.pdf (accessed May 2016).

85 Virginia Garrard-Burnett, *Terror in the Land of the Holy Spirit: Guatemala under General Efrain Rios Montt 1982–1983* (Oxford: Oxford University Press, 2010), 152.

86 Ibid., 154.

87 Garland, "US Seeks New Aid for Guatemala."

88 Malkin, "Trial on Guatemalan Civil War Carnage Leaves Out U.S. Role."

89 United States Department of State, "Analysis of Human Rights Reports on Guatemala by Amnesty International, WOLA/NISGUA, and Guatemala Human Rights Commission," Department of State, Confidential Cable, http://nsarchive.gwu.edu/NSAEBB/NSAEBB11/docs/ (accessed May 2016).

90 Ibid.

91 Ibid.

92 Ibid.

93 Commission for Historical Clarification, *Guatemala*, 42.

94 United States Department of State, "Guatemala: Reports of Atrocities Mark Army Gains," Secret Report Circa late-1982, Department of State, Secret report, http://nsarchive.gwu.edu/NSAEBB/NSAEBB11/docs/doc17.pdf (accessed May 2016).

95 Quoted in Daniel Wilkinson, *Silence on the Mountain: Stories of Terror, Betrayal, and Forgetting in Guatemala* (Durham, NC: Duke University Press, 2004), 327.

96 United States Central Intelligence Agency, "Ríos Montt Gives Carte Blanche to Archivos to Deal with Insurgency," http://nsarchive.gwu.edu/NSAEBB/NSAEBB11/docs/doc18.pdf (accessed August 14, 2017).

97 Robert Parry, "Reagan's Hand in Guatemala's Genocide," *Consortium News*, https://consortiumnews.com/2012/01/23/reagans-hand-in-guatemalas-genocide/ (accessed May 2016).

98 Greg Grandin, "Guatemalan Slaughter was Part of Reagan's Hard Line."

99 Ronald Reagan, "Question-and-Answer Session with Reporters on the President's Trip to Latin America," www.presidency.ucsb.edu/ws/index.php?pid=42070 (accessed August 14, 2017).

100 Ibid.

101 Ibid.

102 Wilkinson, *Silence on the Mountain*, 327.

103 Ibid.

104 Garrard-Burnett, *Terror in the Land of the Holy Spirit*, 157.

105 Counterspin, "On Guatemala, 'The Press has Blood on its Hands," *Fairness and Accuracy in Reporting*, http://fair.org/extra/on-guatemala-the-press-has-blood-on-its-hands/ (accessed May 2016).

106 International Court of Justice, Summary of the Judgment of 26 February 2007.

107 Garrard-Burnett, *Terror in the Land of the Holy Spirit*, 157.

108 Juan Mendez, "Preface: Genocide in Guatemala," in *Quiet Genocide: Guatemala 1981–1983*, ed. Etelle Higonnet (New Brunswick, NJ: Transaction Publishers, 2009), xix.

109 Ibid.

110 Malkin, "Trial on Guatemalan Civil War Carnage Leaves Out U.S. Role."

111 Democracy Now, "Exclusive: Allan Nairn Exposes Role of U.S. and New Guatemalan President in Indigenous Massacres," *Democracy Now*, www.democracynow.org/2013/4/19/exclusive_allan_nairn_exposes_role_of (accessed May 2016).

112 Broder and Lambek, "Military Aid to Guatemala," 130.

Genocide in Bangladesh and Guatemala 119

113 Lauren Carasik, "Justice Postponed in Guatemala: Ríos Montt and the United States Evade Reckoning with the Past," *The Boston Review*, www.truth-out.org/opinion/item/16604-justice-postponed-in-guatemala-rios-montt-and-the-rios united-states-evade-reckoning-with-the-past (accessed May 2016).
114 Ajamu Baraka, "United States Guilty of Genocide in Guatemala Should Be Real Headline," *Institute for Policy Studies,* www.ips-dc.org/united_states_genocide_guatemala/ (accessed May 2016).
115 In the case of Guatemala, Adam Jones believes documents that currently remain classified may also show to what extent the US conspired with South Korea and Israel to transfer arms to Guatemala. Jones, personal communication, August 2, 2017.
116 Bass, *The Blood Telegram*, xii.
117 Banerjee, "Explaining the American 'Tilt' in the 1971 Bangladesh Crisis," 202.
118 Garrard-Burnett, *Terror in the Land of the Holy Spirit*, 145–146.
119 Ibid.
120 Irma Alicia Velasquez Nimatuj, "Guatemala Suffered for U.S. Foreign Policy," *New York Times*, www.nytimes.com/roomfordebate/2013/05/19/what-guilt-does-the-us-bear-in-guatemala/guatemala-suffered-for-us-foreign-policy (accessed May 2016).
121 Quoted in William Blum, *Killing Hope: US Military & CIA Interventions since World War II* (London: Zed Books, 2003), 194.
122 Samantha Power, *"A Problem from Hell": American and the Age of Genocide* (New York: Harper Perennial, 2002), 82.

Bibliography

Ahmed, Feroz, Aijaz Ahmad, and Eqbal Ahmad. "Pakistan, Bangladesh, India: 1970–1973." *MERIP Reports* 16 (1973): 9.
Allison, Mike. "The Myth of the Squeaky-Clean US." *Al Jazeera*. Accessed May 15, 2016. www.aljazeera.com/indepth/opinion/2013/10/myth-squeaky-clean-us-2013101393636747448.html.
Banerjee, Sanjoy. "Explaining the American 'Tilt' in the 1971 Bangladesh Crisis: A Late Dependency Approach." *International Studies Quarterly* 31, no. 2 (1987): 201–216.
Baraka, Ajamu. "United States Guilty of Genocide in Guatemala Should be Real Headline." *Institute for Policy Studies*. Accessed May 12, 2016. www.ips-dc.org/united_states_genocide_guatemala/.
Bass, Gary J. *The Blood Telegram: Nixon, Kissinger, and a Forgotten Genocide*. New York: Vintage Books, 2013.
Beit-Hallahmi, Benjamin. *The Israeli Connection: Whom Israel Arms and Why*. London: I.B. Tauris & Co, 1988.
Blum, William. *Killing Hope: US Military & CIA Interventions since World War II*. London: Zed Books, 2003.
Broder, Tanya, and Bernard D. Lambek. "Military Aid to Guatemala: The Failure of U.S. Human Rights Legislation." *Yale Journal of International Law* 13, no. 111 (1988): 111–145.
Carasik, Lauren. "Justice Postponed in Guatemala: Rios Montt and the United States Evade Reckoning with the Past." *The Boston Review*. Accessed May 12, 2016. www.truth-out.org/opinion/item/16604-justice-postponed-in-guatemala-rios-montt-and-the-united-states-evade-reckoning-with-the-past.
Chesterman, Simon. *Just War or Just Peace?: Humanitarian Intervention and International Law*. Oxford: Oxford University Press, 2003.

120 *Genocide in Bangladesh and Guatemala*

Choudhury, G.W. *India, Pakistan, Bangladesh and the Major Powers*. New York: Free Press, 1976.

Cohen, Stephen. *The Pakistan Army*. Oakland, CA: University of California Press, 1984.

Commission for Historical Clarification. *Guatemala: Memory of Silence*. Accessed May 15, 2016. www.aaas.org/sites/default/files/migrate/uploads/mos_en.pdf.

Counterspin. "On Guatemala, 'The Press Has Blood on Its Hands.'" *Fairness and Accuracy in Reporting*. Accessed May 12, 206. http://fair.org/extra/on-guatemala-the-press-has-blood-on-its-hands/.

Democracy Now. "Exclusive: Allan Nairn Exposes Role of U.S. and New Guatemalan President in Indigenous Massacres." Accessed May 12, 2016. www.democracynow.org/2013/4/19/exclusive_allan_nairn_exposes_role_of.

Doyle, Kate. "Operation Sofia: Documenting Genocide in Guatemala." National Security Archive Electronic Briefing Book No. 297. Accessed May 15, 2016. http://nsarchive.gwu.edu/NSAEBB/NSAEBB297/.

Drouin, Marc. "Understanding the 1982 Guatemalan Genocide." In *State Violence and Genocide in Latin America*, edited by Marcia Esparza, Henry H. Huttenbach and Daniel Feierstein, 81–103. London: Routledge, 2010.

Fein, Helen. *Human Rights and Wrongs: Slavery, Terror, Genocide*. Boulder, CO: Paradigm Publishers, 2007.

Garland, Susan. "US Seeks New Aid for Guatemala." *The Christian Science Monitor*. Accessed May 10, 2016. www.csmonitor.com/1982/0429/042918.html.

Garrard-Burnett, Virginia. *Terror in the Land of the Holy Spirit: Guatemala under General Efrain Rios Montt 1982–1983*. Oxford: Oxford University Press, 2010.

Grandin, Greg. "Guatemalan Slaughter Was Part of Reagan's Hard Line." *New York Times*. Accessed May 10, 2016. www.nytimes.com/roomfordebate/2013/05/19/what-guilt-does-the-us-bear-in-guatemala/guatemalan-slaughter-was-part-of-reagans-hard-line.

Grandin, Greg. "Politics by Other Means: Guatemala's Quiet Genocide." In *Quiet Genocide: Guatemala 1981–1983*, edited by Etelle Higonnet, 1–16. New Brunswick, NJ: Transaction Publishers, 2009.

Harff, Barbara. "No Lessons Learned from the Holocaust? Assessing Risks of Genocide and Political Mass Murder since 1955." *American Political Science Review* 97, no. 1 (2003): 57–73.

Hoge, Warren. "Repression in Guatemala Increases as U.S. Is Seeking to Improve Ties." *New York Times*. Accessed August 14, 2017. www.nytimes.com/1981/05/03/world/repression-in-guatemala-increases-as-us-is-seeking-to-improve-ties.html?pagewanted=all.

International Commission of Jurists. "The Events in East Pakistan, 1971." A Legal Study by the Secretariat of the International Commission of Jurists, Geneva, 1972.

International Court of Justice. Summary of the Judgment of 26 February 2007.

Islam, Suhail, and Syed Hassan. "The Wretched of the Nations: The West's Role in Human Rights Violations in the Bangladesh War of Independence." In *Genocide, War Crimes and the West: History and Complicity*, edited by Adam Jones, 201–213. London: Zed Books 2004.

Ispahani, Farahnaz. *Purifying the Land of the Pure: A History of Pakistan's Religious Minorities*. Oxford: Oxford University Press, 2017.

Jones, Adam. *Genocide: A Comprehensive Introduction*, 2nd ed. London: Routledge, 2011.

Jones, Adam. *Genocide: A Comprehensive Introduction*, 3rd ed. London: Routledge, 2017.

Kiernan, Ben. *Blood and Soil: A World History of Genocide and Extermination from Sparta to Darfur*. New Haven, CT: Yale University Press, 2007.

Kinzer, Stephen. *Reset: Iran, Turkey, and America's Future*. New York: St. Martin's Press, 2010.

Kuper, Leo. *Genocide: Its Political Use in the Twentieth Century*. New Haven: Yale University Press, 1982.

Malkin, Elisabeth. "Trial on Guatemalan Civil War Carnage Leaves Out U.S. Role." *New York Times*. Accessed May 10, 2016. www.nytimes.com/2013/05/17/world/americas/trial-on-guatemalan-civil-war-carnage-leaves-out-us-role.html?_r=0.

McMahon, Robert. *The Cold War on the Periphery: The United States, India, and Pakistan*. New York: Columbia University Press, 1996.

Meierhenrich, Jens. "Introduction: The Study and History of Genocide." In *Genocide: A Reader*, edited by Jens Meierhenrich, 3–55. Oxford: Oxford University Press, 2014.

Meislin, Richard J. "U.S. Military Aid for Guatemala Continuing Despite Official Curbs." *New York Times*. Accessed May 10, 2016. www.nytimes.com/library/world/americas/121982guatemala-us.html.

Mendez, Juan. "Preface: Genocide in Guatemala." In *Quiet Genocide: Guatemala 1981–1983*, edited by Etelle Higonnet, xiii–xx. New Brunswick, NJ: Transaction Publishers, 2009.

Milanovic, Mark. "State Responsibility for Genocide." *The European Journal of International Law* 17, no. 3 (2006): 553–604.

Muskie, Edmund. "Pakistan." Congressional Record – Senate. Accessed August 14, 2017. www.gpo.gov/fdsys/pkg/GPO-CRECB-1971-pt30/pdf/GPO-CRECB-1971-pt30-3-1.pdf.

Nimatuj, Irma Alicia Velasquez. "Guatemala Suffered for U.S. Foreign Policy." *New York Times*. Accessed May 12, 2016. www.nytimes.com/roomfordebate/2013/05/19/what-guilt-does-the-us-bear-in-guatemala/guatemala-suffered-for-us-foreign-policy.

Parry, Robert. "Reagan's Hand in Guatemala's Genocide." *Consortium News*. Accessed May 15, 2016. https://consortiumnews.com/2012/01/23/reagans-hand-in-guatemalas-genocide/.

Power, Samantha. *"A Problem from Hell": American and the Age of Genocide*. New York: Harper Perennial, 2002.

Rabe, Stephen. *The Killing Zone: The United States Wages Cold War in Latin America*. Oxford: Oxford University Press, 2016.

Raghavan, Srinath. *1971: A Global History of the Creation of Bangladesh*. Cambridge, MA: Harvard University Press, 2013.

Reagan, Ronald. "Question-and-Answer Session with Reporters on the President's Trip to Latin America." Accessed August 14, 2017. www.presidency.ucsb.edu/ws/index.php?pid=42070.

Santos, Anne Noronha Dos. *Military Intervention and Secession in South Asia: The Cases of Bangladesh, Sri Lanka, Kashmir, and Punjab*. Westport, CT: Praeger Security International, 2007.

Sikkink, Kathryn. *Mixed Signals: U.S. Human Rights Policy and Latin America*. Ithaca, NY: Cornell University Press, 2004.

Sisson, Richard, and Leo E. Rose. *War and Secession: Pakistan, India, and the Creation of Bangladesh*. Berkeley, CA: University of California Press, 1990.

122 *Genocide in Bangladesh and Guatemala*

United Nations Security Council. Official Record of the 1606th Meeting, 4 December 1971. Accessed May 15, 2016. http://dag.un.org/bitstream/handle/11176/74490/S_PV.1606-EN.pdf?sequence=17&isAllowed=y.

United Nations Security Council. Official Record of the 1608th Meeting, 6 December 1971. Accessed May 15, 2016. http://dag.un.org/bitstream/handle/11176/74492/S_PV.1608-EN.pdf?sequence=13&isAllowed=y.

United Nations Security Council. Official Record of the 1611th Meeting, 12 December 1971. Accessed May 15, 2016. http://dag.un.org/bitstream/handle/11176/74495/S_PV.1611-EN.pdf?sequence=13&isAllowed=y.

United Nations Security Council. Official Record of the 1613th Meeting, 13 December 1971. Accessed May 15, 2016. http://dag.un.org/bitstream/handle/11176/74497/S_PV.1613-EN.pdf?sequence=13&isAllowed=y.

United Nations Security Council. United States: Draft Resolution. December 4, 1971.

United States Central Intelligence Agency. "Counterinsurgency Operations in El Quiché." Accessed May 12, 2016. http://nsarchive.gwu.edu/NSAEBB/NSAEBB11/docs/doc14.pdf.

United States Central Intelligence Agency. "Ríos Montt Gives Carte Blanche to Archivos to Deal with Insurgency." Accessed August 14, 2017. http://nsarchive.gwu.edu/NSAEBB/NSAEBB11/docs/doc18.pdf.

United States Central Intelligence Agency. "The Indo-Pakistani Crisis: Six Months Later." Foreign Relations, 1969–1976, Volume E-7, South Asia, 1969–1972. Accessed August 14, 2017. https://2001–2009.state.gov/r/pa/ho/frus/nixon/e7txt/50136.htm.

United States Department of State. "Analysis of Human Rights Reports on Guatemala by Amnesty International, WOLA/NISGUA, and Guatemala Human Rights Commission." Accessed May 10, 2016. http://nsarchive.gwu.edu/NSAEBB/NSAEBB11/docs/.

United States Department of State. "Guatemala: Reports of Atrocities Mark Army Gains." Accessed May 12, 2016. http://nsarchive.gwu.edu/NSAEBB/NSAEBB11/docs/doc7.pdf.

United States Department of State. "Transcript of Telephone Conversation between President Nixon and His Assistant for National Security Affairs." Foreign Relations, 1969–1976, Volume XI, South Asia Crisis, 1971. Accessed August 14, 2017. https://2001–2009.state.gov/r/pa/ho/frus/nixon/xi/45607.htm.

Wilkinson, Daniel. *Silence on the Mountain: Stories of Terror, Betrayal, and Forgetting in Guatemala.* Durham, NC: Duke University Press, 2004.

6 A history of genocide in Iraq

In his important work, *The Deaths of Others: The Fate of Civilians in America's Wars*, John Tirman labels Iraq America's "Twenty Years' War." He explains how the US began this war with "Operation Desert Storm," which forcibly ejected Iraq from Kuwait following its illegal invasion and occupation of Kuwait in August 1990. This was followed by a twelve-year span during which the US maintained and enforced economic sanctions, repeatedly called for regime change, and occasionally launched acts of military aggression.[1] "Those twelve years," writes Tirman,

> gave way in March 2003 to an invasion of Iraq, allegedly to protect America from Iraq's supposed capability to attack with chemical, biological, or nuclear weapons. Operation Iraqi Freedom did destroy the regime of Saddam Hussein, but in so doing it unleashed an orgy of violence that has caused hundreds of thousands of Iraqi deaths, millions of displaced people, and a society in shambles.[2]

The West Asia-North Africa (WANA) Institute describes Iraq as a place of "chronic conflict." It divides the conflict into three parts—the Iran–Iraq War (1980–1988), Iraq's invasion of Kuwait and the subsequent Gulf War (1990–1991), and the US invasion and occupation of Iraq (2003).[3] During all three stages of Iraq's chronic conflict, Iraqis have been the victims of genocide. The methods by which they have been killed and the perpetrators responsible have changed, but the massive loss of life has been a constant. In this chapter, I focus on the first two phases of genocide in Iraq. The chapter is divided into two main sections. It begins with a discussion of the US relationship with Iraq prior to and during the Kurdish genocide. I conclude that the US provided Iraq with the means to commit genocide, as well as other material and diplomatic support, with knowledge of Iraq's intent to commit genocide. Thus, according to the Bosnia v. Serbia Precedent, the US is responsible for complicity in Iraq's genocide. Next, it evaluates the impact of the economic sanctions on the Iraqi people. I conclude that the US was fully aware of the death and human suffering caused by the sanctions. Yet, despite this knowledge, the US worked deliberately to maintain and enforce

124 *A history of genocide in Iraq*

them. Therefore, based on my definition of genocide, the US is responsible for genocide during both conflict phases.

Iraq's Kurdish genocide

Iraq first used chemical weapons against Kurds in April 1987. On April 15, seven Kurdish villages in the Sulaimania province were attacked with mustard gas. The next day, another seven villages were attacked in the Balisan Valley. In the village of Shaikwasan, 121 people were killed, including 76 children under the age of eight. In six days of poison gas attacks, hundreds of people were killed.[4] These were the first of as many as forty separate attacks perpetrated against Iraq's Kurdish population between April 1987 and August 1988.[5]

The poison gas attacks against the Kurdish population of Iraq were part of a systematic plan to permanently remove the Kurds from their ancestral lands.[6] In response to the presence of armed Kurdish rebels, especially in Iraq's rural and mountainous areas, Saddam viewed all Kurds as a threat. As Samantha Power notes, "Hussein decided that the best way to stamp out rebellion was to stamp out Kurdish life."[7] Thus, while Iraq's genocide was presented by Saddam as a counter-insurgency campaign, it in fact targeted "every man, woman, and child who resided in the new no-go areas."[8]

Following its 1990 investigation, Human Rights Watch (HRW) concluded that Saddam's government held the requisite intent to destroy part of Iraq's Kurdish population through mass murder in order to achieve its military objective.[9] The intent behind the attacks on Iraqi Kurds was made clear in a June 1987 official directive given to the Leadership of the Zakho Section Committee of Organizing National Defense Battalions. It stated,

> Existence is totally taboo in the forbidden villages of the first stage.... On 21/6/87 begins the second stage...After harvesting the winter crops which ends before the 15th of July, cultivation is forbidden for the following summer and winter seasons. Animal grazing is also forbidden in these areas. It is the duty of military forces...to kill any human being or animal that exists in these areas which are considered totally forbidden.[10]

This was not the only evidence of genocidal intent. Ali Hassan al-Majid, also known as "Chemical Ali," vowed in 1987 on a tape obtained by HRW,

> I will kill them all with chemical weapons! Who is going to say anything? The international community? Fuck them! The international community, and those who listen to them! I will not attack them with chemicals just one day, but I will continue to attack them with chemicals for fifteen days.[11]

A history of genocide in Iraq 125

The majority of the victims of the Anfal Campaign were killed between February and August 1988. HRW estimates that 50,000–100,000 people, many of them women and children, were killed during this seven-month period. According to HRW,

> Their deaths did not come in the heat of the battle—'collateral damage' in the military euphemism. Nor were they acts of aberration by individual commanders whose excesses passed unnoticed, or unpunished, by their superiors. Rather, these Kurds were systematically put to death in large numbers on the orders of the central government in Baghdad—days, sometimes weeks, after being rounded up in villages marked for destruction or else while fleeing from army assaults in 'prohibited areas.'[12]

The most well-known attack occurred in Halabja in March 1988, killing as many as 5,000 people. Iraq's use of chemical weapons against members of its own population drew significant international attention. In its report, *Iraq's Crime of Genocide*, HRW notes,

> Thousands of civilians died...Their photographs, mainly of women, children, and elderly people huddled inertly in the streets or lying on their backs with mouths agape, circulated widely, demonstrating eloquently that the great mass of the dead had been Kurdish civilian noncombatants.[13]

Despite the international attention the Halabja attack received, the international response was mainly limited to words of disapproval. As Vera Saeedpour notes,

> Unfortunately, even then, despite worldwide revulsion and rhetorical condemnation, neither the United States nor the United Nations acted. Official reluctance to impose sanctions against the Iraqi regime gave Saddam the green light to again deploy chemical weapons on a larger scale against the Kurds little more than five months later.[14]

Indeed, five months after the Halabja attack, a UN-brokered ceasefire brought an end to the Iran–Iraq War on August 20, 1988. Less than one week later, Iraq resumed its offensive against members of its Kurdish population. Iraqi troops that had previously been engaged in the war effort were redeployed to carry out the final Anfal operation. This began on August 25, 1988, and lasted only a matter of days.[15]

In addition to HRW's pronouncement, there is also general agreement among scholars that Iraq committed genocide against members of its Kurdish population.[16] The Kurdish victims are members of a distinct ethnic group, of the type protected by the Genocide Convention and included in

126 *A history of genocide in Iraq*

most, if not all, scholarly definitions of genocide, including my own. There is also evidence that Iraq attacked Kurds with the intent to destroy as much of the Kurdish population as needed to achieve its objective of cleansing Iraqi Kurdistan of Kurdish people.

US–Iraq relations

The US relationship with Iraq evolved during the Iran–Iraq War. The Iran–Iraq War began in September 1980, when Saddam ordered a full-scale invasion of Iran. Though Iraq achieved initial success in its campaign, Iran had fought the invading forces to a stalemate by 1982. According to Mark Phythian, official US policy in the Iran–Iraq War was one of neutrality. However, hidden from the public, the US favored Iraq. When Iran demonstrated its ability to counter Iraqi attacks, the Reagan administration moved toward normalization of relations with Iraq in order to open up new channels through which it could provide assistance.[17]

One of the first indicators of the US "tilt" toward Iraq in the Iran–Iraq War came when the Reagan administration removed Iraq from the US list of state sponsors of terrorism in November 1983.[18] This change in policy was essential for the opening-up of avenues to support Iraq as a counter-weight to Iran's regional influence, as well as to wean Iraq off its reliance on the Soviet Union. Iraq's removal from the list allowed it to receive US government-backed credit and US military and dual-use technologies, and foreshadowed a resumption of full diplomatic relations, which occurred in late 1984.[19]

Soon after Iraq was removed from the list of state sponsors of terrorism, economic aid began to flow. The US granted Iraq access to its Agriculture Department's Commodity Credit Corporation (CCC) program.[20] According to the US Government Accountability Office, "export credit guarantees approved for Iraq under the programs increased from about $400 million in fiscal year (FY) 1983 to about $1.1 billion in FY 1988 and FY 1989, and $500 million in FY 1990."[21] From 1987 to 1989, a period that bracketed the Kurdish genocide, the amount of financial assistance Iraq received accounted for 23 percent, 25 percent, and 21 percent of the entire Export Credit Guarantee Programs, respectively.[22] Additionally, the US exponentially increased its import of Iraqi crude oil during the period surrounding the genocide. In 1983, the US imported 10,000 barrels per day. By 1987, that number increased to 82,000 barrels. In 1988 and 1989, the US imported 343,000 and 441,000 barrels, respectively.[23]

Removal of Iraq from the list of state sponsors of terrorism also enabled the US to provide Iraq with dual-use technologies. This included the sale of helicopters manufactured in the US. In 1983, Iraq was sold sixty Hughes MD-500 'Defender' helicopters and ten Bell UH–IS helicopters. Of course, the helicopters were sold to Iraq based on Saddam's promise that they would only be used for civilian purposes.[24] This was part of the

A history of genocide in Iraq   127

attraction of providing Iraq with dual-use commodities. They could be sold to Iraq under the pretense that they were for civilian purposes, but could then be transferred or modified for military purposes.

In 1984, Saddam purchased 45 Bell 214ST helicopters that were originally designed for military use. He claimed that some would be used to transport VIPs while others would be used for crop-dusting. A member of the US House of Representatives, Howard Berman, protested the sale of the helicopters, writing in a letter, "It is beyond belief that Iraq, with its foreign exchange reserves depleted by its conflict with Iran, would purchase forty-five helicopters at $5 million apiece simply to transport civilian VIPs."[25] W. Tapley Bennett Jr., Assistant Secretary of State for Legislative Affairs, responded by noting that the "civilian model" Bell helicopter was not on the list of items prohibited from sale.[26] Berman's suspicions were warranted. An eyewitness account published in *Aviation Week and Space Technology* asserted that at least 30 of the 45 helicopters were being used for military training exercises.[27] Further, helicopters fitted for crop dusting were allegedly used to spray Kurds with chemical weapons.[28]

Even prior to Iraq's removal from the state sponsors of terrorism list, an October 1983 classified memo recommended that the US selectively lift restrictions on "third-party transfers of U.S.-licensed military equipment to Iraq."[29] Relatedly, Howard Teicher, a former National Security Council staffer, confirmed the existence of a national security directive based on which the US "actively supported the Iraqi war effort by...closely monitoring third country arms sales to Iraq to make sure that Iraq had the military weaponry required."[30] Following this advice, the Reagan administration "began secretly allowing Jordan, Saudi Arabia, Kuwait and Egypt to transfer United States weapons, including howitzers, Huey helicopters, and bombs to Iraq."[31] These countries were not alone. Italy received a direct request from the US that it help funnel arms to Iraq.[32] Once again, as in the case of Guatemala, the Reagan administration enlisted other states to provide the support it was unable to at the time.

Iraq also benefited from US intelligence sharing. The US offered Iraq satellite intelligence as early as 1982. In 1984, President Reagan signed a national security directive that formally authorized a "limited intelligence-sharing program with Iraq."[33] The intelligence included "satellite reconnaissance photographs of strategic Iranian sites for targeting bomb raids, data on Iranian air force and troop positions...and communication intercepts."[34] Sharing increased exponentially in 1987 and 1988, even after Iraq's genocide against its Kurdish population began, and continued until as late as May 1990.

The US provided this intelligence despite having thoroughly documented Iraq's chemical weapons capabilities and its repeated use of such weapons. The US maintains that Iraq never informed the US of its plans to use chemical weapons. However, such an explicit admission was unnecessary. In a 2013 interview with *Foreign Policy*, retired Air Force Colonel Rick

128   *A history of genocide in Iraq*

Francona stated, "The Iraqis never told us that they intended to use nerve gas. They didn't have to. We already knew."[35] Shane Harris and Matthew Aid, the authors of the *Foreign Policy* article, support Francona's assertion with the inclusion of a series of recently declassified CIA documents that further demonstrate US knowledge of Iraq's illicit program and its use of prohibited weapons. This exemplifies the problems associated with a "double-edged sword"; the ability of the US to provide Iraq with substantial operational intelligence in its conflict with Iran meant that the US was also well informed of Iraq's actions and capabilities.

A 1980 US Defense Intelligence Agency report stated that Iraq had been actively acquiring a chemical warfare capability since the 1970s.[36] On November 1, 1983, the US confirmed that Iraq was using chemical weapons "almost daily" against Iran.[37] A few weeks later, a background cable on Iraq's use of chemical weapons stated that Iraq had used chemical weapons against Kurdish insurgents.[38] A series of memos from 1984 further establish US knowledge. A February 24 memo identifies Iraq's first use of nerve agents against Iran and armed Kurds—July 1982 and July 1983 respectively.[39] A March 13 memo predicted Iraq would employ the future widespread use of mustard gas.[40] A memo circulated a mere ten days later shows that the CIA knew Iraq would be capable of using "militarily significant quantities" of nerve agents by fall 1984.[41] The same memo also offers the first evidence that the US believed Saddam was willing to use chemical weapons against strictly civilian populations: "Attacks on civilian areas, such as Qom, in an attempt to force Tehran to the negotiating table, cannot be ruled out."[42]

At the latest, the US knew by August 1987 that Iraq was using chemical weapons against its Kurdish civilian population. Commenting on US intelligence, Larry Pope, former State Department officer director for Iran and Iraq, asserts, "There was a lag of a couple weeks at most. We knew that something dreadful was going on. We knew al-Majid was running the show. We had the satellite overhead that showed villages razed."[43] According to an August 4 memo from the Joint Chiefs of Staff to the Defense Intelligence Agency, Iraq was flattening villages and destroying civilian areas with frequent air raids, employing "ruthless repression," and using "chemical agents."[44] In an April 1988 memo, it states that a military campaign "waged to eradicate village bases of support" for armed Kurdish groups began in April 1987, which coincides directly with the start of Iraq's Kurdish genocide.[45] Further, according to the memo, Iraq had demonstrated a willingness to use chemical weapons "against Kurdish population centers" and that the "prospect of further civilian casualties" would not dissuade their continued use.[46] Thus, Harris and Aid conclude, "The U.S. knew Hussein was launching some of the worst chemical attacks in history—and still gave him a hand."[47]

Notably, a number of the memos cited above primarily attribute Iraq's successful chemical weapons program to Western Europe. For example, the November 1, 1983 memo states that "Iraq has acquired a CW production

A history of genocide in Iraq   129

capability, presumably from Western firms, including possibly a U.S. foreign subsidiary."[48] According to the February 24, 1984 memo, "Chemical agent precursors, munitions, equipment and expertise were purchased in Western Europe and Egypt with a view toward development of both mustard and nerve agents."[49] However, the US treated chemical agents as another type of dual-use technology, because of their potential civilian applications. In May 1994, Senators Riegle and D'Amato submitted their report, "U.S. Chemical and Biological Warfare-Related Dual Use Exports to Iraq and their Possible Impact on the Health Consequences of the Gulf War," also known as "The Riegle Report." As is evident from the title, the report was primarily concerned with the potential impact of Saddam's chemical and biological weapons on American forces in the aftermath of the Gulf War. Nonetheless, the report offers important insights into Iraq's development and use of chemical weapons, as well as materials provided by the US that may have been used in Saddam's weapons program.

According to the report,

> Records available from the supplier for the period from 1985 until the present show that during this time, pathogenic (meaning 'disease producing'), toxigenic (meaning 'poisonous'), and other biological research materials were exported to Iraq pursuant to application and licensing by the U.S. Department of Commerce.[50]

The report also notes that Iraq had been developing mustard gas, sarin gas, and the nerve agent VX since the early 1980s, along with the capability to experiment with hydrogen cyanide, cyanogen chloride, and lewisite—a capability that was enhanced by the assistance of foreign firms.[51] In passing, the report notes, "According to some sources, Iraq used mixed agent weapons combining cyanogen, mustard gas, and tabun against the Kurds."[52] Nonetheless, during the years surrounding the genocide, the Reagan administration continued to approve licenses for the export of dual-use goods with the knowledge that the licensed equipment could be used for military purposes, while also knowing that Iraq had used and was continuing to use chemical weapons against members of Iran's military and civilian population, and armed Kurds and Kurdish civilians. During the last two years of the Reagan administration, the US refused only six of 247 license applications. At least a dozen major Iraqi weapons facilities received dual-use import licenses, including at least one that was involved in the major production of chemical and biological weapons.[53]

In addition to the material support already described, the US also provided Iraq with political cover at the Security Council for its war crimes and genocide. As a permanent member with veto power, the US was able to wield significant influence on behalf of Iraq. Iran first accused Iraq of using chemical weapons in a letter submitted to the United Nations Secretary-General on November 3, 1983.[54] Following Iran's accusation, the

130 *A history of genocide in Iraq*

first of many, the Secretary-General authorized a fact-finding mission. The results of the investigation were submitted to the Security Council in March 1984. The experts who conducted the investigation unanimously concluded that chemical weapons had been used. Nonetheless, the Security Council only authorized its president to deliver a statement that did not identify who was responsible for the use of chemical weapons. Instead, the statement said only that the Security Council was concerned about "the unanimous conclusions of the specialists that chemical weapons have been used" and that it "strongly condemns the use of chemical weapons reported by the mission of specialists."[55] Thus, the Security Council issued only a limited response via a watered-down presidential statement, which is a far weaker response than a Security Council resolution would have been.

Obfuscation like this was part of a deliberate US strategy. According to Juan Cole, in response to Iran's attempt to attribute to Iraq the use of chemical weapons, the US "wanted to protect Hussein from condemnation by a motion of 'no decision,' and hoped to get U.S. allies aboard. If that ploy failed and Iraq were to be castigated, he ordered that the U.S. just abstain from the vote."[56] The US also argued that the use of chemical weapons ought to be a matter for the United Nations Human Rights Commission.[57]

Empty and lukewarm Security Council responses would become something of a pattern leading up to Iraq's genocidal use of chemical weapons against members of its Kurdish population in 1987 and 1988. In April 1985, the Security Council received the results of an investigation that concluded that: (1) chemical weapons were used in March 1985; (2) they were used against Iranian soldiers; and (3) the chemical weapons were delivered via bombs dropped from aircraft.[58] Once again, Iraq's use of chemical weapons was met with a presidential statement rather than a resolution. In February 1986, the Security Council unanimously passed Resolution 582, which condemned the use of chemical weapons. However, the resolution failed to indicate who was employing chemical weapons; instead, it noted that "both the Islamic Republic of Iran and Iraq are parties to the Protocol for the Prohibition of the Use in War of Asphyxiating, Poisonous or Other Gases, and of Bacteriological Methods of Warfare."[59] Prior to the vote on Resolution 582, the US placed blame on Iran for the continuing conflict, and expressed its concern over the use of chemical weapons, similarly failing to identify who was responsible for their use.[60]

On March 21, 1986, the Security Council moved to issue a presidential statement declaring that its

> members are profoundly concerned by the unanimous conclusion of the specialists that chemical weapons on many occasions have been used by Iraqi forces against Iranian troops, and the members of the Council strongly condemn this continued use of chemical weapons in clear violation of the Geneva Protocol of 1925, which prohibits the use in war of chemical weapons.

A history of genocide in Iraq   131

Of the fifteen Security Council members, only the US voted against the statement, effectively vetoing it, not because it was factually inaccurate, but because it specifically named Iraq as responsible.[61]

In May 1987, the Security Council acknowledged that Iraq had used chemical weapons against Iranian civilians.[62] Nonetheless, when the Security Council unanimously passed Resolution 598 in July 1987, it once again failed to specify who was responsible for the use of chemical weapons. Even as Iraq's use of chemical weapons in its genocidal campaign against members of its Kurdish population intensified, the Security Council response seemingly weakened. Less than two months after the chemical attack on Halabja that killed as many as 5,000 Kurds, the Security Council unanimously adopted Resolution 612 on May 9, 1988. The resolution noted that an investigation concluded that "chemical weapons continue to be used in the conflict and that their use has been on an even more intensive scale than before."[63] The resolution also condemned "vigorously the use of chemical weapons in the conflict between the Islamic Republic of Iran and Iraq" and stated the expectation that "both sides refrain from the future use of chemical weapons."[64]

Resolution 612 was consistent with US State Department policy. The US was growing concerned with increasingly vocal criticism of Iraq, and sought evidence that would implicate Iran. In an internal directive, the State Department issued guidelines for how US diplomats should respond to queries regarding the chemical attack on Halabja. These included, among others: Iran and Iraq are both parties to the 1925 Protocol that bans the use of chemical weapons; the US has condemned Iraq for its chemical attack on Halabja; both Iran and Iraq used chemical weapons around Halabja; and there is convincing evidence of Iranian use of chemical weapons, but the US is not ready to discuss the evidence publicly.[65]

One week after Resolution 612 was passed, as part of an effort to pressure the Security Council to recognize Iraq's responsibility for the Halabja attack, Iran submitted a letter to the Secretary-General. In it, Iran explicitly referred to the attack on Halabja as genocide, and accused the UN of failing to respond appropriately. Instead of taking proactive measures, the UN "allowed the lapse of two weeks following the legitimate request of this Mission to dispatch a team of experts."[66] Thus, argued Iran,

> The team was dispatched at a time when the evidence…had to a degree worn off due to the passage of time; a great number of the wounded had by then died or been discharged from the hospital after treatment. Such was the United Nations procrastinative reaction to the Halabja genocide.[67]

Iran then accused the "dominant powers" of pressuring the Security Council into its insufficient response. Chief among these dominant powers was the

132 *A history of genocide in Iraq*

US. Despite being fully aware of who was responsible, the US blocked Iran from seeking explicit recognition of Iraq's responsibility for the attack.[68]

There is overwhelming evidence that suggests that the US is responsible for one or more of genocide's ancillary acts. The US maintained close relations with Iraq throughout most of its war with Iran, which included the time directly preceding and during Iraq's Kurdish genocide. The US continued to support Iraq even after genocide was committed.[69] In the following sections, the evidence is evaluated to determine whether the US failed to uphold a responsibility to prevent genocide in Iraq and whether the US was complicit it.

Did the US uphold its obligation to prevent genocide in Iraq?

It is evident in the US relationship with Iraq that it incurred an obligation to prevent genocide in Iraq. Declassified documents show that the US was aware of Iraq's repeated use of chemical weapons against Iran during the Iran–Iraq War. The US also knew Iraq had used chemical weapons not only against Iran's military, but against Iranian civilians, Kurdish insurgents, and Kurdish civilians. In Bosnia v. Serbia, the ICJ found that Serbia should have been aware that something like the genocide at Srebrenica was possible, because of its knowledge of the hostility that existed between Bosnian Serbs and Bosnian Muslims. The US was similarly aware of the tension that existed between Iraq and its Kurdish population. Significantly, the genocide at Srebrenica was perpetrated during an approximately two-week period. Thus, the ICJ based its findings primarily on its belief that Serbia was aware that a Srebrenica was possible. Iraq's Kurdish genocide, however, was committed over a period of seventeen months, beginning in April 1997 and ending in August 1998. Thus, not only should the US have been aware that a Kurdish genocide was possible, but it had seventeen months to conclude that one was underway.

The US also maintained close financial, military, and political relations with Iraq. Once the US made its "tilt" toward Iraq, the aid flowed rapidly. Iraq was removed from the US list of state sponsors of terrorism in November 1983 even though the US was fully aware that it was committing war crimes by attacking Iran with chemical weapons. In late 1984, the US restored full diplomatic relations. In 1983, Iraq received $400 million in export credit guarantees. By 1988, this had increased to $1.1 billion.[70] During the two years in which Iraq committed genocide (1987–1988), Iraq accounted for 23 percent and 25 percent of the entire US Export Credit Guarantee Program.[71] The US also exponentially increased its consumption of Iraqi crude oil during the genocide, thus providing Iraq with additional economic support.[72]

US military aid to Iraq came in the form of military equipment and dual-use technologies. Helicopters were a popular item. In 1983 and 1984, the US sold Iraq more than one hundred.[73] The helicopters were provided

A history of genocide in Iraq 133

for "civilian" use, but were used by Iraq for military purposes. The US became aware of Iraq's efforts to modify the helicopters for military purposes by June 1983, when evidence emerged that Iraq was militarizing its Hughes helicopters.[74] As previously noted, some of the helicopters are even believed to have been used to spray Kurds with chemical agents.[75] The US also helped negotiate third-party transfers of weapons to Iraq.[76]

Perhaps most significantly, the US treated chemical agents as a type of dual-use technology with full knowledge of the extent of Iraq's chemical weapons program and its repeated use of such weapons. During the last two years of the Reagan administration, a period that overlapped with Iraq's Kurdish genocide, the US refused only six of 247 license applications. At least a dozen major Iraqi weapons facilities received dual-use export licenses, including at least one that was involved in the major production of chemical and biological weapons.[77]

In addition to financial and military aid, the US also provided Iraq with diplomatic aid. It did so through a combination of the diplomatic and political tactics employed during the genocides in Pakistan and Guatemala. As it did during Pakistan's genocide, the US used its seat at the Security Council to provide Iraq with political cover for its actions. As with Guatemala, the US worked to give the impression that it was unsure what was happening. It presented the chemical attacks committed during the Iran–Iraq War as having an ambiguous perpetrator. The US repeatedly obstructed attempts at the Security Council to name Iraq as the party responsible for the use of chemical weapons, including vetoing a presidential statement in 1986. The US even blocked Iran's effort aimed at getting the Security Council to attribute the Halabja attack to Iraq. As declassified documents show, the US partook in this shameful diplomacy with full knowledge of who was responsible for the chemical attacks throughout the 1980s.

It is clear from the evidence that the US had significant means of influence over Iraq, and that it chose not to use its influence to deter Iraq from committing genocide against members of its Kurdish population. As Samantha Power notes, "The United States had tremendous leverage with Iraq.... But the Reagan administration viewed U.S. influence as something to be stored, not squandered."[78] The US provided Iraq with various forms of assistance, including in each of the areas identified by the ICJ in Bosnia v. Serbia—political, military, and financial—prior to, during, and subsequent to the genocide. In many respects, the assistance peaked during the time directly surrounding Iraq's genocidal campaign. Therefore, it is evident that the US failed to uphold its obligation to prevent genocide.

Recall that the ICJ determined that the obligation to prevent genocide was one of conduct and not one of result. While the US was not under an obligation to succeed in preventing genocide in Iraq, it was obligated to employ all reasonable means available to do so. As the ICJ noted,

134   *A history of genocide in Iraq*

A State does not incur responsibility simply because the desired result is not achieved; responsibility is however incurred if the State manifestly failed to take all measures to prevent genocide which were within its power, and which might have contributed to preventing the genocide.

Just as the ICJ found that Serbia did nothing to prevent the Srebrenica massacres, the US did nothing to prevent Iraq's massacres of members of its Kurdish population.

Was the US complicit in Iraq's Kurdish genocide?

The evidence summarized above has significant implications regarding whether the US was also complicit in Iraq's genocide. To find that the US was complicit in Iraq's genocide, it is not necessary for the US to have shared Iraq's intent to commit genocide. The US did not even need to support Iraq's broader repressive policies aimed at its Kurdish population. It would be enough for the US to have been aware of Iraq's genocidal intent when it was providing Iraq with aid that facilitated the commission of genocide.

Based on declassified documents, US efforts to provide Iraq with political cover, the seventeen-month duration of the genocide, and the fact that only six of 247 license applications for dual-use technologies—or approximately .025 percent—were refused between 1987 and 1988, there is overwhelming evidence, even if circumstantial in some cases, that the US was complicit in Iraq's Kurdish genocide. Declassified documents show that the US knew about Iraq's illicit weapons program as early as the 1970s.[79] The US also knew Iraq was using chemical weapons against Iran and Kurdish insurgents by 1983, and Kurdish civilians by August 1987.[80] According to Joyce Battle,

> Chemical warfare was viewed as a potentially embarrassing public relations problem that complicated efforts to provide assistance. The Iraqi government's repressive internal policies, though well known to the US government at the time, did not figure at all in the presidential directives that established US policy toward the Iran–Iraq war.[81]

The US also provided Iraq with military intelligence during the Iran–Iraq War. The intelligence shared included satellite reconnaissance photographs, Iranian troop positions, and communication intercepts.[82] US intelligence sharing increased exponentially in 1987 and 1988.[83] It would be disingenuous to accept that the US was aware of Iraq's chemical weapons program and its use of chemical weapons, while also having the technology to monitor what was happening via satellite and communication intercepts, but reject that the US was aware that Iraq was attacking Kurds with the intent to commit genocide at some point during the campaign's seventeen-month duration.

A history of genocide in Iraq   135

Despite its knowledge of Iraq's use of chemical weapons against its Kurdish population, the US continued to provide Iraq with political cover even after the March 1988 Halabja attack. As Mark Milanovic notes, complicit acts include covering up evidence of the crime.[84] There is little reason to believe the US shared Iraq's intent to commit genocide. Therefore, I cannot conclude the US conspired with Iraq to commit genocide. However, there is more than enough evidence to conclude that the US was complicit in Iraq's genocide: it was aware of Iraq's intent to commit genocide, and provided it with the means to commit it.

A note on Samantha Power's analysis of the US role in Iraq

In her chapter on Iraq in *"A Problem from Hell": America and the Age of Genocide*, Power makes a significant contribution to our understanding of the US relationship with Iraq, some of which is cited in this chapter. It is not the thoroughness or analysis in Power's work that falls short; rather, time and again, Power's conclusions are simply insufficient. For example, Power cites declassified documents and former US officials, demonstrating that the US was aware of Iraq's repeated use of chemical weapons against Iran and Kurdish insurgents, and their use against Kurdish civilians. Yet, Power claims, "In Washington skepticism greeted gassing reports. Americans were so hostile toward Iran that they mistrusted Iranian sources."[85] Similarly, Power makes multiple references to a lack of incontrovertible evidence of Iraq's responsibility. For example, according to Power, "U.S. officials reluctant to criticize Iraq again took refuge in the absence of perfect information."[86] In contradictory fashion, Power lends legitimacy to US "skepticism" by citing distrust of Iranian sources and a lack of "perfect information," while providing evidence that the US knew what Iraq was doing, *according to US sources*.

Power also spends considerable time emphasizing Senator Claiborne Pell's effort to pass the Prevention of Genocide Act. In September 1988, Pell introduced this legislation, which would have cut Iraq off from receiving agricultural and manufacturing credits. According to Power, "Influenced by his foreign policy aide Peter Galbraith, Pell argued that not even a U.S. ally could get away with gassing his own people."[87] In this narrative, Pell is portrayed as morally outstanding for his effort. This is clear in Power's subsequent criticism of the Bush administration for failing to suspend "the CCC [credits] program or any of the other perks extended to the Iraqi regime, in 1989, a year *after* [emphasis in original] Hussein's savage gassing attack."[88] Instead, writes Power, the Bush administration "doubled its commitment to Iraq, hiking annual CCC credits above $1 billion. Pell's Prevention of Genocide Act, which would have penalized Hussein, was torpedoed."[89] While the Bush administration, and the Reagan administration before it, deserve the criticism, and much more, Power propagates a narrative that celebrates Pell, a US Senator from 1961 to 1997, as heroic and morally upstanding for

136 *A history of genocide in Iraq*

introducing legislation *after* Iraq had carried out its last act of the Kurdish genocide—seventeen months after it began and six months after the Halabja attack. Further, in drawing a line at "gassing his own people," it appears Pell was unconcerned about Iraq being an ally while using chemical weapons against Iran.

Ultimately, Power might conclude, based on the Bosnia v. Serbia Precedent, that the US had an obligation to prevent genocide in Iraq, and failed to uphold it. However, it is unlikely that Power would find the US complicit in the genocide. This is evident in how she gives the US the benefit of the doubt, leaving readers with the false impression that the US chose not to get involved due to geostrategic interests and a lack of "perfect information."[90] According to Power, rather than "send a strong message that genocide would not be tolerated...special interests, economic profit, and a geopolitical tilt toward Iraq thwarted humanitarian concerns."[91] Thus, Power concludes not that the US was complicit in genocide, but that the US "punted on genocide, and the Kurds paid the price."[92]

Economic sanctions and the collective punishment of Iraqis

In August 1990, Iraq illegally invaded and occupied Kuwait. Within days, the Security Council approved the most comprehensive sanctions regime in history. The sanctions banned all economic exchanges between Iraq and other states until Iraq withdrew from Kuwait. At the time, Iraq was importing 70 percent of its food, relying on the sale of oil to fund the imports.[93] Though the sanctions were initially implemented as a response to Iraq's violation of the United Nations Charter's Article 2(4) prohibition against the use of force against the territorial integrity of another state, they were renewed in April 1991—after the US-led coalition successfully ejected Iraqi forces from Kuwait. During the Gulf War, the US deliberately targeted Iraq's civilian infrastructure, including electricity and sanitation facilities.[94] These attacks exacerbated the effects of the initial sanctions and made the subsequent sanctions that much more destructive.

The sanctions had a near-immediate effect on public health in Iraq. They prohibited Iraq from importing "dual-use" goods, including those necessary to purify Iraq's drinking water and repair and maintain its infrastructure, especially in communication, transportation, and electricity generation, which was badly damaged during the Gulf War. Additionally, the sanctions significantly impeded purchases of medicines and foodstuffs.[95] Water supply shortages and the limited power supply degraded the functional capacity of Iraq's health care system. Communicable diseases reached epidemic proportions in 1993 and became endemic to life in Iraq for years to come. These included water-borne diseases and malaria, both of which were previously under control.[96] Immediately prior to the Gulf War, typhoid and cholera were nearly nonexistent—11.3 and zero per 100,000 people, respectively. By 1994, there were 142 cases of typhoid per 100,000 Iraqis and 1,344

A history of genocide in Iraq 137

cases of cholera per 100,000.[97] Iraqis, especially children, died of diarrhea, dysentery, and other normally preventable and survivable maladies that were not found in Iraq prior to the imposition of sanctions. This was due to untreated water and sewage, and because Iraq lacked access to medicines.[98]

In 1995, Sarah Zaidi and Mary C. Smith Fawzi conducted a community survey in Baghdad under the sponsorship of the United Nations Food and Agricultural Organization. Zaidi and Fawzi found a threefold increase in diarrheal-disease-related mortality in children under five years of age. Overall, they found a twofold increase in infant mortality compared with the year prior to the implementation of the economic sanctions. The twofold increase in infant mortality was sustained during the four years subsequent to the end of the Gulf War in 1991. Additionally, Zaidi and Fawzi found rates of malnutrition among children in Baghdad to be similar to those in less developed countries.[99] Child mortality rates in rural areas of Iraq were even higher than those in Baghdad.[100] Zaidi and Fawzi concluded that their data was "consistent with the economic and social realities seen in Iraq."[101] As a result of the sanctions, Iraqis were subjected to conditions of life that included high food prices, low purchasing power, failing water and sanitation systems, and hospitals operating at 40 percent capacity.[102]

Between 1994 and 1999, Iraqi children under five had a mortality rate of 131 per 1,000 live births. This was more than twice the rate of 56 per 1,000 recorded between 1984 and 1989, during which time Iraq was in the midst of an armed conflict with Iran. Similarly, infant mortality increased from 47 per 1,000 live births between 1984 and 1989 to 109 per 1,000 births between 1994 and 1999. The International Child Health Group concluded, "The reasons for the excess deaths are clear—economic collapse with plummeting wages, soaring food prices, poor sanitation, lack of safe water, and inadequate provision of healthcare."[103] The World Health Organization (WHO) and United Nations Children's Fund (UNICEF) reported that deaths of Iraqi children under five caused by the sanctions ranged from 5,000 to 7,000 per month. Additionally, it was not unusual for births in rural areas to go unregistered immediately after birth. If an infant died before being registered, the birth was never recorded. Therefore, the WHO in Baghdad considered the above range to be an underestimate.[104] The estimated number of Iraqis killed by or in connection with the sanctions varies and has generated considerable controversy. The total number of Iraqis killed could range from 1 to 2 million.[105] A conservative estimate regarding the number of children under the age of five who were killed is 300,000, with other estimates reaching 700,000.[106]

Did the US commit genocide in Iraq?

The economic sanctions imposed on Iraq caused massive death and human suffering. According to medical professionals and researchers, as well as intergovernmental organizations, the sanctions were the direct cause of the

138 *A history of genocide in Iraq*

death and suffering. Whether the US is responsible for genocide in Iraq, resulting from the initiation, maintenance, and enforcement of the sanctions, is dependent on three key factors. First, can the sanctions be attributed to the US? If not, answers to the subsequent questions are immaterial.[107] Second, did the sanctions qualify as a method of genocide and, therefore, a prohibited act? Finally, were the sanctions employed with the intent to commit genocide?

Attribution to the US

Though the sanctions were administered under the auspices of the United Nations, they were authorized and maintained primarily at the behest of the US.[108] Paul Conlon, a former Iraq Sanctions Committee official, acknowledged that US officials drafted every Security Council Resolution that dealt with sanctions against Iraq and their enforcement during the first few years of the sanctions regime.[109] Additionally, the US worked vigorously to maintain the sanctions regime, even as other members of the international community raised questions about their consequences. All this led George Bisharat to conclude, "Absent promotion by the United States, the sanctions may well have been abandoned years [before], perhaps even immediately following the cease-fire in the Gulf War in 1991."[110]

Official US statements also indicate that the US implicitly accepted a form of ownership over the maintenance and enforcement of the sanctions, though not the associated death and human suffering. In the following examples, the US situated itself between Iraq and sanctions relief, while placing responsibility for the death and human suffering with Iraq. US representatives even portrayed the US role as humanitarian, while justifying the continuation of the sanctions. In October 1992, Ambassador Edward Perkins stated that Iraq's refusal to comply with Security Council resolutions "has prevented its own population from receiving humanitarian relief."[111] In April 1995, Ambassador Madeleine Albright stated,

> The United States believes that Iraq's compliance with all the Security Council resolutions is the only way in which it will prove to the international community that its intentions are peaceful. Then, and only then, can this Council move to modify the sanctions regime.[112]

Of course, this was a distortion of reality. The only thing impeding an end to the sanctions regime was the US and those it successfully lobbied for support. Further, Albright proclaimed, "Our work on this new resolution is based on our humanitarian concern that the people of Iraq are suffering as a result of the policies of their Government."[113] Notably, Albright limits the effects of the sanctions by 1995 to "suffering," omitting the tens of thousands, if not hundreds of thousands, of Iraqi children who had already been killed.

A history of genocide in Iraq 139

The US also played a significant role in enforcement of the sanctions as a member of the Iraq Sanctions Committee. In this role, the US deliberately delayed or blocked the provision of humanitarian goods, including those for which there were clear exceptions in the sanctions regime. The combination of the sanction regime prohibitions and the cumbersome process by which exceptions were considered significantly impeded "*all* [emphasis in original] purchases by Iraq," even those that were clearly permitted, such as medicine and food.[114] Dual-use goods were also generally prohibited throughout the duration of the sanctions. The designation included just about anything that could have been used to rehabilitate and maintain Iraq's infrastructure, especially for transportation, communication, and generation of electricity.[115] Additionally, it is clear the US viewed items that could be used to promote public health in Iraq as dual-use. In a 2004 report titled "Suspected WMD-Related Dual-Use Goods and Procurement Transactions," the CIA listed attempted transactions that it believes violated the sanctions regime. These included, as labeled by the CIA, "chemical warfare raw materials"; "mobile laboratory trucks"; "chemical equipment and precursors"; "dual-use autoclaves"; and "biological dual-use" procurements.[116] Each of these "dual-use" items had important civilian applications, including chemical treatment for water and sewage; research on herbicides, pesticides, and other agriculture-related issues; sterilization of medical equipment; and research for breeding animals, such as cows and sheep, and crops.[117] It is bitterly ironic that the US provided Iraq with dual-use goods when Iraq was using them to commit war crimes and genocide during the 1980s, but denied Iraq access to such goods when they were needed to save the lives of Iraqis.

On September 12, 1997, Russia indirectly accused the US of preventing humanitarian aid from reaching the Iraqi people. According to Ambassador Sergey Lavrov, by August 1997, Iraq was receiving only 9.5 percent of the needed amount of medicine and medical supplies, and no agricultural products or water purifying agents. Iraq was also struggling to produce electrical energy, because of the damage done to its infrastructure and its inability to import the supplies needed to make repairs due to the sanctions. Lavrov noted that this was part of a "trend of blocking medical supplies and food contracts" required to meet urgent needs in Iraq. Lavrov accused "relevant delegations" of blocking requests without demonstrating cause for doing so.[118] In response to Lavrov's accusation, Ambassador Bill Richardson once again blamed Iraq for the humanitarian crisis. Richardson chastised Russia for attempting to insert language into a Security Council resolution "that seeks to blame the United Nations for actions solely the fault of the Government of Iraq."[119]

On December 4, 1997, China questioned the humanitarian nature of the Oil for Food Program, which was launched with the stated intention of alleviating human suffering. According to Ambassador Qin Huasun, the oil sales permitted were far from sufficient to meet Iraq's basic humanitarian needs. Additionally,

140   *A history of genocide in Iraq*

owing to the slow pace of review and approval procedures, at the conclusion of phase II there are still deliveries outstanding under phase I, and the overwhelming majority of phase II import applications have yet to be approved. Such a situation, in which the import of humanitarian goods lags far behind the export of oil, is unacceptable.[120]

Even more significantly, China directed attention to the systematic failure of the "humanitarian" response to the death and suffering in Iraq caused by the sanctions. Ambassador Huasun stated,

At the same time, I also wish to point out that if the revenue from oil exports cannot be speedily used to meet humanitarian needs, then, no matter how much oil is exported, it will not ease Iraq's humanitarian plight.[121]

In response, after seven years of maintaining and enforcing the sanctions, and with hundreds of thousands of Iraqi children dead, Ambassador Richardson again proclaimed the US' humanitarian credentials, asserting, "I think by now it should be clear to all where genuine concern for the welfare of the Iraqi people resides."[122]

Economic sanctions as a method of genocide

In my definition of genocide, I include three different means by which genocide can be committed. These include killing members of the group; deliberately imposing conditions that are likely to cause the deaths of members of the group; and enacting policies that seek to erase the group's cultural identity, also known as cultural genocide. Clearly, the first two methods apply to the economic sanctions in Iraq. Some scholars might reject the applicability of the first method, because the US was not physically murdering the Iraqis that its policy killed. Their deaths would be viewed as an "indirect" consequence of the sanctions. However, it is indisputable that the sanctions imposed conditions that caused the deaths of a national group—Iraqis. The length of time that the sanctions were administered with knowledge of the death and human suffering they caused is also evidence of their deliberate nature.

Scholars who reject "indirect" genocide wrongly treat policies that deliberately kill members of a group as less severe than murdering members of a group. But whether a perpetrator murders members of a protected group or deliberately creates and/or maintains conditions that kill them, members of the group die. The immediacy of murdering members of a group makes such acts more visible. Yet, deliberately starving or denying access to potable water will also kill group members; it just takes longer. Notably, the exclusion of indirect means of genocide is far from unanimous. For example, Jack Porter's definition includes starvation and, along with Isidor Walliman and Michael Dobkowski's, economic subjugation. Helen Fein includes the imposition of conditions that cause increasing infant mortality.[123] All these apply to the conditions created in Iraq by the sanctions.

The sanctions on Iraq were directly responsible for the precipitous decline in public health and the resulting death and human suffering. Before the sanctions, Iraq had an excellent and still-improving public health record. In 1980, Iraq initiated a program with the goal of reducing infant and child mortality by more than 50 percent over the next 10 years. According to a 1990 UNICEF survey, the program was largely successful.[124] Relatedly, a WHO study found that prior to the Gulf War, Iraqis had good vaccination coverage, access to clean water and electricity, and a marked decline in infant and under-five mortality rates.[125] Iraq achieved these standards despite its war with Iran between 1980 and 1988. As Tirman notes, "Even after the deprivations of the Iran–Iraq War, Iraq was a relatively modern society, with good electricity, sewage, water treatment, and health care infrastructure."[126] By the end of 1991, the Center for Economic and Social Rights reported that 70,000 children had already died.[127] As already detailed, communicable diseases, including water-borne diseases and malaria, had reached epidemic proportions by 1993.[128] By 1994, cases of typhoid and cholera had gone from being virtually nonexistent to significant.[129] Iraqi children died from diarrhea, dysentery, and other normally preventable and survivable maladies. Death from such ailments, too, was nearly absent in Iraq before the imposition of sanctions.[130] Infant mortality and mortality among children under five increased exponentially under the sanctions. The WHO and UNICEF estimate that 5,000–7,000 Iraqi children died each month.[131] The total number of children killed ranges from the conservative estimate of 300,000 to a high-end estimate of 700,000.[132] The number typically cited is 500,000.

In 1999, Dr. Richard Garfield published an assessment of the impact of the Gulf War and economic sanctions on public health in Iraq. He concluded that the rate of mortality among children under five had not been seen in Iraq in 20 years, "representing a loss of several decades of progress in reducing mortality."[133] The number of Iraqis killed under the sanctions regime were both avoidable and foreseeable. The cumulative effect of the sanctions left Iraqi children and their parents powerless to fend off the resulting plight. Had it not been for the US insistence that the sanctions continue, despite the very public death and suffering they caused, the Security Council might have lifted them as early as 1991, after Iraq was ejected from Kuwait.[134] Instead, they were maintained and enforced for twelve more years, until the US launched its war of aggression in 2003. A 1999 UNICEF report starkly concluded that had the public health trends of the previous three decades continued, there would have been half a million fewer deaths in Iraq.[135] The US was responsible for the sanctions, and the sanctions were responsible for the death and human suffering. Therefore, the US was responsible for the death and suffering, which was caused by a recognized means of genocide. The only question that remains is whether the US maintained and enforced the sanctions with the intent to commit genocide.

142 *A history of genocide in Iraq*

Economic sanctions and genocidal intent

My definition of genocide includes a moderated intent requirement. I define genocide as the attempt to eliminate, in whole or in part, a national, political, social, ethnic, racial, cultural, or socioeconomic group with the purpose of destroying it as such or achieving a political, social, or economic objective. Therefore, under my definition, genocide can be committed with the specific intent to destroy the targeted group. It can also be committed as part of a plan to achieve a particular objective when the plan involves employment of one of the methods of genocide against members of a protected group.

In an important analysis, Joy Gordon rejects allegations that the US committed genocide in Iraq via the economic sanctions based on the absence of evidence of specific intent. Gordon points to public statements made by US officials that express the opposite of intent to commit genocide—alleged concern for the well-being of Iraqis. For example, Gordon quotes a 1999 US policy report that claims that sanctions were "not intended to harm the people of Iraq."[136] The same report stated, "We want to see Iraq return as a respected and prosperous member of the international community."[137] Madeleine Albright even went so far as to present the US as a good humanitarian actor, even as it worked to maintain the sanctions. According to Albright, "The United States, in the person of me, in fact authored a resolution because I was concerned about the children of Iraq."[138] Albright's statement was delivered before the Chicago Council on Foreign Relations in late 1999, after upwards of 500,000 Iraqi children had been killed.

Gordon also highlights the alleged purpose of the sanctions proffered by the US—the maintenance of international peace and security. By invoking international peace and security to justify the economic sanctions regime, the US claimed the intent behind the sanctions was not to kill Iraqis due to their membership in a national group. Therefore, according to this defense, the deaths of 500,000 Iraqi children were a tragic byproduct of US efforts to maintain international peace and security. Relatedly, the argument goes, because the US was only trying to maintain international peace and security, to which Iraq was a threat, agency for the deaths of Iraqi children rests not with the US, but with Saddam Hussein. If only Saddam had cooperated, the sanctions would have been lifted, bringing an end to the death and human suffering. Though Gordon questions the persuasiveness of these defenses, she remains steadfastly committed to a specific intent requirement. The stated US justification was something other than the destruction of the Iraqi people as such; therefore, "whatever the unspoken intent may be," even though

> there may be acts which have harmed the innocent, and they may have been done quite deliberately ... the intent concerned political or legal goals regarding the enforcement of international security (or, as some might suggest, concerned the U.S. interest in protecting its access to Saudi oil).[139]

A history of genocide in Iraq   143

Clearly, Gordon gives the US the benefit of the doubt. The US is far from the only perpetrator of genocide to avoid leaving behind evidence of specific intent. As Josef Kunz notes, "governments, less stupid than that of National Socialist Germany, will never admit the intent to destroy a group as such, but will tell the world that they are acting against traitors and so on."[140]

While the US offered other explanations for why it sought to maintain and enforce the devastating sanctions, there is evidence of an implicit intent to kill Iraqis—both as members of a national group and in order to achieve its political objectives. Using a hybrid version of my intent requirement that includes both a specific intent criterion and the less restrictive requirement that acts of genocide be committed against a protected group with the purpose of achieving a particular objective, US intentions undoubtedly satisfy the intent requirement. Beginning with the former, intent can be inferred based on what knowledge the responsible party had of the likely and, if applicable, real consequences of its actions, along with whether the actions were continued despite this knowledge. As Adam Jones notes, using as an example the removal of indigenous populations from their land,

> if the coveting of native lands led to the removal of indigenous populations to territories incapable of sustaining life; if this unsustainability was 'reasonably foreseeable,' and confirmed when the deported population started to die *en masse,* and if the policies were not promptly reversed or ameliorated, then genocidal intent may still be said to have existed—albeit in a general form.[141]

Thanks to the publication in 1999 of a previously classified Defense Intelligence Agency memorandum from 1991, we know that the US was fully aware of the likely consequences of the sanctions *before* they were implemented. The content of the memo made clear that the US was aware that the impending military action and ongoing sanctions would have disastrous consequences for Iraqis. The memo demonstrates that the US knew all the following information and related consequences. Iraq was dependent on imported specialized equipment and chemicals to purify its water. Sanctions would impede Iraq's access to the equipment and chemicals it needed. Failure to acquire the supplies it needed would result in a shortage of potable water for much of Iraq's population; shortage of clean water could lead to epidemics of disease. Surface water in Iraq contained high levels of minerals such as carbonates, sulfates, chlorides, and nitrates, and if not treated could result in diarrhea and the formation of kidney stones. Iraq's rivers also contained biological pollutants and bacteria. If not purified with chlorine, consumption of river water could cause cholera, hepatitis, and typhoid epidemics. Additionally, pure-water-dependent industries would be incapacitated, including pharmaceuticals and food processing plants.[142]

The Defense Intelligence Agency memo predicted what has already been shown were the actual outcomes of the sanctions for the Iraqi people. The

144 *A history of genocide in Iraq*

fact that the US foresaw the consequences of enacting economic sanctions on Iraq, but designed them, advocated for them, and maintained and enforced them is illustrative of intent. The death and suffering caused by the sanctions were well documented. There was no shortage of studies that showed dramatic increases in preventable and curable diseases. As John Quigley notes, the US, along with its fellow Security Council members, was well aware of the death and human suffering caused by the sanctions, yet repeatedly voted to extend them.[143] Numerous published studies, many of which have been cited in this chapter, made public the death and human suffering in Iraq, attributing it to the sanctions. Security Council meetings regularly discussed the humanitarian situation in Iraq. Perhaps the most damning evidence of US intent to commit genocide came from then-US Secretary of State Madeleine Albright. In May 1996, while being interviewed on *60 Minutes*, Albright was asked by Lesley Stahl: "We have heard that a half million children have died. I mean, that's more children than died in Hiroshima. And, you know, is the price worth it?" Albright responded, "I think this is a very hard choice, but the price–we think the price is worth it."[144]

Two UN supervisors of the Oil for Food program—Denis Halliday and Hans von Sponeck—resigned in protest in 1998 and 2000, respectively. Halliday explained his resignation, stating that during his thirteen months in Baghdad he had come to consider the sanctions as "nothing less than genocidal."[145] Two years before Halliday resigned his post, former US Attorney General Ramsey Clark participated in a citizen's tribunal in Madrid, submitting a "criminal complaint" against the US. In his complaint, Clark alleged the US, aided and abetted by the Security Council, imposed, maintained, and enforced

> extreme economic sanctions and a strict military blockade on the people of Iraq for the purpose of injuring the entire population, killing its weaker members, infants, children, the elderly and the chronically ill, by depriving them of medicines, drinking water, food, and other essentials.[146]

In 2000, Iraq, itself no stranger to the crime, accused the US of genocide in an official complaint. Iraq stated,

> The comprehensive sanctions that have been maintained against Iraq for more than 10 years...have prevented the people of Iraq from enjoying the exercise of its economic, social, cultural, civil and political rights, chief among them the right to life and the right to development. This is to be considered as tantamount to genocide, whose perpetrators are to be punished by the international community under the terms of the 1948 Convention on the Prevention and Punishment of the Crime of Genocide.[147]

A history of genocide in Iraq   145

The US might not have bombed Iraq's civilian infrastructure and enforced the sanctions with the sole purpose of killing Iraqis. However, in knowing the likely impact of the sanctions before they were initiated, combined with knowledge of the real human consequences, the US demonstrated an intent to systematically kill large numbers of Iraqis. Whatever its other intentions might have been, the US killed 500,000 children and more than one million Iraqis in all to achieve its political objectives. Iraqis were treated as a means to an end. In this regard, Jones concludes that "an accusation of genocide founded on willful and malignant negligence" is justified.[148] Similarly, Elias Davidsson argues that "the degree of premeditation available to the defendants, the foreseeability of the consequences, the feedback received regularly by the defendants regarding the consequences of their deeds," along with the years during which they were maintained, all point to a prima facie case of genocide.[149]

Conclusion

Throughout most of the 1980s, the US openly and materially supported Iraq in its war with Iran. This support came in the form of military and economic aid, as well as direct financial support through an exponential increase in the consumption of Iraqi oil. During this period, the US was fully aware of Iraq's illicit chemical and biological weapons programs. The US also knew full well that Iraq was using chemical weapons against Iran and Kurdish insurgents, as well as their use on Kurdish civilians. This did not stop the US from providing Iraq with tactical intelligence, which is tantamount to "complicity in some of the most gruesome chemical weapons attacks ever launched."[150]

Nonetheless, the US continued to deliver aid to Iraq, including chemical agents that were used by Iraq in its weapons program. Beginning in April 1997, Iraq began its genocidal campaign against members of its Kurdish population. Over the next seventeen months, Iraq launched as many as forty separate attacks on Iraqi Kurds.[151] Most of the victims—an estimated 50,000–100,000 people—were killed between February and August 1988.[152] Over the two-year period during which Iraq committed genocide, the US overwhelmingly approved license applications for dual-use technologies. Based on the strength of US intelligence and the lengthy duration of the genocide, the US was aware of Iraq's intent to commit genocide while the US was supplying Iraq with aid that facilitated the crime. Therefore, it is clear the US was complicit in Iraq's genocide.

Only a few short years later, the US initiated a genocidal campaign of its own through its primary role in the design, implementation, and enforcement of an immensely destructive economic sanctions regime. The economic sanctions imposed at the behest of the US caused the deaths of Iraqis in three mutually reinforcing ways. First, the sanctions prevented Iraqis from having access to potable water, causing epidemics to emerge.

146 *A history of genocide in Iraq*

Second, the lack of pure water and access to ingredients needed to produce medicines impeded the production of pharmaceuticals that could be used to fight diseases. Third, the sanctions impeded Iraq from directly importing the supplies it needed to protect its citizens.

The public health record that existed prior to the imposition of sanctions, as compared to the one that emerged concurrently with the maintenance of the sanctions, clearly demonstrates that the sanctions inflicted upon Iraqis conditions of life that led to the deaths of hundreds of thousands of children and more than one million people altogether. Additionally, these conditions were deliberately created. A declassified CIA memorandum shows that the US knew the likely consequences of the sanctions. The US also knew the actual consequences of the sanctions. The fact that tens of thousands of children were dying each year from causes related to the sanctions was well documented. Nonetheless, the sanctions were maintained for more than a decade. This is evidence of implied intent to cause the death and suffering. The US attempted to use Saddam Hussein's authoritarian rule and previous violence—including genocidal treatment of his own people—to redirect the blame for the genocidal sanctions onto Saddam. Saddam's authoritarian rule in Iraq, however, does not preclude a finding that the US committed genocide in Iraq. In fact, it is unequivocal that the US enacted a form of collective punishment against the Iraqi people. The US continued to collectively punish the Iraqi people when it was clear the sanctions were causing a massive death toll and immense human suffering, especially among children.

The US was responsible for sanctions that were, in turn, responsible for massive deaths and human suffering. Even if the primary *purpose* was not to destroy Iraqi lives, the destruction was nevertheless *deliberate* and *intentional*. The US used Iraqis as nothing more than pawns in its effort to achieve a political objective. Therefore, the US is directly responsible for the commission of genocide in Iraq. Yet, from a survey of much of the genocide studies and human rights literatures, one would not know that the US was complicit in and directly responsible for two separate cases of genocide over a 16-year period in the same country.

Notes

1 John Tirman, *The Deaths of Others: The Fate of Civilians in America's Wars* (Oxford: Oxford University Press, 2011), 192.
2 Ibid.
3 Sean D. Thomas, "Chronic Conflict: A Case Study of Iraq," *WANA Institute.* Part 1 available at http://wanainstitute.org/sites/default/files/fact_sheets/Iraq_part_1.pdf; Part 2 available at http://wanainstitute.org/sites/default/files/fact_sheets/Iraq-part-2.pdf; Part 3 available at http://wanainstitute.org/sites/default/files/fact_sheets/Iraq-part-3.pdf (accessed June 6, 2017).
4 Vera Beaudin Saeedpour, "Establishing State Motives for Genocide: Iraq and the Kurds," in *Genocide Watch,* ed. Helen Fein (New Haven, CT: Yale University Press, 1992), 65.

A history of genocide in Iraq 147

5 Human Rights Watch, *Genocide in Iraq: The Anfal Campaign against the Kurds,* www.refworld.org/cgi-bin/texis/vtx/rwmain?page=printdoc&docid=47fdfb1d0 (accessed May 10, 2016).
6 Saeedpour, "Establishing State Motives for Genocide," 60.
7 Samantha Power, *"A Problem from Hell": American and the Age of Genocide* (New York: Harper Perennial, 2002), 171.
8 Ibid., 172.
9 Human Rights Watch, *Genocide in Iraq*.
10 Quoted in Saeedpour, "Establishing State Motives for Genocide," 64.
11 The tape is dated May 26, 1988, but from the context HRW believes it was recorded in 1987. Human Rights Watch, *Genocide in Iraq*, Appendix A: The Ali Hassan Al-Majid Tapes.
12 Ibid.
13 Human Rights Watch, *Iraq's Crime of Genocide*, www.hrw.org/report/1994/05/01/iraqs-crime-genocide-anfal-campaign-against-kurds (accessed May 10, 2016).
14 Saeedpour, "Establishing State Motives for Genocide," 60.
15 Ibid.
16 William Schabas, Leila Nadya Sadat, Beth Van Schaack, and Samuel Totten were interviewed, and Helen Fein's and Ben Kiernan's works were reviewed. All except Schabas agreed that Iraq committed genocide against members of its Kurdish population between 1987 and 1988. William Schabas, Interview, 17 September 2011; Leila Nadya Sadat, Interview, 26 September 2011; Beth Van Schaack, Interview, 19 September 2011; Totten, interview, 17 September 2011; Ben Kiernan, *Blood and Soil: A World History of Genocide and Extermination from Sparta to Darfur* (New Haven, CT: Yale University Press, 2007), 585; Helen Fein, *Human Rights and Wrongs: Slavery, Terror, Genocide* (Boulder, CO: Paradigm Publishers, 2007), 112.
17 Mark Phythian, *Arming Iraq: How the U.S. and Britain Secretly Built Saddam's War Machine* (Boston: Northeastern University Press, 1997), 33.
18 Ibid., 34.
19 Ibid.; Joyce Battle, "Shaking Hands with Saddam Hussein: The U.S. Tilts toward Iraq, 1980–1984," *National Security Archives Electronic Briefing Book No. 82* (2003), http://nsarchive.gwu.edu/NSAEBB/NSAEBB82/ (accessed May 10, 2016).
20 Power notes that the US provided Iraq with an average of $500 million per year in credits between 1983 and 1988. In Power, *"A Problem from Hell"*, 173.
21 United States Government Accountability Office, "Iraq's Participation in the Commodity Credit Corporation's GSM 102/103 Export Credit Guarantee Programs." www.gao.gov/products/T-NSIAD-91-13 (accessed May 10, 2016).
22 Ibid.
23 United States Energy Information Administration, "Petroleum & Other Liquids: U.S. Imports from Iraq of Crude Oil." www.eia.gov/dnav/pet/hist/LeafHandler.ashx?n=PET&s=MCRIMIZ2&f=A (accessed May 10, 2016).
24 Bruce W. Jentleson, *With Friends like These: Reagan, Bush and Saddam 1982–1999* (New York: W.W. Norton, 1994), p. 44.
25 Henry Weinstein and William C. Rempel, "Iraq Arms: Big Help from U.S.: Technology Was Sold with Approval–and Encouragement–from the Commerce Department but Often Over Defense Officials' Objections," *Los Angeles Times*. http://articles.latimes.com/1991-02-13/news/mn-1097_1_commerce-department-approved-millions/3 (accessed May 10, 2016).
26 Ibid.
27 Murray Waas, "What Washington Gave Saddam for Christmas," in *The Iraq War Reader: History, Documents, Opinions*, eds. Micah L. Sifry and Christopher Cerf (New York: Simon & Schuster, 2003), 35.

148 *A history of genocide in Iraq*

28 Phythian, *Arming Iraq*, 38.
29 Waas, "What Washington Gave Saddam for Christmas," 31.
30 Quoted in Juan Cole, "US Protected Iraq at UN from Iranian Charges of Chemical Weapons Use," *Informed COMMENT*, www.juancole.com/2013/08/protected-charges-chemical.html (accessed August 16, 2017).
31 Waas, "What Washington Gave Saddam for Christmas," 35.
32 Ibid., 36.
33 Ibid., 40.
34 Ibid.
35 Shane Harris and Matthew M. Aid, "Exclusive: CIA Files Prove America Helped Saddam as He Gassed Iran," *Foreign Policy*, http://foreignpolicy.com/2013/08/26/exclusive-cia-files-prove-america-helped-saddam-as-he-gassed-iran/ (accessed May 16, 2016).
36 Cited in Valerie Adams, *Chemical Warfare, Chemical Disarmament: Beyond Gethsemane* (London: MacMillan Press, 1989), 85.
37 United States Department of State, "Iraq Use of Chemical Weapons," Bureau of Politico-Military Affairs Information Memorandum from Jonathan T. Howe to George P. Schultz, November 1, 1983.
38 United States Department of State, "Iraqi Use of Chemical Weapons," Office of the Assistant Secretary for Near Eastern and South Asian Affairs Action Memorandum from Jonathan T. Howe to Lawrence S. Eagleburger, November 21, 1983.
39 United States Central Intelligence Agency, "Prospects for Use of Chemical Weapons by Iraq against Iran Over the Next Six Months," https://ia800202.us.archive.org/0/items/CIA-Iraq-Chemical-Weapons-1980s/163047754-Memo-Predicts-Use-of-Nerve-Agents.pdf (accessed August 16, 2017), 1.
40 United States Central Intelligence Agency, "Monthly Warning Meetings for February 1984," https://ia600202.us.archive.org/0/items/CIA-Iraq-Chemical-Weapons-1980s/163048262-CIA-Predicts-Widespread-Use-of-Mustard-Agents-and-Use-of-Nerve-Agent-by-Late-Summer.pdf (accessed August 16, 2017), 1.
41 United States Central Intelligence Agency, "Iraq: Use of Nerve Agent," https://ia800202.us.archive.org/0/items/CIA-Iraq-Chemical-Weapons-1980s/163048832-CIA-Confirms-Iraq-Used-Nerve-Agent.pdf (accessed August 16, 2017), 1. By 1985, according to a January 1985 memo, Iraq held a stockpile of artillery shells containing mustard agents estimated at several thousand. See United States Central Intelligence Agency, "The Iraqi Chemical Weapons Program in Perspective," https://ia600202.us.archive.org/0/items/CIA-Iraq-Chemical-Weapons-1980s/163050054-Intelligence-Assessment-of-Iraqi-Chemical-Weapons-Program.pdf (accessed August 16, 2017), iv.
42 Ibid., 3.
43 Quoted in Power, *"A Problem from Hell"*, 186.
44 United States Joint Chiefs of Staff, "The Internal Situation in Iraq," https://search.proquest.com/dnsa/docview/1679071168/3453DE88E05D4FCCPQ/1?-accountid=8285 (accessed August 16, 2017), 2.
45 United States Central Intelligence Agency, "Impact and Implications of Chemical Weapons Use in the Iran–Iraq War," www.cia.gov/library/reading-room/docs/DOC_0001079783.pdf (accessed August 16, 2017), 6.
46 Ibid.
47 Harris and Aid, "Exclusive."
48 United States Department of State, "Iraq Use of Chemical Weapons."
49 United States Central Intelligence Agency, "Prospects for Use of Chemical Weapons by Iraq against Iran," 1.
50 Donald W. Riegle, Jr. and Alfonse M. D'Amato, "The Riegle Report: U.S. Chemical and Biological Warfare-Related Dual Use Exports to Iraq and Their

A history of genocide in Iraq 149

Possible Impact on the Health Consequences of the Gulf War," www.gulfweb. org/report/riegle1.html (accessed May 11, 2016), 10.

51 Ibid.
52 Ibid., 4.
53 See Table 2.3 in Phythian, *Arming Iraq*, 44.
54 United Nations Security Council, Letter Dated 3 November 1983 from the Charge D'Affaires A.I. of the Permanent Mission of the Islamic Republic of Iran to the United Nations Addressed to the Secretary-General, www.un.org/en/ga/search/view_doc.asp?symbol=S/16128 (accessed May 15, 2016).
55 United Nations Security Council, Official Record of the 2524th Meeting, 30 March 1984, http://repository.un.org/bitstream/handle/11176/64537/S_PV.2524-EN.pdf?sequence=16&isAllowed=y (accessed May 15, 2016).
56 Cole, "US Protected Iraq at UN."
57 Ibid.
58 United Nations Security Council, Official Record of the 2576th Meeting, 25 April 1985, http://repository.un.org/bitstream/handle/11176/62755/S_PV.2576-EN.pdf?sequence=19&isAllowed=y (accessed May 15, 2016).
59 United Nations Security Council, Resolution 582 (1986) of 24 February 1986, www.un.org/en/ga/search/view_doc.asp?symbol=S/RES/582(1986) (accessed May 15, 2016).
60 United Nations Security Council, Provisional Record of the 2666th Meeting, 24 February 1986, www.securitycouncilreport.org/atf/cf/%7B65BFCF9B-6D2 7-4E9C-8CD3-CF6E4FF96FF9%7D/Chap%20VII%20SPV%202666.pdf (accessed August 17, 2017).
61 I was unable to locate primary documentation. Excerpts of the statement and the US vote are cited in a number of reputable sources. See Brian M. Mazanec, *The Evolution of Cyber War: International Norms for Emerging-Technology Weapons* (Lincoln, NE: Potomac Books, 2015), 63; Mike Wells and Nick Fellows, *History for the IB Diploma: Causes and Effects of 20th Century Wars*, 2nd ed. (Cambridge: Cambridge University Press, 2016), 244; Joy Gordon, *Invisible War: The United States and the Iraq Sanctions* (Cambridge, MA: Harvard University Press, 2010), 258.
62 United Nations Security Council, Note by the President of the Security Council, 14 May 1987, https://documents-dds-ny.un.org/doc/UNDOC/GEN/N87/122/05/IMG/N8712205.pdf?OpenElement (accessed May 15, 2016).
63 United Nations Security Council, Resolution 612 (1988) of 9 May 1988, www.un.org/en/ga/search/view_doc.asp?symbol=S/RES/612(1988) (accessed May 15, 2016).
64 Ibid.
65 Joost R. Hiltermann, *A Poisonous Affair: America, Iraq, and the Gassing of Halabja* (Cambridge: Cambridge University Press, 2007), 126–127.
66 United Nations Security Council, Letter Dated 16 May 1988 from the Charge D'Affaires A.I. of the Permanent Mission of the Islamic Republic of Iran to the United Nations Addressed to the Secretary-General, 16 May 1988, https://documents-dds-ny.un.org/doc/UNDOC/GEN/N88/132/79/IMG/N8813279. pdf?OpenElement (accessed May 15, 2016), 1–2.
67 Ibid.
68 Power, *"A Problem from Hell"*, 195.
69 Ibid.
70 United States Government Accountability Office, "Iraq's Participation in the Commodity Credit Corporation's GSM."
71 Ibid.
72 United States Energy Information Administration, "Petroleum & Other Liquids."

150   *A history of genocide in Iraq*

73 Jentleson, *With Friends like These*, 44; Weinstein and Rempel, "Iraq Arms."
74 Hiltermann, *A Poisonous Affair*, 45.
75 Phythian, *Arming Iraq*, 38.
76 Waas, "What Washington Gave Saddam for Christmas," 31.
77 Phythian, *Arming Iraq*, 44.
78 Power, *"A Problem from Hell"*, 223.
79 Adams, *Chemical Warfare, Chemical Disarmament*, 85.
80 United States Department of State, "Iraq Use of Chemical Weapons"; United States Joint Chiefs of Staff, "The Internal Situation in Iraq."
81 Joyce Battle, "Shaking Hands with Saddam Hussein."
82 Phythian, *Arming Iraq*, 40.
83 Ibid.
84 Mark Milanovic, "State Responsibility for Genocide," *The European Journal of International Law* 17, no. 3 (2006): 573.
85 Power, *"A Problem from Hell,"* 190.
86 Ibid., 208.
87 Ibid., 173.
88 Ibid.
89 Ibid.
90 Ibid., 208.
91 Ibid., 173.
92 Ibid., 172–173.
93 Tirman, *The Death of Others*, 205.
94 Roger Normand, "Sanctions against Iraq: Is It Genocide?" *Guild Practitioner* 58 (2001): 27.
95 Joy Gordon, "When Intent Makes All the Difference in the World: Economic Sanctions on Iraq and the Accusation of Genocide," *Yale Human Rights and Development Journal* 5, no. 2 (2014): 71.
96 Mohamed M. Ali and Iqbal H. Shah, "Sanctions and Childhood Mortality in Iraq," *The Lancet* 355 (2000): 1856.
97 Gordon, "When Intent Makes All the Difference in the World," 71–72.
98 Normand, "Sanctions against Iraq," 27.
99 Sarah Zaidi and Mary C. Smith Fawzi, "Health of Baghdad's Children," *The Lancet* 346 (1995): 1485.
100 Ali and Shah, "Sanctions and Childhood Mortality in Iraq," 1856.
101 Zaidi and Fawzi, "Health of Baghdad's Children," 1485.
102 Ibid.
103 Roger Dobson, "Sanctions against Iraq 'Double' Child Mortality," *BMJ* 321 (2000): 1490.
104 Denis J. Halliday, "The Impact of Sanctions on the People of Iraq," *Journal of Palestine Studies* 28, no. 2 (1999): 30.
105 George E. Bisharat, "Sanctions as Genocide," *Transnational Law & Contemporary Problems* 11 (2001): 381.
106 Normand, "Sanctions against Iraq," 28.
107 They would be irrelevant to an analysis of a uniquely US role. If evidence shows that the sanctions represent a prohibited act and were maintained with genocidal intent, whoever the sanctions can be attributed to would be implicated in the commission of genocide.
108 See Gordon, "When Intent Makes All the Difference in the World," 58; Bisharat, "Sanctions as Genocide," 389–390; Adam Jones, *Genocide: A Comprehensive Introduction*, 2nd ed. (London: Routledge, 2011), 44.
109 Gordon, "When Intent Makes All the Difference in the World," 58, n.1.
110 Bisharat, "Sanctions as Genocide," 390.

A history of genocide in Iraq 151

111 United Nations Security Council, Provisional Record of the 3117th Meeting, 2 October 1992, http://dag.un.org/bitstream/handle/11176/54483/S_PV.3117-EN.pdf?sequence=3&isAllowed=y (accessed May 15, 2017).

112 United Nations Security Council, Provisional Record of the 3519th Meeting, 14 April 1995, www.un.org/en/ga/search/view_doc.asp?symbol=S/PV.3519 (accessed May 15, 2017).

113 Ibid.

114 Gordon, "When Intent Makes All the Difference in the World," 71.

115 Ibid., 70–71.

116 United States Central Intelligence Agency, "Suspected WMD-Related Dual-Use Goods and Procurement Transactions," www.cia.gov/library/reports/general-reports-1/iraq_wmd_2004/chap2_annxI.html (accessed June 3, 2017).

117 Ibid.

118 United Nations Security Council, Provisional Record of the 3817th Meeting, 12 September 1997, www.un.org/en/ga/search/view_doc.asp?symbol=S/PV.3817 (accessed May 15, 2017).

119 Ibid.

120 United Nations Security Council, Provisional Record of the 3840th Meeting, 4 December 1997, www.un.org/en/ga/search/view_doc.asp?symbol=S/PV.3840 (accessed May 15, 2017).

121 Ibid.

122 Ibid.

123 All cited in Jones, *Genocide*, 2nd edition, 17–18.

124 Gordon, "When Intent Makes All the Difference in the World," 71.

125 Ibid.

126 Tirman, *The Deaths of Others*, 205.

127 Normand, "Sanctions against Iraq," 30.

128 Ali and Shah, "Sanctions and Childhood Mortality in Iraq," 1856.

129 Gordon, "When Intent Makes All the Difference in the World," 71–72.

130 Normand, "Sanctions against Iraq," 27.

131 Halliday, "The Impact of Sanctions on the People of Iraq," 30.

132 Roger Normand, "Sanctions against Iraq," 28.

133 Richard Garfield, "Morbidity and Mortality among Iraqi Children from 1990 through 1998: Assessing the Impact of the Gulf War and Economic Sanctions," www.casi.org.uk/info/garfield/dr-garfield.html (accessed May 1, 2016).

134 Bisharat, "Sanctions as Genocide," 390.

135 Gordon, "When Intent Makes All the Difference in the World," 72.

136 Ibid., 74.

137 Ibid.

138 Ibid.

139 Quoted in Gordon, "When Intent Makes All the Difference in the World," 76.

140 Josef Kunz, "The United Nations Convention on Genocide," *The American Journal of International Law* 43, no. 4 (1949): 743.

141 Jones, *Genocide*, 2nd edition, 38.

142 United States Defense Intelligence Agency, "Iraq Water Treatment Vulnerabilities," www.gulflink.osd.mil/declassdocs/dia/19950901/950901_511rept_91.html (accessed 3 June 2017).

143 John Quigley, *The Genocide Convention: An International Law Analysis* (Burlington, VT: Ashgate, 2006), 204.

144 Quoted in Gordon, *Invisible War*, 157.

145 Denis J. Halliday, "US Policy and Iraq: A Case of Genocide?" in *Genocide, War Crimes and the West*, ed. Adam Jones (London: Zed Books, 2004), 264.

152 *A history of genocide in Iraq*

146 Ramsey Clark, "Criminal Complaint against the United States and Others for Crimes against the People of Iraq," in *Genocide, War Crimes and the West*, ed. Adam Jones (London: Zed Books, 2004), 271.
147 Quoted in Quigley, *The Genocide Convention*, 204.
148 Jones, *Genocide*, 61.
149 Quoted in Gordon, "When Intent Makes All the Difference in the World," 74.
150 Harris and Aid, "Exclusive."
151 Human Rights Watch, *Genocide in Iraq*.
152 Ibid., 3.

Bibliography

Adams, Valerie. *Chemical Warfare, Chemical Disarmament: Beyond Gethsemane*. London: MacMillan Press, 1989.

Ali, Mohamed M., and Iqbal H. Shah. "Sanctions and Childhood Mortality in Iraq." *The Lancet* 355 (2000): 1851–1857.

Battle, Joyce. "Shaking Hands with Saddam Hussein: The U.S. Tilts toward Iraq, 1980–1984." *National Security Archives Electronic Briefing Book No. 82*, 2003. Accessed May 10, 2016. http://nsarchive.gwu.edu/NSAEBB/NSAEBB82/.

Bisharat, George E. "Sanctions as Genocide." *Transnational Law & Contemporary Problems* 11 (2001): 379–425.

Clark, Ramsey. "Documents 2 and 3: Criminal Complaint against the United States and Others for Crimes against the People of Iraq (1996) and Letter to the Security Council (2001)." In *Genocide, War Crimes and the West: History and Complicity*, edited by Adam Jones, 270–275. London: Zed Books, 2004.

Cole, Juan. "US Protected Iraq at UN from Iranian Charges of Chemical Weapons Use." *Informed COMMENT*. Accessed August 16, 2017. www.juancole.com/2013/08/protected-charges-chemical.html.

Dobson, Roger. "Sanctions against Iraq 'Double' Child Mortality." *BMJ* 321 (2000): 1490.

Fein, Helen. *Human Rights and Wrongs: Slavery, Terror, Genocide*. Boulder, CO: Paradigm Publishers, 2007.

Garfield, Richard. "Morbidity and Mortality among Iraqi Children from 1990 through 1998: Assessing the Impact of the Gulf War and Economic Sanctions." Accessed May 1, 2016. www.casi.org.uk/info/garfield/dr-garfield.html.

Gordon, Joy. *Invisible War: The United States and the Iraq Sanctions*. Cambridge, MA: Harvard University Press, 2010.

Gordon, Joy. "When Intent Makes All the Difference in the World: Economic Sanctions on Iraq and the Accusation of Genocide." *Yale Human Rights and Development Journal* 5, no. 2 (2014): 57–84.

Halliday, Denis J. "The Impact of Sanctions on the People of Iraq." *Journal of Palestine Studies* 28, no. 2 (1999): 29–37.

Halliday, Denis J. "US Policy and Iraq: A Case of Genocide?" In *Genocide, War Crimes and the West*, edited by Adam Jones, 264–269. London: Zed Books, 2004.

Harris, Shane, and Matthew M. Aid. "Exclusive: CIA Files Prove America Helped Saddam as He Gassed Iran." *Foreign Policy*. Accessed May 16, 2016. http://foreignpolicy.com/2013/08/26/exclusive-cia-files-prove-america-helped-saddam-as-he-gassed-iran/.

Hiltermann, Joost R. *A Poisonous Affair: America, Iraq, and the Gassing of Halabja*. Cambridge: Cambridge University Press, 2007.

A history of genocide in Iraq 153

Human Rights Watch. *Genocide in Iraq: The Anfal Campaign against the Kurds.* Accessed May 10, 2016. www.refworld.org/cgi-bin/texis/vtx/rwmain?page=printdoc&docid=47fdfb1d0.

Human Rights Watch. *Iraq's Crime of Genocide.* Accessed May 10, 2016. www.hrw.org/report/1994/05/01/iraqs-crime-genocide-anfal-campaign-against-kurds.

Jentleson, Bruce W. *With Friends like These: Reagan, Bush and Saddam 1982–1999.* New York: W.W. Norton, 1994.

Jones, Adam. *Genocide: A Comprehensive Introduction*, 2nd ed. London: Routledge, 2011.

Kiernan, Ben. *Blood and Soil: A World History of Genocide and Extermination from Sparta to Darfur.* New Haven, CT: Yale University Press, 2007.

Kunz, Josef. "The United Nations Convention on Genocide." *The American Journal of International Law* 43, no. 4 (1949): 738–746.

Mazanec, Brian M. *The Evolution of Cyber War: International Norms for Emerging-Technology Weapons.* Lincoln, NE: Potomac Books, 2015.

Milanovic, Mark. "State Responsibility for Genocide." *The European Journal of International Law* 17, no. 3 (2006): 553–604.

Normand, Roger. "Sanctions against Iraq: Is It Genocide?" *Guild Practitioner* 58 (2001): 27–31.

Phythian, Mark. *Arming Iraq: How the U.S. and Britain Secretly Built Saddam's War Machine.* Boston, MA: Northeastern University Press, 1997.

Power, Samantha. *"A Problem from Hell": American and the Age of Genocide.* New York: Harper Perennial, 2002.

Quigley, John. *The Genocide Convention: An International Law Analysis.* Burlington, VT: Ashgate, 2006.

Riegle, Donald W., and Alfonse M. D'Amato. "The Riegle Report: U.S. Chemical and Biological Warfare-Related Dual Use Exports to Iraq and Their Possible Impact on the Health Consequences of the Gulf War." Accessed May 11, 2016. www.gulfweb.org/report/riegle1.html.

Saeedpour, Vera Beaudin. "Establishing State Motives for Genocide: Iraq and the Kurds." In *Genocide Watch,* edited by Helen Fein, 59–69. New Haven, CT: Yale University Press, 1992.

Thomas, Sean D. "Chronic Conflict: A Case Study of Iraq Part 1." *WANA Institute.* Accessed June 6, 2017. http://wanainstitute.org/sites/default/files/fact_sheets/Iraq_part_1.pdf.

Thomas, Sean D. "Chronic Conflict: A Case Study of Iraq Part 2." *WANA Institute.* Accessed June 6, 2017. http://wanainstitute.org/sites/default/files/fact_sheets/Iraq-part-2.pdf.

Thomas, Sean D. "Chronic Conflict: A Case Study of Iraq Part 3." *WANA Institute.* Accessed June 6, 2017. http://wanainstitute.org/sites/default/files/fact_sheets/Iraq-part-3.pdf.

Tirman, John. *The Deaths of Others: The Fate of Civilians in America's Wars.* Oxford: Oxford University Press, 2011.

United Nations Security Council. Letter Dated 3 November 1983 from the Charge D'Affaires A.I. of the Permanent Mission of the Islamic Republic of Iran to the United Nations Addressed to the Secretary-General. Accessed May 15, 2016. www.un.org/en/ga/search/view_doc.asp?symbol=S/16128.

United Nations Security Council. Letter Dated 16 May 1988 from the Charge D'Affaires A.I. of the Permanent Mission of the Islamic Republic of Iran to the United

154 *A history of genocide in Iraq*

Nations Addressed to the Secretary-General. Accessed May 15, 2016. https:// documents-dds-ny.un.org/doc/UNDOC/GEN/N88/132/79/IMG/N8813279. pdf?OpenElement.

United Nations Security Council. Note by the President of the Security Council, 14 May 1987. Accessed May 15, 2016. https://documents-dds-ny.un.org/doc/ UNDOC/GEN/N87/122/05/IMG/N8712205.pdf?OpenElement.

United Nations Security Council. Official Record of the 2524th Meeting, 30 March 1984. Accessed May 15, 2016. http://repository.un.org/bitstream/handle/11176/ 64537/S_PV.2524-EN.pdf?sequence=16&isAllowed=y.

United Nations Security Council. Official Record of the 2576th Meeting, 25 April 1985. Accessed May 15, 2016. http://repository.un.org/bitstream/handle/11176/62755/S_ PV.2576-EN.pdf?sequence=19&isAllowed=y.

United Nations Security Council. Provisional Record of the 2666th Meeting, 24 February 1986. Accessed August 17, 2017. www.securitycouncilreport.org/atf/ cf/%7B65BFCF9B-6D27-4E9C-8CD3-CF6E4FF96FF9%7D/Chap%20VII%20 SPV%202666.pdf.

United Nations Security Council. Provisional Record of the 3117th Meeting, 2 October 1992. Accessed May 15, 2017. http://dag.un.org/bitstream/handle/11176/54483/S_PV. 3117-EN.pdf?sequence=3&isAllowed=y.

United Nations Security Council. Provisional Record of the 3519th Meeting, 14 April 1995. Accessed May 15, 2017. www.un.org/en/ga/search/view_doc.asp?symbol=S/ PV.3519.

United Nations Security Council. Provisional Record of the 3817th Meeting, 12 September 1997. Accessed May 15, 2017. www.un.org/en/ga/search/view_doc. asp?symbol=S/PV.3817.

United Nations Security Council. Provisional Record of the 3840th Meeting, 4 December 1997. Accessed May 15, 2017. www.un.org/en/ga/search/view_doc.asp? symbol=S/PV.3840.

United Nations Security Council. Resolution 582 (1986) of 24 February 1986. Accessed May 15, 2016. www.un.org/en/ga/search/view_doc.asp?symbol=S/RES/582(1986).

United Nations Security Council. Resolution 612 (1988) of 9 May 1988. Accessed May 15, 2016. www.un.org/en/ga/search/view_doc.asp?symbol=S/RES/612(1988).

United States Central Intelligence Agency. "Impact and Implications of Chemical Weapons Use in the Iran–Iraq War." Accessed August 16, 2017. www.cia.gov/ library/readingroom/docs/DOC_0001079783.pdf.

United States Central Intelligence Agency. "Iraq: Use of Nerve Agent." Accessed August 16, 2017. https://ia800202.us.archive.org/0/items/CIA-Iraq-Chemical-Weapons-1980s/163048832-CIA-Confirms-Iraq-Used-Nerve-Agent.pdf.

United States Central Intelligence Agency. "Monthly Warning Meetings for February 1984." Accessed August 16, 2017. https://ia600202.us.archive.org/0/items/CIA-Iraq-Chemical-Weapons-1980s/163048262-CIA-Predicts-Widespread-Use-of-Mustard-Agents-and-Use-of-Nerve-Agent-by-Late-Summer.pdf.

United States Central Intelligence Agency. "Prospects for Use of Chemical Weapons by Iraq against Iran Over the Next Six Months." Accessed August 16, 2017. https:// ia800202.us.archive.org/0/items/CIA-Iraq-Chemical-Weapons-1980s/163047754-Memo-Predicts-Use-of-Nerve-Agents.pdf.

United States Central Intelligence Agency. "Suspected WMD-Related Dual-Use Goods and Procurement Transactions." Accessed June 3, 2017. www.cia.gov/library/ reports/general-reports-1/iraq_wmd_2004/chap2_annxI.html.

United States Central Intelligence Agency. "The Iraqi Chemical Weapons Program in Perspective." Accessed August 16, 2017. https://ia600202.us.archive.org/0/items/CIA-Iraq-Chemical-Weapons-1980s/163050054-Intelligence-Assessment-of-Iraqi-Chemical-Weapons-Program.pdf.

United States Defense Intelligence Agency. "Iraq Water Treatment Vulnerabilities." Accessed June 3, 2017. www.gulflink.osd.mil/declassdocs/dia/19950901/950901_511rept_91.html.

United States Department of State. "Iraq Use of Chemical Weapons." Bureau of Politico-Military Affairs Information Memorandum from Jonathan T. Howe to George P. Schultz, November 1, 1983.

United States Department of State. "Iraqi Use of Chemical Weapons." Office of the Assistant Secretary for Near Eastern and South Asian Affairs Action Memorandum from Jonathan T. Howe to Lawrence S. Eagleburger, November 21, 1983.

United States Energy Information Administration. "Petroleum & Other Liquids: U.S. Imports from Iraq of Crude Oil." Accessed May 10, 2106. www.eia.gov/dnav/pet/hist/LeafHandler.ashx?n=PET&s=MCRIMIZ2&f=A.

United States Government Accountability Office. "Iraq's Participation in the Commodity Credit Corporation's GSM 102/103 Export Credit Guarantee Programs." Accessed May 10, 2016. www.gao.gov/products/T-NSIAD-91-13.

United States Joint Chiefs of Staff. "The Internal Situation in Iraq." Accessed August 16, 2017. https://search.proquest.com/dnsa/docview/1679071168/3453DE88E05D4FCCPQ/1?accountid=8285.

Waas, Murray. "What Washington Gave Saddam for Christmas." In *The Iraq War Reader: History, Documents, Opinions*, edited by Micah L. Sifry and Christopher Cerf, 30–40. New York: Simon & Schuster, 2003.

Weinstein, Henry, and William C. Rempel. "Iraq Arms: Big Help from U.S.: Technology Was Sold with Approval—and Encouragement—from the Commerce Department but Often Over Defense Officials' Objections." *Los Angeles Times*. Accessed May 10, 2016. http://articles.latimes.com/1991-02-13/news/mn-1097_1_commerce-department-approved-millions/3.

Wells, Mike, and Nick Fellows. *History for the IB Diploma: Causes and Effects of 20th Century Wars*, 2nd ed. Cambridge: Cambridge University Press, 2016.

Zaidi, Sarah, and Mary C. Smith Fawzi. "Health of Baghdad's Children." *The Lancet* 346 (1995): 1485.

7   Genocide in Vietnam

Incorporated in my definition of genocide is a nexus between aggressive war and genocide. The nexus is formed in part by including protection for political groups, along with national groups—the two groups most likely to be victims of aggressive war. My revised intent requirement completes the nexus: it defines genocide as the attempt to eliminate a group with the purpose of destroying it as such or achieving a political, social, or economic objective, and includes unarmed and armed members of the targeted group as victims of genocide. The nexus is limited to aggressive war, because this involves the illegitimate use of force. Thus, every death that results from aggressive war is also illegitimate. Participation in war to defend against an aggressor, too, can amount to genocide. However, this would be determined by the means of mounting the defense, rather than the act of participation itself. After all, states have a customary right to self-defense, as well as a legal one under Article 51 of the United Nations Charter.

Under Article 2(4) of the Charter, the threat or use of force by one state against another is prohibited. There are only two exceptions to this rule. First, states can use force when authorized by the Security Council under its Chapter VII powers. Second, as noted above, states can use force in self-defense. Beyond these exceptions, the use of force constitutes an act of aggression. Following World War II, the Charter of the International Military Tribunal defined aggression as the "planning, preparation, initiation or waging of a war of aggression, or a war in violation of international treaties, agreements or assurances, or participation in a common plan or conspiracy for the accomplishment of any of the foregoing."[1]

Since then, there have been numerous efforts to articulate a clear definition of aggression. In 1951, the International Law Commission (ILC) offered the following definition:

> Aggression is the use of force by a State or Government against another State or Government, in any manner, whatever the weapons used and whether openly or otherwise, for any reason or for any purpose other than individual or collective self-defence or in pursuance of a decision or recommendation by a competent organ of the United Nations.[2]

Genocide in Vietnam 157

Importantly, the ILC defined aggression by the nature of the act, rather than the means by which it is conducted. Further, the ILC essentially defined aggression as an attempt to use force to achieve an objective that has some purpose other than one explicitly endorsed by the United Nations.

In 1974, the General Assembly expanded on the United Nations Charter's prohibition on the use of force by enumerating specific acts that constitute aggression. Under General Assembly Resolution 3314 (XXIX), the first use of force in contravention of the Charter's provisions "shall constitute prima facie evidence of an act of aggression," regardless of whether there was a "declaration of war."[3] Acts of aggression include, *inter alia*: (1) the invasion or attack by one state against another; (2) the military occupation, however temporary, resulting from an invasion or attack; (3) the bombardment of one state by another; and (4) the blockade of one state's ports or coasts by another state.[4] Finally, the General Assembly defined a war of aggression as "a crime against international peace" that "gives rise to international responsibility."[5]

The US engaged in a decade-long series of aggressive acts against Vietnam that together constituted a war of aggression against the Vietnamese people. The US bombarded Vietnam relentlessly and attacked the country and its people by various other means. The US did so in violation of the United Nations Charter, and for its own political purposes. The context in which the US initiated its attacks offers ample evidence of this. The US used two "false flag" events in the Gulf of Tonkin to portray its impending war of aggression as one of self-defense. The purpose of the war, however, was not to defend the US; it was to keep from "losing" Vietnam to the communists. The US sought to manipulate the narrative to justify its war of aggression. These events were also used to secure Congressional support, which the Johnson administration received when the Gulf of Tonkin resolution authorized it "to take all necessary measures to repel any armed attack against the forces of the United States and to prevent further aggression."[6]

The first "false flag" incident took place on August 2, 1964. The US claimed that North Vietnamese torpedo boats launched an "unprovoked attack" against the USS Maddox, which had been on a "routine patrol" of the Gulf of Tonkin. However, the Maddox, a destroyer, had in fact been gathering intelligence to support attacks against North Vietnam carried out by the South Vietnamese navy and the Laotian air force.[7] Whereas the facts surrounding the first incident were manipulated to aid in making the case for war in Vietnam, the second incident never even occurred. On August 4, the Pentagon claimed that North Vietnam had launched a second unprovoked attack in the Gulf of Tonkin. That same evening, Johnson announced on national television that he was authorizing "retaliatory" air strikes against North Vietnam.[8] Less than a week later, Congress passed the Gulf of Tonkin resolution with a near-unanimous vote of 504 in favor, including every voting member of the House of Representatives, and two against, both in the Senate.

158 *Genocide in Vietnam*

That November, Johnson won the presidential election. On March 2, 1965, the US initiated a sustained and massively destructive bombing campaign in "self-defense" against a country 8,500 miles from its borders. In an interview in 1967 with an Australian journalist, North Vietnam's Foreign Minister Nguyen Duy Trinh presented a very different picture than that propagated by the US—one that explicitly identified the US as perpetrator of an aggressive war, using the most brutal tactics, in pursuit of its own objectives. According to Trinh,

> The U.S. imperialists are waging the most barbarous war of aggression against our country.... The people of North Vietnam have not been and will never be cowed by the barbarous bombing raids of the U.S. imperialists and have dealt them well-deserved counterblows.[9]

Further, Trinh demanded that the US "stop its war of aggression in Vietnam and let the Vietnamese people settle their own affairs themselves."[10]

In this chapter, I revisit the contentious debate in genocide studies regarding whether the US is responsible for committing genocide in Vietnam. Applying my definition of genocide, I provide a unique contribution to this debate by offering a perspective that takes into account the methods by which the US fought its war of aggression, the purpose of the war, and the intent of the violence, along with the fact that the victims were members of a political group. Previous allegations of genocide have been generally limited to the indiscriminate nature of the war and the massacres of civilians. Most genocide scholars reject genocide allegations. However, the combination of the methods used, the purpose and intent of the war of aggression, and the membership of the victims in a political group implicates the US in the commission of genocide in Vietnam.

The remainder of this chapter is divided into three parts. First, I provide a brief summary of the methods by which the US waged its war of aggression. As will be shown, it is undeniable that the US committed prohibited acts against the people of Vietnam. Second, I present evidence that the purpose of the war of aggression was to destroy the viability of communism in Vietnam, and that the intent of the massive violence inflicted on the Vietnamese people was to kill as many real or perceived communists as was necessary to achieve the objective of eliminating communism in Vietnam. Finally, I explain why all the victims of the US war of aggression were also victims of genocide.

Genocidal acts

During the so-called "Vietnam War," known in Vietnam as the "Resistance War against America," the US unleashed a massive wave of destruction, committing atrocities against members of the National Liberation Front (NLF) and its real and perceived supporters in South Vietnam. Beginning in 1965, the US launched a full-scale invasion, ultimately sending more than

500,000 troops to Vietnam to fight the NLF and members of North Vietnam's regular forces. From 1965 to 1975, the US dropped upwards of eight million tons of bombs and other munitions on South and North Vietnam, equaling the explosive force of approximately 640 atomic bombs of the kilotonnage dropped on Hiroshima.[11] When laid crater to crater, the US destroyed an area the size of Maine.[12] As Adam Jones stresses, "This was more than was dropped by all countries in all theaters of the Second World War."[13] The US also used eight million tons of other ordnance and 400,000 tons of napalm, an incendiary weapon.[14]

Along with the massive bombing campaigns, a network of what were essentially concentration camps was created in South Vietnam. Large areas of land were also designated as "free-fire zones." Of these zones, Howard Zinn wrote: "all persons remaining within them—civilians, old people, children—were considered an enemy, and bombs were dropped at will."[15] When combined, free-fire zones covered approximately three-fourths of South Vietnam.[16] People who refused to evacuate their villages risked being slaughtered by air and land units of the US and South Vietnamese militaries. "The most infamous such event," writes Jones,

> was the My Lai massacre—a four-hour-long rampage by US troops on March 16, 1968, in the village of Son My and its constituent hamlets of My Lai, My Khe, and Co Luy in Quang Ngai province. Infuriated by guerrilla attacks, US troops of Charlie Company, 1st Battalion slaughtered, raped, and wreaked material destruction. The My Lai memorial plaque today lists 504 victims.[17]

The My Lai massacre may have been the largest of such attacks, but it was far from the only one of a genocidal nature.[18]

Estimates of the total number of Vietnamese killed during the duration of the US war against Vietnam range from 1.5 million to 3.8 million.[19] However, the death and destruction attributable to the US does not end with these direct casualties. As many as 74 million liters of "tactical" herbicides were used in Vietnam between 1961 and 1971.[20] In 1970, before the long-term consequences of US chemical and biological warfare on the people of Vietnam became known, Orville Schell and Barry Weisberg described them as follows:

> The near complete destruction of the living landscape and the human society...is proceeding at such a staggering rate that it is really impossible to estimate its true scope, severity or long-range consequences....So far reaching is the destruction that finally one is forced to ask whether or not the American military has not in fact found a way of dealing with wars of national liberation: the destruction of the people and the land itself.[21]

The chemicals were sprayed over one-seventh of South Vietnam, with effects that endure to this day.[22] At 43 million liters, Agent Orange accounted for

160   *Genocide in Vietnam*

nearly 60 percent of the herbicides used.[23] Agent Orange contains a form of dioxin called TCCD, which is believed to be responsible for significant ongoing health complications in Vietnam. In 2003, Cathy Scott-Clark and Adrian Levy wrote,

> Evidence has also emerged that the US government not only knew that Agent Orange was contaminated, but was fully aware of the killing power of its contaminant dioxin, and yet still continued to use the herbicide in Vietnam for 10 years of the war and in concentrations that exceeded its own guidelines by 25 times.[24]

It is an incontrovertible fact that the US is responsible for acts in Vietnam that are prohibited under my definition of genocide, along with most scholarly definitions of genocide, and by the Genocide Convention. The US deliberately killed large numbers of Vietnamese; caused serious bodily or mental harm; and inflicted upon the Vietnamese people conditions of life calculated to bring about their physical destruction in whole or in part. Thus, as Hugo Adam Bedau writes,

> The charge of genocide in Vietnam against the United States has an undeniable rhetorical appropriateness. No other single word so well captures the magnitude of the offensiveness of the war in light of the methods used to fight it, the purposes advanced as its justification, the facts of the political and social realities in Southeast Asia, and the complex but not entirely elusive intentions of the Johnson (and Nixon) administrations in fighting it as they did.[25]

Nonetheless, accusations against the US of genocide in Vietnam have been rather few, and those levied have been persistently challenged and dismissed, including by Bedau, primarily on the grounds that the US lacked genocidal intent.

Genocidal intent

Scholars who reject genocide accusations found their objections on a specific intent requirement for genocide. This limited conception of genocidal intent permits massive violence to be committed by one state against the population of another state so long as it is under the guise of "war." For example, Matthew Lippman notes,

> American decision-makers certainly realized that their terror tactics entailed a substantial likelihood of decimating large numbers of Vietnamese and shattering civil society. Yet, most scholars argued that allegations of genocide could not be sustained absent proof of specific criminal intent.[26]

Relatedly, Helen Fein dismisses attempts to label US actions in Vietnam as genocide as a conflation of war crimes with genocide.[27]

French philosopher Jean-Paul Sartre disagreed. Sartre argued, "The genocidal intent is implicit in the facts."[28] For Sartre, these include the premeditated nature of US attacks and the attacks themselves, with "villages burned, the population subjected to massive bombing, livestock shot, vegetation destroyed by defoliants, crops ruined by toxic aerosols, and everywhere indiscriminate shooting, murder, rape and looting. This is genocide in the strictest sense: massive extermination."[29] In response to Sartre, a number of scholars acknowledge that methods of genocide were employed; in the acts Sartre described, this includes killing members of a group and deliberately imposing on members of the group conditions of life calculated to bring about its physical destruction in whole or in part. However, according to Joy Gordon, "This is evidence of ordinary intent only—that the acts were voluntary, deliberate, and chosen."[30] Similarly, in an essay written in direct response to Sartre, Bedau asserts,

> Yet this is insufficient to assure us that the intention with which such actions have been done is the intention relevant to genocide. From the fact that a certain series of actions are intentional actions, it does not follow that they are done with genocidal intention.[31]

More dismissive of Sartre's accusation, Louis Pollack, former Dean of the Yale Law School, writes,

> I don't find it very useful to talk about those alleged offenses as genocide. We have nothing that indicates the definition of that offense has been met...I doubt if we have crimes of genocide, but undoubtedly we have crimes of murder and violations of the rules of war which are treatable by courts.[32]

As discussed in Chapter 2 and exemplified by Pollack's assessment, some genocide scholars insist on a clear delineation between war and genocide. Unwavering commitment to such a hard distinction can only be sustained when war is depicted as a legitimate means of violence, and when the genocidal nature of aggressive war is unrecognized. For some, war retains a "legitimate" role in the modern world. It has its critics, of course; but most of the criticism is limited to whether the war was "justified," and whether the means by which it was conducted exceeded those permitted under international humanitarian law. Meanwhile, no rules govern genocide beyond those that prohibit it. Central to the legitimation of war, and to its distinction from genocide, is the insistence that war is justified—all who wage war and who support it will find a defense for it—and that the intent behind the violence was to "win" the war. In discussions of the Genocide Convention's intent requirement at the Sixth Committee, the US made this very point,

162 *Genocide in Vietnam*

arguing that "in times of war, the motive for the act was not to destroy a group as such, but to impair the military strength of the enemy."[33]

The emphasis on intent would continue during the Korean War. From 1950 to 1953, the US dropped 635,000 tons of bombs and 32,557 tons of napalm on the Korean Peninsula, with little regard for civilian casualties.[34] During the Korean War, upwards of three million civilians were killed, most of them in the North.[35] During an interview, Curtis LeMay, head of Strategic Air Command during the war, asked rhetorically, "Over a period of three years or so, we killed off—what—20 percent of the population of Korea as direct casualties of war, or from starvation and exposure?"[36] The massive death and destruction in the Korean War is generally treated as an unfortunate, but justifiable, consequence of war. The harm to noncombatants from the violence was "a tragedy of war but not a crime."[37] Thus, intent allows perpetrators of war, even wars of aggression, to kill millions of people, while differentiating them from perpetrators of genocide. This involves a "stunning contradiction between lethal consequences and proclaimed scrupulousness" in which less importance is placed on "whether civilians were killed than on whether they were killed intentionally."[38]

Israel Charny has argued that the definition of genocide must reflect the "reality of masses of dead people."[39] Treating war as somehow conceptually distinct from genocide privileges the death and destruction that is war's inevitable consequence. It unjustifiably distinguishes the illegitimate act of aggressive war, which can kill as many or more people than genocide, from the illegitimate act of genocide. In doing so, it denies the victims of war their group membership, whether national, political, or other; erases the purpose of aggressive war; and negates victims' right to resist their own destruction.

The US war of aggression perpetrated against the people of Vietnam displayed genocidal intent in two mutually reinforcing ways. The purpose of the war was to destroy communism in Vietnam. The intent of the violence was to kill as many communists in Vietnam as required to achieve the war's political objective. Therefore, the US launched a war of aggression with the intent of destroying the communist political group in Vietnam. This constitutes genocide.

US policy prior to its unleashing massive violence and destruction on the Vietnamese people demonstrated the purpose of its aggressive war. Following the Viet Minh's defeat of the French at Dien Bien Phu in May 1954, the US, the Soviet Union, France, the United Kingdom, and China met in Geneva to discuss the future of Vietnam (as well as Korea). With France's defeat in the so-called "First Indochina War," known in Vietnam as the "Anti-French Resistance War," Vietnam's independence was inevitable. However, the question remained whether its government would be communist. Rather than allowing for self-determination, the powers agreed that Cambodia and Laos would become independent kingdoms, while Vietnam would be partitioned like Korea and Germany. As part of the agreement, Vietnam was partitioned along the 17th parallel, with the communists holding the North and the South aligning itself with the US.

The partition was intended to be temporary, with elections to be held in two years' time. Article 6 of the Final Declaration declared,

> The Conference recognizes that the essential purpose of the agreement relating to Vietnam is to settle military questions with a view to ending hostilities and that the military demarcation line is provisional and should not in any way be interpreted as constituting a political or territorial boundary.[40]

On the issue of elections, then-US Under Secretary of State Walter Bedell Smith said,

> In connection with the statement in the Declaration concerning free elections in Vietnam, my government wishes to make clear its position which it has expressed in a Declaration made in Washington on 29 June 1954, as follows: 'In the case of nations now divided against their will, we shall continue to seek unity through fair elections, supervised by the United Nations to ensure they are conducted fairly.'[41]

Despite alleged US support for free elections in Vietnam as part of a reunification process, the US refused to sign the Geneva Agreement, relieving the US of any legal obligation to respect it.[42] It became clear that neither South Vietnam nor the US had any intention of supporting elections so long as the communists were likely to win. Having taken control of South Vietnam in 1955, Ngo Dinh Diem rejected elections, instead launching a campaign to crush the communist opposition.[43] Jonathan Neale describes Diem's South Vietnam as a police state in which repressive measures were used to suppress a majority peasant and worker population that opposed him. "In 1956," writes Neale,

> anybody who had agitated for elections was arrested—about 50,000 people, of whom roughly 12,000 were executed...The terror smashed half the Communist cells in Tay Ninh province by late 1955, and 90 percent of the party cells in Tay Ninh were gone by the end of 1956.[44]

Diem's brutal repression of communists in South Vietnam was carried out with full US support.

In response to Diem's refusal to hold elections and his increasingly repressive policies, South Vietnamese opposed to Diem formed the NLF political party at a conference in 1960. The NLF was composed of around twenty sociopolitical organizations; hence it constituted a political group. The government in Saigon dubbed the NLF the "Viet Cong," a pejorative formed by shortening Viet Nam Cong San (Vietnamese Communists). In his book *War, Peace, and the Viet Cong*, Douglas Pike describes the political role played by the NLF in South Vietnam. He writes,

164   *Genocide in Vietnam*

Political power, all the political power if possible, quite clearly represents the NLF's objective. It regards itself as the sole, genuine, legitimate representative of the South Vietnamese people and labels the Saigon government 'rebel' and illegitimate. The language it speaks, although militant and sloganized, is the language of government and politics.[45]

Citing a document issued in 1967, Pike lists the NLF's four major policies as: (1) to save the nation from the US aggressors; (2) to reunify South and North Vietnam; (3) to build an independent, neutral, peaceful, and democratic Vietnam; and (4) to implement a neutral, peaceful foreign policy.[46]

The US worked against a political process that would have seen Vietnam reunited based on the results of the planned elections. Simultaneously, the US supported Diem as he violently repressed political opposition. After the political opposition formed the NLF in 1960 and Diem was murdered in a coup by his own generals in 1963, the US used two "false flag" events to justify its war of aggression as a "war of self-defense." When the US initiated that war, it did so because it feared the communists, as represented by the NLF, were poised to win control of the country, whether through a legitimate vote or through an armed struggle. Officials stressed the implications for US elsewhere. At the time, the US was deeply invested in anti-communist governments, such as South Korea and, as discussed in Chapter 4, Indonesia. The Kennedy and Johnson administrations both cited the "domino theory," formulated by President Eisenhower in 1954, as the reason for US involvement in Vietnam. According to the theory, if Vietnam ("French Indochina" during the Eisenhower administration) "went communist," so too would the rest of Southeast Asia. In a 1956 speech, then-Senator Kennedy asserted, "Vietnam represents the cornerstone of the Free World in Southeast Asia. It is our offspring. We cannot abandon it, we cannot ignore its needs."[47]

This line of thinking did not change in subsequent years. In a November 1964 intelligence assessment on the situation in South Vietnam, the National Security Council warned that the "political situation remains critical and extremely fragile."[48] The assessment notes that "the loss of South Vietnam to Communist control, in any form, would be a major blow to our basic policies. US prestige is heavily committed to the maintenance of a non-Communist South Vietnam" and that the US may need to "take forceful enough measures in the situation so that we emerge from it, even in the worst case, with our standing as the principal helper against Communist expansion as little impaired as possible."[49] Here, it was clearly stated that the US might need to involve itself directly in the South Vietnamese political conflict—to physically attack the Communist opposition—in order to, as in Indonesia, prevent communist control.

Relatedly, in March 1965, Assistant Secretary of Defense John MacNaughton wrote in a memo to Secretary of Defense Robert McNamara that the US objective in Vietnam was principally to avoid a humiliating defeat; in other words, to avoid damage to the US "reputation as a guarantor" and

Genocide in Vietnam 165

to keep South Vietnam out of communist hands.[50] And in May 1966, Henry Cabot Lodge, Jr., US Ambassador to South Vietnam, "praised the decision to deploy U.S. troops to Vietnam. The recent overthrow of the Communists in Indonesia is a direct result of our having taken a firm stand in Vietnam."[51] This claim has been disputed, but it nonetheless reflected the dominant mentality at the time.

From the so-called "Pentagon Papers," published by the *New York Times* in 1971, Bedau extrapolated four interlocking principles that dominated the thinking of the civilian and military leadership during the early years of the Johnson administration. These principles demonstrate a connection between the purpose of the aggressive war and the intent to destroy communists as a political group, in whole or part. According to Bedau, they included the need to prop up the non-communist government in Saigon; the belief that this could not be accomplished unless the communist NLF was prevented from taking control of South Vietnam; and the conviction that the only way to prevent this from happening was to destroy the NLF's political power by separating the people from the NLF through force.[52] It is clear that the US intended to eliminate the NLF and its supporters to the degree necessary to destroy the viability of communism in the South. In its attempt to prevent Vietnam from "going communist," the US helped to impede national elections that would have almost certainly resulted with a unified communist Vietnam, and physically attacked real and perceived members of the communist political group with the intent to eliminate the political opposition to the Saigon government.

Interestingly, perhaps the best case that has been made for the US intent to commit genocide against a political group in South Vietnam was Bedau's, in arguing against a genocidal intent underlying US actions. According to Bedau,

> The methods used were undertaken as a last resort, and would never have been used at all if the people of South Vietnam had shown both a nominal loyalty to Saigon and some sustained resistance to the blandishments and threats of the Viet Cong. In any case, the genocide-like acts were not genocidal, because they were not done with the intention of killing *any part* [emphasis in original] of the people of South Vietnam 'as such.' These were acts done with the intention of killing people who were simply in the way, simply there, because, in the judgment of field officers, they might at a later point prove to be Viet Cong or because they were in a zone or area of South Vietnam where one could not be sure that any of the natives were loyal to the Saigon government.[53]

Bedau concludes that the people who were killed, wounded, and forced to become refugees by the US were not victimized with the intent to destroy them. Rather, the intent behind US actions was to ensure that all of the people of South Vietnam were ruled by a government in Saigon that was not

166   *Genocide in Vietnam*

"anti-Western [and] pro-Communist."[54] Thus, had the people killed shown loyalty to the government in Saigon and disavowed communism, they might still be alive today. In other words, those perceived to be "in the way" of preserving an anti-communist South Vietnam were in fact targeted as members of a group as such, just not one of the groups protected by the Genocide Convention, due to the omission of political groups during the treaty's drafting process. They were targeted as supporters of the NLF with the intent to destroy communism's base of support in South Vietnam.

Killing members of a political group with the intent to destroy the group as such clearly satisfies a specific intent requirement. Genocide against a political group seeks to eliminate the targeted group's ability to function as a viable political entity. "Thus," according to Barbara Harff, genocides against political groups (what Harff and Gurr refer to as 'politicide') "typically attempt to destroy the ability of opposition groups to challenge or resist the regime by targeting their potential supporters."[55] Similarly, Jason Campbell identifies the following as indicators of genocidal intent against a political group: (1) potential victims are reluctant to accept state-endorsed ideology; (2) the state's ideology seeks to eliminate a part of the population within the state's jurisdiction; and (3) a refusal to accept the state's ideology is punishable by death or forced emigration.[56]

What Bedau describes as lacking genocidal intent fits neatly into the above conceptions of specific intent to commit genocide against members of a political group. The purpose of the US war of aggression and the intent behind its killing of Vietnamese was to rid Vietnam of communists as a viable political group. Simply being, or being perceived to be, communist was punishable by death or forced emigration. In 1988, Harff and Ted Gurr developed a typology of 'politicides.' It includes retributive politicide, repressive politicide, and revolutionary politicide. Retributive politicides target a previously dominant or influential group in response to past abuses perpetrated by the group. Repressive politicides target political groups, parties, or other politically based factions because of their oppositional activities. Revolutionary politicides target political enemies who are acting in the service of a revolutionary ideology.[57] The US attack against North Vietnam, the NLF, and its real and perceived supporters can be described as repressive and revolutionary politicide. The US targeted a political group in Vietnam because its ideologically infused activities stood in opposition to US interests in Vietnam and the broader region. Harff and Gurr's typology does not seem to leave room for interstate politicide. Yet, an international dimension seems clear. The same relationships can exist between the perpetrators of aggressive war and a victimized group in the state being attacked. Aggressive war waged by one state against a political group located in another state, in order to destroy the political group as such, contains the elements that define genocide against a political group just as does an intrastate conflict in which the state victimizes a group within its own polity.

Victims of genocide

The US war of aggression against Vietnam was launched with the intention of destroying the viability of communism in Vietnam. Therefore, the victims of the war, both unarmed and armed, were real and perceived members of a communist political group, or were ascribed membership by the perpetrators. In this regard, the victims can be divided into four categories—those who were killed as members of North Vietnam's regular armed forces; those killed as members of the organized resistance in South Vietnam, meaning the armed wing of the NLF; those killed because of their real or perceived support of the NLF; and those killed based solely on the view, rooted in racism, that all Vietnamese were members of the armed resistance. As Sartre noted,

> In the confused minds of the American soldiers, 'Vietcong' and 'Vietnamese' tend to increasingly blend into one another. They often say to themselves, 'The only good Vietnamese is a dead Vietnamese,' or what amounts to the same thing, 'A dead Vietnamese is a Vietcong.'[58]

Therefore, Sartre concluded, US armed forces tortured and killed "men, women and children in Vietnam merely *because they are Vietnamese* [emphasis in original]."[59] Put another way, the intent was to kill communists in Vietnam. All Vietnamese were essentially viewed as the same. Therefore, all Vietnamese were viewed as communists, especially those who were killed.

Incredibly, in his study of democide—"the murder of any person or people by a government, including genocide, politicide, and mass murder"—R.J. Rummel claimed that "the U.S. democide in Vietnam seems to have killed at least 4,000 Vietnamese civilians, POWs, or enemy seeking to surrender, maybe as many as 10,000 Vietnamese. A prudent figure may be 5,500 overall."[60] Thus, according to Rummel's utterly implausible calculation, of the approximately 1.5 million to 3.8 million Vietnamese killed during the US war of aggression, all but a few thousand deaths were attributable to some other actor, or were justified. In other words, in Rummel's view, 5,000–10,000 Vietnamese were killed in US war crimes, while the remaining victims were either "legitimate" casualties of war or "collateral damage." Zinn stated that the CIA, as part of "Operation Phoenix" peaking in 1968–1969, executed at least 20,000 civilians in South Vietnam "who were suspected of being members of the Communist underground," further evidence of an intent to commit genocide against members of a political group.[61] Relatedly, in an understatement, Maynard Parker wrote in *Foreign Affairs* in January 1975, "Although the Phoenix program did undoubtedly kill or incarcerate many innocent civilians, it did also eliminate many members of the Communist infrastructure."[62] In what essentially meets the definition of genocide against a political group, it is unclear whether Parker believes unarmed communists were "innocent civilians."

168 *Genocide in Vietnam*

Because the US perpetrated a war of aggression with the intent of eliminating communism in South Vietnam, the victims of the genocide against political groups include not only those group members who were unarmed; it also includes those who constituted the armed resistance to the group's destruction—in other words, North Vietnam's regular forces and the armed wing of the NLF. As Carl Clausewitz puts it, "The fighting forces must be *destroyed*: that is, they must be *put in such a condition that they can no longer carry on the fight* [emphases in original]."[63] Similarly, Shaw states that war is an act of force that seeks to "destroy the power of an enemy and its will to resist."[64] Additionally, according to Shaw, "in waging war, the intention is to *destroy the real or imputed power of the enemy group* [emphasis in original], including its economic, political, cultural and ideological power, together with its ability to resist this destruction."[65] To destroy communism in South Vietnam, the US sought to destroy the ability of communists, as members of a political group, to resist their subjugation. This required that the armed resistance be eliminated, as well as destroying a sufficient portion of the group to render its resistance futile. Thus, destruction of the armed resistance was a means to the end of destroying communism in Vietnam.

Conclusion

There has been some debate regarding whether the US committed genocide during its war of aggression against Vietnam. The general consensus is that the US is not guilty of genocide, because it lacked specific genocidal intent in waging the war. While some might argue that US actions cannot be both war and genocide, such a claim cannot withstand scrutiny. In its war of aggression, the US committed acts of genocide with genocidal intent against members of a political group in pursuance of its objective of eliminating communism from Vietnam.

To achieve its political and economic objectives, the US attacked real and perceived members of the communist political group in Vietnam with the intent to destroy the group as such. Because the genocide in Vietnam was carried out under the guise of war, everyone the US killed was a victim of genocide. This includes members of communist North Vietnam's regular forces, who were attacked without provocation simply because they were the armed representatives of the communist political party in control of North Vietnam. It includes the members of the NLF's armed resistance in South Vietnam. Finally, it includes all those killed who were strictly civilians, whether they were killed as real or perceived supporters of the NLF, or killed because all Vietnamese were depicted as members of the armed resistance, or were killed "unintentionally."

My conclusion that the US is guilty of genocide in Vietnam is based on a combination of traditional definitions of genocide, which include a specific intent requirement, and my own definition that includes protection for political groups and a nexus between aggressive war and genocide. This finding has significant implications for the study of war and genocide. War retains a "legitimate" role in international politics. As argued in Chapter 2, this is primarily due to war being a tool employed by democratic and pseudo-democratic states. As Irving Horowitz implies, democratic states only use war with just intentions, in a "struggle between good and evil" with authoritarian states.[66] Horowitz essentially justifies wars of aggression, so long as the perpetrator is a democratic state facing off with an "evil" authoritarian one. However, the only type of war that is legitimate is a defensive war limited to the means strictly necessary to fend off the aggressor. Aggressive war is never legitimate; it is always prohibited. And, as demonstrated in Chapter 2 and in this chapter, aggressive war is a means of achieving a political, economic, or social objective that involves perpetrating violence against anyone who impedes that objective. Depending on the purpose, scale, and victims of this violence, it could amount to genocide, as in the US war of aggression against Vietnam. It is my hope that others will recognize the nexus between aggressive war and genocide and, as they do, that war will lose its aura of legitimacy. Genocide scholars will no longer insist on a hard distinction between war and genocide; other wars will be revisited to determine whether the aggressors were guilty of genocide; restitution will be paid by aggressors to their victims; and those responsible for the genocidal wars will be held to account.

Notes

1 Quoted in Steven R. Ratner and Jason S. Abrams, *Accountability for Human Rights Atrocities in International Law: Beyond the Nuremberg Legacy* (Oxford: Oxford University Press, 2001), 124.
2 International Law Commission, *Yearbook of the International Law Commission 1951, Volume 1*, http://legal.un.org/ilc/publications/yearbooks/english/ilc_1951_v1.pdf (accessed May 7, 2017), 116.
3 United Nations General Assembly, *Resolution 3314 (XXIX) of 14 December 1974*, www.un.org/ga/search/view_doc.asp?symbol=A/RES/3314(XXIX)(accessed May 7, 2017), 143.
4 Ibid.
5 Ibid., 144.
6 Mike Gravel, *The Pentagon Papers*, Gravel Edition, Volume 3 (Boston, MA: Beacon Press, 1972), 722.
7 Jeff Cohen and Norman Solomon, "30-Year Anniversary: Tonkin Gulf Lie Launched Vietnam War," *Fair and Accuracy in Reporting*, July 27, 1994. Accessed May 12, 2016. http://fair.org/media-beat-column/30-year-anniversary-tonkin-gulf-lie-launched-vietnam-war/.
8 Ibid.
9 George C. Herring, *The Secret Diplomacy of the Vietnam War: The Negotiating Volumes of the Pentagon Papers* (Austin, TX: University of Texas Press, 1983), 422.
10 Ibid., 423.
11 Adam Jones, *Genocide: A Comprehensive Introduction*, 2nd ed. (London: Routledge, 2011), 74; Jonathan Neale, *A People's History of the Vietnam War* (New York: The New Press, 2003), 75.

170   *Genocide in Vietnam*

12 S. Brian Wilson, "Bob Kerrey's Atrocity, the Crime of Vietnam and the Historic Pattern of US Imperialism," in *Genocide, War Crimes & the West*, ed. Adam Jones (London: Zed Books, 2004), 167.

13 Jones, *Genocide*, 2nd ed., 74.

14 Wilson, "Bob Kerrey's Atrocity," 167.

15 Howard Zinn, *A People's History of the United States, 1492-Present* (New York: Harper Perennial, 2005), 477.

16 Wilson, "Bob Kerrey's Atrocity," 167.

17 Jones, *Genocide*, 2nd ed., 75.

18 Ibid.

19 John Tirman, "Why Do We Ignore the Civilians Killed in America's Wars?" *The Washington Post*, www.washingtonpost.com/opinions/why-do-we-ignore-the-civilians-killed-in-american-wars/2011/12/05/gIQALCO4eP_story.html?utm_term=.843088ec6931 (accessed May 15, 2016).

20 Blue Water Navy Vietnam Veterans and Agent Orange Exposure, Committee on Blue Water Navy Vietnam Veterans and Agent Orange Exposure, Board on the Health of Select Populations, Institute of Medicine of the National Academies (Washington, DC: The National Academies Press, 2011). Available www.nap.edu/catalog/13026/blue-water-navy-vietnam-veterans-and-agent-orange-exposure (accessed May 21, 2016), 49.

21 Orville Schell and Barry Weisberg, "Ecocide in Indochina," in *Ecocide in Indochina: The Ecology of War*, ed. Barry Weisberg (San Francisco, CA: Canfield Press, 1970), 32.

22 Wilson, "Bob Kerrey's Atrocity," 167.

23 Blue Water Navy Vietnam Veterans and Agent Orange Exposure, 7.

24 Cathy Scott-Clark and Adrian Levy, "Spectre Orange," *The Guardian*, March 28, 2003. Accessed June 3, 2016. www.theguardian.com/world/2003/mar/29/usa.adrianlevy.

25 Hugo Adam Bedau, "Genocide in Vietnam?" in *Philosophy, Morality, and International Affairs*, eds. Virginia Held, Sidney Morgenbesser, and Thomas Nagel (Oxford: Oxford University Press, 1974), 43–44.

26 Matthew Lippman, "The Convention on the Prevention and Punishment of the Crime of Genocide: Fifty Years Later," *Arizona Journal of International and Comparative Law* 15, no. 2 (1998), 480.

27 Helen Fein, "Genocide, Terror, Life Integrity, and War Crimes: The Case for Discrimination," in. *Genocide: Conceptual and Historical Dimensions*, ed. George J. Andreopoulos (Philadelphia, PA: University of Pennsylvania Press, 1997), 99.

28 Jean-Paul Sartre, *On Genocide* (Boston, MA: Beacon Press, 1968), 78.

29 Ibid., 73.

30 Joy Gordon, "When Intent Makes All the Difference in the World: Economic Sanctions on Iraq and the Accusation of Genocide," *Yale Human Rights and Development Journal* 5, no. 2 (2014): 66.

31 Bedau, "Genocide in Vietnam," 21–22.

32 Quoted in Richard Falk, "Ecocide, Genocide, and the Nuremberg Tradition of Individual Responsibility," in *Philosophy, Morality, and International Affairs*, eds. Virginia Held, Sidney Morgenbesser, and Thomas Nagel (Oxford: Oxford University Press, 1974), 124.

33 Hirad Abtahi and Philippa Webb, *The Genocide Convention: The Travaux Préparatoires* (Leiden: Martinus Nijhoff Publishers, 2008), 864.

34 Bruce Cumings, *The Korean War: A History* (New York: Random House, 2011), 149.

35 Mehdi Hasan, "Why Do North Koreans Hate Us? One Reason—They Remember the Korean War," *The Intercept*, May 3, 2017, https://theintercept.com/2017/05/03/why-do-north-koreans-hate-us-one-reason-they-remember-the-korean-war/.

36 Richard H. Kohn and Joseph P. Harahan, *Strategic Air Warfare: An Interview with Generals Curtis LeMay, Leon W. Johnson, David A. Burchinal, and Jack J. Catton* (Washington, DC: Office of Air Force History, 1988), 88.
37 Sahr Conway-Lanz, "Bombing Civilians after World War II: The Persistence of Norms against Targeting Civilians in the Korean War," in *The American Way of Bombing: Changing Ethical and Legal Norms, from Flying Fortresses to Drones*, eds. Matthew Evangelista and Henry Shue (Ithaca, NY: Cornell University Press, 2014), 58.
38 Ibid.
39 Israel W. Charny, "Toward a Generic Definition of Genocide," in *Genocide: Conceptual and Historical Dimensions*, ed. George J. Andreopoulos (Philadelphia, PA: University of Pennsylvania Press, 1997), 64.
40 Quoted in Baladas Ghoshal, "Regional Fallout: Vietnam," in *Superpower Rivalry and Conflict: The Long Shadow of the Cold War on the Twenty-First Century*, ed. Chandra Chari (London: Routledge, 2010), 51.
41 Ibid.
42 Neale, *A People's History of the Vietnam War*; Ghoshal, "Regional Fallout: Vietnam," 34.
43 Ghoshal, "Regional Fallout: Vietnam," 51.
44 Neale, *A People's History of the Vietnam War*, 38.
45 Douglas Pike, *War, Peace, and the Viet Cong* (Cambridge, MA: The M.I.T. Press, 1969), 4.
46 Ibid.
47 Quoted in Neale, *A People's History of the Vietnam War*, 67.
48 Edward C. Keefer and Charles S. Sampson, "Paper Prepared by the National Security Council Working Group," in *Foreign Relations of the United States, 1964–1968, Volume I, Vietnam, 1964* (Washington, DC: United States Government Printing Office), 916.
49 Ibid., 917–918.
50 Quoted in Neale, *A People's History of the Vietnam War*, 69.
51 David C. Humphrey, "Summary Notes of the 557th Meeting of the National Security Council," in *Foreign Relations of the United States, 1964–1968, Volume IV, Vietnam, 1966* (Washington, DC: United States Government Printing Office), 382.
52 Bedau, "Genocide in Vietnam," 42–43.
53 Ibid.
54 Ibid., 43.
55 Barbara Harff, "No Lessons Learned from the Holocaust? Assessing Risks of Genocide and Political Mass Murder since 1955," *American Political Science Review* 97, no. 1 (2003): 59.
56 Jason Campbell, *On the Nature of Genocidal Intent* (Lanham, MD: Lexington Books, 2013), 7.
57 Barbara Harff and Ted Gurr, "Toward Empirical Theory of Genocides and Politicides: Identification and Measurement of Cases since 1945," *International Studies Quarterly* 32, no. 3 (1988): 363.
58 Sartre, *On Genocide*, 80.
59 Ibid., 82.
60 Rummel, R. J. *Death by Government* (London: Transaction Publishers, 1994), 277.
61 Zinn, *A People's History*, 478.
62 Maynard Parker, "Vietnam: The War that Won't End," *Foreign Affairs*, January 1975. Accessed July 13, 2016. www.foreignaffairs.com/articles/vietnam/1975-01-01/vietnam-war-wont-end.
63 Carl Clausewitz, *On War* (Oxford: Oxford University Press, 2007), 90.

172   *Genocide in Vietnam*

64 Martin Shaw, *War & Genocide* (Malden, MA: Polity Press, 2003), 18.
65 Martin Shaw, *What Is Genocide?* (Malden, MA: Polity Press, 2007), 35.
66 Irving L. Horowitz, "Science, Modernity and Authorized Terror," in *Studies in Comparative Genocide*, eds. Levon Chorbajian and George Shirinian (London: Palgrave Macmillan, 1999), 22.

Bibliography

Abtahi, Hirad, and Philippa Webb. *The Genocide Convention: The Travaux Préparatoires*. Leiden: Martinus Nijhoff Publishers, 2008.

Andreopoulos, George J. "Introduction: The Calculus of Genocide." In *Genocide: Conceptual and Historical Dimensions*, edited by George J. Andreopoulos, 1–28. Philadelphia, PA: University of Pennsylvania Press, 1997.

Bedau, Hugo Adams. "Genocide in Vietnam?" In *Philosophy, Morality, and International Affairs*, edited by Virginia Held, Sidney Morgenbesser, and Thomas Nagel, 5–46. Oxford: Oxford University Press, 1974.

Blue Water Navy Vietnam Veterans and Agent Orange Exposure. Committee on Blue Water Navy Vietnam Veterans and Agent Orange Exposure, Board on the Health of Select Populations, Institute of Medicine of the National Academies. Washington, DC: The National Academies Press, 2011. Accessed May 21, 2016. www.nap.edu/catalog/13026/blue-water-navy-vietnam-veterans-and-agent-orange-exposure.

Campbell, Jason. *On the Nature of Genocidal Intent*. Lanham, MD: Lexington Books, 2013.

Charny, Israel. "Toward a Generic Definition of Genocide." In *Genocide: Conceptual and Historical Dimensions*, edited by George J. Andreopoulos, 64–94. Philadelphia, PA: University of Pennsylvania Press, 1997.

Clausewitz, Carl. *On War*. Oxford: Oxford University Press, 2007.

Cohen, Jeff, and Norman Solomon. "30-Year Anniversary: Tonkin Gulf Lie Launched Vietnam War." *Fair and Accuracy in Reporting*. Accessed May 12, 2016. http://fair.org/media-beat-column/30-year-anniversary-tonkin-gulf-lie-launched-vietnam-war/.

Conway-Lanz, Sahr. "Bombing Civilians after World War II: The Persistence of Norms against Targeting Civilians in the Korean War." In *The American Way of Bombing: Changing Ethical and Legal Norms, from Flying Fortresses to Drones*, edited by Matthew Evangelista and Henry Shue, 47–63. Ithaca, NY: Cornell University Press, 2014.

Cumings, Bruce. *The Korean War: A History*. New York: Random House, 2011.

Falk, Richard. "Ecocide, Genocide, and the Nuremberg Tradition of Individual Responsibility." In *Philosophy, Morality, and International Affairs*, edited by Virginia Held, Sidney Morgenbesser, and Thomas Nagel, 123–137. Oxford: Oxford University Press, 1974.

Fein, Helen. "Genocide, Terror, Life Integrity, and War Crimes: The Case for Discrimination." In *Genocide: Conceptual and Historical Dimensions*, edited by George J. Andreopoulos, 95–107. Philadelphia, PA: University of Pennsylvania Press, 1997.

Ghoshal, Baladas. "Regional Fallout: Vietnam." In *Superpower Rivalry and Conflict: The Long Shadow of the Cold War on the Twenty-First Century*, edited by Chandra Chari, 50–56. London: Routledge, 2010.

Gordon, Joy. "When Intent Makes All the Difference in the World: Economic Sanctions on Iraq and the Accusation of Genocide." *Yale Human Rights and Development Journal* 5, no. 2 (2014): 57–84.

Genocide in Vietnam 173

Gravel, Mike. *The Pentagon Papers*, Gravel Edition, Volume 3. Boston, MA: Beacon Press, 1972.

Harff, Barbara. "No Lessons Learned from the Holocaust? Assessing Risks of Genocide and Political Mass Murder since 1955." *American Political Science Review* 97, no. 1 (2003): 57–73.

Harff, Barbara, and Ted Gurr. "Toward Empirical Theory of Genocides and Politicides: Identification and Measurement of Cases since 1945." *International Studies Quarterly* 32, no. 4 (1988): 359–371.

Hasan, Mehdi. "Why Do North Koreans Hate Us? One Reason—They Remember the Korean War." *The Intercept*. Accessed June 24, 2017. https://theintercept.com/2017/05/03/why-do-north-koreans-hate-us-one-reason-they-remember-the-korean-war/.

Herring, George C. *The Secret Diplomacy of the Vietnam War: The Negotiating Volumes of the Pentagon Papers*. Austin, TX: University of Texas Press, 1983.

Horowitz, Irving L. "Science, Modernity and Authorized Terror." In *Studies in Comparative Genocide*, edited by Levon Chorbajian and George Shirinian, 15–30. London: Palgrave Macmillan, 1999.

Humphrey, David C. "Summary Notes of the 557th Meeting of the National Security Council." In *Foreign Relations of the United States, 1964–1968, Volume IV, Vietnam, 1966*. Washington, DC: United States Government Printing Office, 1998.

International Law Commission. *Yearbook of the International Law Commission 1951, Volume 1*. Accessed May 7, 2017. http://legal.un.org/ilc/publications/yearbooks/english/ilc_1951_v1.pdf.

Jones, Adam. *Genocide: A Comprehensive Introduction*, 2nd ed. London: Routledge, 2011.

Keefer, Edward C., and Charles S. Sampson. "Paper Prepared by the National Security Council Working Group." In *Foreign Relations of the United States, 1964–1968, Volume I, Vietnam, 1964*. Washington, DC: United States Government Printing Office.

Kohn, Richard H., and Joseph P. Harahan. *Strategic Air Warfare: An Interview with Generals Curtis LeMay, Leon W. Johnson, David A. Burchinal, and Jack J. Catton*. Washington, DC: Office of Air Force History, 1988.

Lippman, Matthew. "The Convention on the Prevention and Punishment of the Crime of Genocide: Fifty Years Later." *Arizona Journal of International and Comparative Law* 15 (1998): 415–514.

Neale, Jonathan. *A People's History of the Vietnam War*. New York: The New Press, 2003.

Parker, Maynard. "Vietnam: The War that Won't End." *Foreign Affairs*, January 1975.

Pike, Douglas. *War, Peace, and the Viet Cong*. Cambridge, MA: The M.I.T. Press, 1969.

Ratner, Steven R., and Jason S. Abrams. *Accountability for Human Rights Atrocities in International Law: Beyond the Nuremberg Legacy*. Oxford: Oxford University Press, 2001.

Rummel, R. J. *Death by Government*. London: Transaction Publishers, 1994.

Sartre, Jean-Paul Sartre. *On Genocide*. Boston, MA: Beacon Press, 1968.

Schell, Orville, and Barry Weisberg. "Ecocide in Indochina." In *Ecocide in Indochina: The Ecology of War*, edited by Barry Weisberg. San Francisco, CA: Canfield Press, 1970.

174 *Genocide in Vietnam*

Scott-Clark, Cathy, and Adrian Levy. "Spectre Orange." *The Guardian*. Accessed June 3, 2016. www.theguardian.com/world/2003/mar/29/usa.adrianlevy.

Shaw, Martin. *War & Genocide*. Malden, MA: Polity Press, 2003.

Shaw, Martin. *What Is Genocide?* Malden, MA: Polity Press, 2007.

Tirman, John. "Why Do We Ignore the Civilians Killed in America's Wars?" *Washington Post*. Accessed May 15, 2016. www.washingtonpost.com/opinions/why-do-we-ignore-the-civilians-killed-in-american-wars/2011/12/05/gIQALCO4eP_story.html?utm_term=.843088ec6931.

United Nations General Assembly. *Resolution 3314 (XXIX) of 14 December 1974*. Accessed May 7, 2017. www.un.org/ga/search/view_doc.asp?symbol=A/RES/3314(XXIX).

Wilson, S. Brian. "Bob Kerrey's Atrocity, the Crime of Vietnam and the Historic Pattern of US Imperialism." In *Genocide, War Crimes & the West*, edited by Adam Jones, 164–180. London: Zed Books, 2004.

Zinn, Howard. *A People's History of the United States, 1492-Present*. New York: Harper Perennial, 2005.

8 Again and again

The US relationship with genocide

It has been nearly seventy years since the Genocide Convention was adopted by the General Assembly on December 9, 1948. Subsequent to its adoption and entry into force, genocide has been committed over and over again. The most well-known and frequently studied cases include the Tutsi genocide in Rwanda in 1994, the genocide at Srebrenica in Bosnia in 1995, and the Darfur genocide in Sudan from 2003 to 2008. Notably, the US did not maintain close relations with any of the governments or actors responsible for the commission of genocide in any of these cases. In *Preventing Genocide: A Blueprint for U.S. Policymakers*, which would have been better titled, *The U.S. and the Prevention of Genocide: Stop Committing It*, Madeleine Albright and William Cohen seize on the common but limited range of cases of genocide that conveniently omit those involving the US. According to Albright and Cohen, "Much depends on the relationship of the target country to its neighboring states as well as world powers. Russia's and China's respective relationships with Serbia and Sudan are recent examples of how a great power patron can complicate diplomacy."[1] Not only do Albright and Cohen give France a pass on its relationship with Rwanda during the Tutsi genocide, but they do the same for the US, despite its close relations with, and the diplomatic cover it gave, numerous governments as they were committing genocide.

This selective recognition contributes to a false narrative that depicts the US as a bystander to genocide due to its inability to muster the political will necessary to prevent it. The US operates in a political culture of impunity, reinforced by the culture of impunity that prevails for the US in genocide studies. In addition to the Armenian Genocide and the Jewish Holocaust, much of the genocide literature focuses on the previously mentioned cases—Rwanda, Bosnia, and Sudan—along with the Cambodian Genocide. Additional research has targeted Soviet policies throughout much of the 20th century and China during Mao's "Cultural Revolution." In *"A Problem from Hell": America and the Age of Genocide*—the most widely read contribution to genocide studies, and a Pulitzer Prize winner—Samantha Power includes lengthy case studies of Cambodia, Iraq, Bosnia, Rwanda, and Kosovo.[2] In her inclusion of Iraq's

176 *The US relationship with genocide*

Kurdish genocide, Power does find room for one chapter on a case in which the US maintained close relations with a government responsible for the commission of genocide, of which she is critical. However, Power merely finds that the US failed to "send a strong message that genocide would not be tolerated," and instead "punted on genocide, and the Kurds paid the price."[3]

The US relationship with genocide that has been exposed in the previous chapters differs markedly from the one typically found in mainstream political and academic discourse. The mythical US relationship with genocide portrays the US as a leader with a mixed record on genocide prevention. As Albright and Cohen describe it:

> Over the span of time, our top officials have been unable to summon the political will to act in a sustained and consistent manner or take timely steps needed to prevent genocide and mass atrocities from occurring. The road to genocide prevention *may* be paved with the best intentions, but our leaders have not always been bold enough in confronting congressional skeptics or reluctant policymakers.[4]

Similarly, Power's overall thesis can be summarized as follows: the US has often played the role of bystander to genocide due to an absence of leadership and of political will to prioritize its proclaimed support for human rights; therefore, the US needs to do more to prevent genocide, i.e. intervene militarily. Greg Grandin whittles down Power's thesis even further: "the problem is not what the United States does...but what it doesn't do: act to stop genocide."[5]

This narrative resonates with those who are proponents of the role the US plays in the world, because it includes a critique of American foreign policy without recognizing the far darker truth beneath the surface. In this narrative, the US has made some mistakes, but nothing that would call into question America's unique "exceptionalism." The problem with this popular narrative is that it conceals the true nature of the US relationship with many of the governments that have committed genocide since the Holocaust, as well as the US' own actions. Based on my definition of genocide and analysis of cases, the US shared responsibility or was directly responsible for the commission of genocide repeatedly during the second half of the 20th century. The US conspired with Indonesia to commit genocide against members of Indonesia's Communist political group. Over a seven-month period, between 500,000 and one million communists were murdered. The US supplied Indonesia with covert support, including communications equipment, small arms, and the names of 5,000 communists, while sharing Indonesia's genocidal intent. The US was complicit in genocide in Bangladesh (then-East Pakistan), Guatemala, and Iraq. In each of these cases, the US provided the genocidal governments with material aid and diplomatic support. The US committed cultural genocide, a crime that is arguably

The US relationship with genocide 177

ongoing, against its indigenous peoples. The US also committed genocide against the people of Vietnam during its war of aggression. Finally, the US committed genocide against the people of Iraq with its design, implementation, maintenance, and enforcement of economic sanctions that killed at least 500,000 children.

Not included in the list of seven cases is the possibility that the US was responsible for genocide during the Korean War. For three years, the US indiscriminately carpet-bombed the north, and areas of the south, with well over 500,000 tons of bombs. Upwards of three million civilians were killed during the war, with most residing in the north.[6] This amounted to approximately 20 percent of the Korean population. In Chapter 2, in establishing the nexus between aggressive war and genocide, I also noted that particular means of warfare can constitute genocide. Examples of genocide typically cited by scholars, such as Leo Kuper, and Eric Markusen and David Kopf, include the firebombing of Dresden and the use of the atomic bombs on Nagasaki and Hiroshima.[7] However, the massive death and destruction that the US indiscriminately wreaked on the Korean people, particularly in the north, could also amount to genocide.

Significantly, only three of the seven cases I documented are even considered controversial. These include cultural genocide against America's indigenous peoples, genocide in Vietnam, and genocide in Iraq resulting from the US-imposed economic sanctions. There is general scholarly agreement that Pakistan, Guatemala, and Iraq committed genocide. With the inclusion of political groups in the definition of genocide, it is also incontrovertible that Indonesia committed genocide. For scholars who include cultural genocide in their definitions, such genocide against America's indigenous peoples, too, is uncontroversial. Finally, US responsibility for genocide caused by the economic sanctions should not be as controversial as it is. The US knowingly imposed conditions on the Iraqi people that were calculated to bring about the deaths of Iraqis. Iraqis were used as nothing more than a means to an end. This leaves only Vietnam, which likewise ought to be less controversial, especially among scholars who include political groups in their definitions. The US launched a war of aggression with the purpose of eliminating communism in Vietnam. To achieve this objective, the US sought to kill as many Vietnamese communists as the success of its objective required. This is genocide.

Despite all the evidence presented, and despite the fact that scholars generally recognize genocide in more than half of the cases I documented, the US has largely been immunized from allegations of genocide. It would be easy to write off US responsibility for genocide as a thing of the past. However, the first two decades of the 21st century belie any verdict that things have changed. Since the turn of the century, the US has been complicit in what appears more and more like an ongoing genocide in Yemen. The US has also failed to uphold its obligation to prevent what Al Jazeera has described as the "hidden genocide" in Myanmar.[8]

Complicity in genocide in Yemen

Substantial US support for the Saudi-led coalition (hereafter, Saudi Arabia) in Yemen is particularly illustrative of the fact that the American foreign policy of supporting governments as they commit egregious crimes is not limited to a specific and past era. What began as apparent Saudi war crimes has escalated into what is arguably genocide. During both phases of Saudi Arabia's crimes in Yemen, the US has provided it with massive amounts of military aid, as well as diplomatic support.

In September 2014, the Houthis, a Shia group from northern Yemen, seized control of Yemen's capital of Sanaa. By January 2015, the Houthis had ousted President Hadi. They next moved south towards the port city of Aden. On March 26, Saudi Arabia led a coalition of nine Arab countries in an aerial bombing campaign against the Houthis and allied forces.[9] By April 2016, a little over a year after the bombings began, at least 3,200 civilians had been killed, more than 5,700 had been injured, and another 2.5 million people had been displaced.[10] Saudi Arabia has used weapons including the MK-84, a "general purpose bomb" that can weigh up to 2,000 pounds and has a substantial blast radius; "bunker buster" bombs; and cluster munitions.[11] The use of such weapons against civilian-populated areas prompted allegations that Saudi Arabia was committing war crimes in Yemen.[12]

In January 2016, the Panel of Experts on Yemen, established pursuant to Security Council Resolution 2140 (2014), issued its final report.[13] The Panel "documented 119 coalition sorties relating to violations of international humanitarian law. Many attacks involved multiple air strikes on multiple civilian objects."[14] According to the report,

> The Panel documented that the coalition had conducted air strikes targeting civilians and civilian objects, in violation of international humanitarian law, including camps for internally displaced persons and refugees; civilian gatherings, including weddings; civilian vehicles, including buses; civilian residential areas; medical facilities; schools; mosques; markets, factories and food storage warehouses; and other essential civilian infrastructure, such as the airport in Sana'a, the port in Hudaydah and domestic transit routes.[15]

Additionally, the Panel of Experts found that the attacks on civilians and civilian infrastructure have been widespread, meaning "massive, frequent, large-scale action, carried out collectively with considerable seriousness and directed against a multiplicity of victims"; and systematic, meaning that there is evidence that such attacks have been of an organized nature, demonstrating the likely existence of an official or de facto policy or plan.[16]

The Panel of Experts is not alone. Human Rights Watch (HRW) and Amnesty International have conducted their own investigations. In March 2016,

HRW documented 36 unlawful airstrikes launched by Saudi Arabia, including "attacks on schools, hospitals, and homes, with no evidence they were being used for military purposes," killing more than 550 civilians.[17] Amnesty International documented at least 32 additional unlawful airstrikes, including attacks on schools, hospitals, markets, and mosques, killing as many as 361 civilians, including 127 children.[18]

The objects of Saudi Arabia's attacks and the disproportionate number of civilians killed, along with their widespread and systematic nature, provide evidence to support allegations of both war crimes and crimes against humanity. Under the Geneva Convention and the Rome Statute of the International Criminal Court, the following are considered war crimes when committed as part of a plan or policy, or as part of a large-scale commission of such crimes: intentionally attacking civilian populations and objects; intentionally launching an attack with knowledge that the attack will result in loss of life and injury disproportionate to the anticipated military gain; intentionally attacking buildings dedicated to religion and education, and hospitals; and attacking towns, villages, dwellings, or buildings which are not military objectives.[19] As noted above, the Panel of Experts, HRW, and Amnesty International documented a substantial number of cases in which Saudi Arabia violated all these prohibitions. As Rasha Mohamed and Rawan Shaif write,

> The facts speak for themselves, and evidence of violations of international humanitarian law cannot be dismissed as mere hearsay...Amnesty International and other organizations have presented compelling evidence over the past year that indicates all parties to the Yemen conflict have committed war crimes. But some countries do not want to see the evidence that is staring them in the face. Flooding the region with arms is akin to adding fuel to the fire.[20]

If Saudi violence in Yemen was limited to its aerial attacks that have killed at least 10,000 civilians by April 2017, Saudi crimes might be limited to war crimes.[21] However, Saudi Arabia has also imposed an air and naval blockade on Yemen since March 2015. The blockade is used to enforce mostly arbitrary regulations and restrictions on imports, including food, fuel, medical supplies, and humanitarian aid. Imports are delayed for extensive periods or denied altogether. [22] According to UN Special Rapporteur on Human Rights and International Sanctions Idriss Jazairy, Yemen imports 80–90 percent of the food, medicines, and fuel necessary for the survival of its people.[23] Denying Yemenis access to food appears to be part of a deliberate strategy. It exacerbates the effects of Saudi Arabia's bombing campaign that has destroyed much of Yemen's agricultural, health, and transportation infrastructure.[24] The UN estimates that 21 million people in Yemen—or about 82 percent of the population—are in need of immediate humanitarian assistance. One-third are suffering from famine.[25]

180 *The US relationship with genocide*

Jazairy asserts that the blockade is one of the main causes of the humanitarian disaster and, therefore, "amounts to an unlawful unilateral coercive measure (UCM) under international law."[26] Further, according to Jazairy, the blockade is a "grave breach of the most basic norms of human rights law" and is responsible for a "man-made famine" in Yemen.[27] The combination of Saudi aerial attacks on Yemen's infrastructure and the blockade of Yemeni ports is comparable to US strategy in Iraq during the 1990s. In 1991, the US deliberately attacked Iraq's vital infrastructure, exacerbating the effects of the sanctions that were initiated the previous year and maintained until 2003. Like Yemen, Iraq imported a significant portion of its food supply. The sanctions on Iraq prevented it from completing the economic exchanges it required to feed and tend to its population; import items necessary to repair its damaged infrastructure; operate its hospitals at required capacity; and purify its drinking water. The US-imposed sanctions on Iraq severely undermined public health in Iraq, killing at least 500,000 Iraqi children.

Though the Saudi blockade has not yet killed Yemenis on the same scale as the US sanctions on Iraq, it is causing a precipitous decline in public health in a country that was already one of the world's most impoverished. According to the UN, by December 2016,

> Nearly 2.2 million children in Yemen are acutely malnourished and require urgent care. At least 462,000 children suffer from Severe Acute Malnutrition (SAM), a drastic increase of almost 200 percent since 2014. An additional 1.7 million children suffer from Moderate Acute Malnutrition.[28]

The grave breaches of human rights law to which Jazairy refers encompass elements of crimes against humanity. As discussed in Chapter 2, crimes against humanity are human rights violations of such an egregious nature, and committed systematically and/or widespread, that they are crimes against the immediate victims, as well as all of humanity. Jones describes crimes against humanity as "crimes against one's fellows, viewed in a universal context," meaning they constitute an assault on all of humanity regardless of whether one is a victim of the assault or a witness to it; whether it is occurring in one's own country or a country half way around the world.[29] Under the Rome Statute of the International Criminal Court, crimes against humanity include, among others, acts, inhumane acts that intentionally cause "great suffering, or serious injury to body or to mental or physical health."[30] Clearly, Saudi Arabia's actions are intentionally causing Yemenis great suffering and serious injury. Yet, based on the intentional aerial attacks on civilians and civilian objects, including essential infrastructure, and the deliberate human suffering caused by the blockade, is it possible that a finding of genocide is also justified?

This book has already emphasized, as does the Genocide Convention and other genocide scholars, that genocide can be committed via indirect means by deliberately imposing conditions that are likely to cause the deaths of members of the group. Evidence indicates that Saudi Arabia is doing exactly that—deliberately inflicting on Yemenis conditions of life calculated to bring about their destruction in whole or in part. The intent is implicit in Saudi Arabia's full knowledge of the humanitarian catastrophe for which it is responsible and its maintenance of the blockade, while simultaneously continuing its bombing campaign. This is not only a war; it is genocide against Yemenis as a national group.

The US has long sold arms to Saudi Arabia, but sales have increased significantly in recent years, including while Saudi Arabia has been committing war crimes, crimes against humanity, and genocide. Beginning in 2010, under the Obama administration, the US sold Saudi Arabia $48 billion in weapons, a "new record for the value of U.S. weapons deals with the Saudi regime."[31] That is three times the sale of arms during the entire eight years of the previous Bush administration.[32] Subsequent to the initiation of the Saudi bombing campaign, the Obama administration made: (1) a $5.4 billion deal in July 2015 to sell to Saudi Arabia 600 Patriot Missiles, and a $500 million deal to sell more than 1,000,000 rounds of ammunition, hand grenades, and other items; (2) an $11.25 billion deal in October 2015 to sell Saudi Arabia up to four Lockheed Littoral Combat Ships; and (3) a $1.29 billion deal in November to sell Saudi Arabia more than 10,000 air-to-surface missiles, "bunker buster" bombs, and MK84 general purpose bombs. As HRW notes, all three of the munitions included in the November deal have been used by Saudi Arabia in Yemen.[33] Since taking office in January 2017, the Trump administration appears set upon outdoing the Obama administration. While an apparent $110 billion arms deal proved to be "a bunch of letters of interest or intent, but not contracts," [34] around one-fourth of the cited $110 billion sale is "in the actual pipeline."[35]

In addition to the sale of arms, the US has also provided Saudi Arabia with logistical and diplomatic support. The US has deployed personnel to the Saudi joint planning and operations cell. According to HRW, "US participation in specific military operations, such as providing advice on targeting decisions and aerial refueling during bombing raids, may make US forces jointly responsible for laws-of-war violations by coalition forces."[36] In addition to the arms sales, perhaps the most significant aid the US has provided Saudi Arabia with is jet fuel and midair refueling. Since March 2015, the US has delivered more than 67 million pounds of fuel and refueled Saudi and coalition aircraft more than 9,000 times.[37] Monthly delivery of fuel reached a record high in January 2017, a month shared by the Obama and Trump administrations. According to journalist Sam Oakford, "Refueling stayed at near-record levels through March (4.03 million) before falling in May and June. During 2017 average monthly totals are up by nearly a third compared to 2015 and 2016."[38]

Saudi Arabia's destruction of Yemen through its bombing campaign and its genocidal blockade of Yemeni ports, which has created conditions of life

182 *The US relationship with genocide*

in Yemen calculated to destroy Yemen's population in whole or part, would not be possible without the aid the US has provided. This has enabled Saudi Arabia to deliberately create famine conditions that have left 2.2 million children in Yemen acutely malnourished. Another 462,000 children are suffering from Severe Acute Malnutrition (SAM), an increase of 200 percent since the US-supported Saudi war began. Another 1.7 million children are suffering from Moderate Acute Malnutrition.[39]

According to the International Court of Justice's two-part test regarding complicity in genocide, the US has been and continues to be complicit in Saudi Arabia's genocide in Yemen. The US has provided Saudi Arabia with the material and diplomatic support that it requires to commit its crimes. The US has done so with full knowledge of the humanitarian consequences of its support. While the Obama administration blocked the sale of precision-guided munitions in October 2016 after Saudi Arabia attacked a funeral in Sanaa, this was little more than a symbolic protest, considering it had already sold Saudi Arabia more than $100 billion in weapons, and continued to provide fuel and midair refueling.[40] Congress has also, at times, attempted to block weapons sales. Nonetheless, US support for Saudi Arabia's war crimes and genocide has persisted from one US administration to the next. Notably, under the Obama administration, the US was represented at the United Nations by Ambassador Samantha Power. This led Dan Kovalik to proclaim,

> Yes, the Obama Administration is knowingly aiding and abetting the Saudis...This is a fact. And, it is a fact which is quite ironic given that the current Obama-appointed U.S. Ambassador to the U.N. is Samantha Power—an individual who came to prominence through her Pulitzer-winning book which condemned the West's failure to respond to genocide throughout the world.[41]

Failure to prevent genocide in Myanmar

In a May 2015 report published by the United States Holocaust Memorial Museum (USHMM), the staff at the Simon-Skjodt Center for the Prevention of Genocide concluded that Rohingya in Myanmar have been

> subject to dehumanization through rampant hate speech, the denial of citizenship, and restrictions on freedom of movement, in addition to a host of other human rights violations that put this population at grave risk of additional mass atrocities and even genocide.[42]

Significantly, following their March 2015 field investigation, the Simon-Skjodt staff left Myanmar

> deeply concerned that so many preconditions for genocide are already in place. With a recent history of mass atrocities and within a pervasive

The US relationship with genocide 183

climate of hatred and fear, the Rohingya may once again become the target of mass atrocities, including genocide.[43]

In March 2014, United to End Genocide conducted a fact-finding mission in Myanmar. In a report documenting the results of this mission, Thomas Andrews and Daniel Sullivan concluded, "Nowhere in the world are there more known precursors to genocide than in Burma today."[44] Andrews and Sullivan came to this conclusion based on evidence of a mounting death toll, a massive population of internally displaced persons (IDPs) and refugees, and the systematic and widespread nature of their afflictions. Andrews and Sullivan found that more than 140,000 IDPs were living in environments tantamount to "concentration camps."[45] Many of the IDP camps are over-crowded and lack adequate food, water, shelter, sanitation, and access to medical care.[46]

The recent history of mass atrocities referenced by the USHMM began in early June 2012, following the rape and murder of a Buddhist woman in late May.[47] In Myanmar's Arakan State, ethnic Arakanese Buddhists clashed with Rohingya, with deadly violence engulfing four townships, killing dozens of people.[48] By July, according to Maung Tun Khin, president of the Burmese Rohingya Organization UK, at least 650 Rohingya had been killed by Arakanese and government forces, and at least 1,200 more were missing.[49]

After a period of relative calm, violence resumed in October 2012 and expanded to nine townships in the Arakan State. The renewed violence was far more organized than in June. According to HRW,

> For months, local Arakanese political party officials and senior Buddhist monks publicly vilified the Rohingya population and de-scribed them as a threat to Arakan State. On October 23, thousands of Arakanese men armed with machetes, swords, homemade guns, Molotov cocktails, and other weapons descended upon and attacked Muslim villages in nine townships throughout the state. State security officials either failed to intervene or participated directly in the violence. In some cases attacks occurred simultaneously in townships separated by considerable distance.[50]

In addition to the physical attacks on Rohingya, HRW found 27 unique areas of destruction using satellite imagery. Images of areas of Sittwe that were affected by the violence in June showed 2,558 destroyed structures. Images of four of the areas affected by violence in October showed an ad-ditional 2,304 destroyed structures. In what was only a partial picture of the violence committed between June and October, at least 4,862 structures were destroyed in Arakan State in mostly residential areas.[51]

The rise in ethnic and religious tensions, and the systematic abuse of human rights, appear to be the result of a well-organized and financed

184 *The US relationship with genocide*

campaign led by extremist nationalist Buddhist Monks, supported and/or tolerated by the government of Myanmar.[52] As noted above, the simultaneous attacks in separate districts offer evidence of a coordinated plan. At the local level, Arakanese political parties, monks' associations, and community groups held regular meetings in full view of local, state, and national authorities. They made public statements and issued pamphlets that typically denied the existence of the Rohingya ethnicity, demonized Rohingyas, and called for their removal from Myanmar.[53]

Despite the open commission of violence against Rohingya and its public incitement, local, state, and national officials have not adequately implemented measures to stop it. Much of the violence has been perpetrated in the presence of state security forces, including local police, Lon Thein riot police, and the interagency border control force. The security forces have stood by rather than protect Rohingya, and have at times directly participated in the violence. In some cases, security forces disarmed Rohingya of the wooden sticks with which they sought to defend themselves.[54] Penny Green asserts that the violence has been orchestrated by Myanmar's security forces, especially the Nasaka border force, with the assistance of Arakan nationalists, paramilitaries, and extremist Buddhist monks. "Together," writes Green, "they have been able to act with impunity."[55]

Green's assessment that the commission of violence against Rohingya is carried out with impunity is consistent with HRW's findings that the Myanmar government has failed to seriously investigate or take legal action against anyone responsible for planning, organizing, or participating in the violence.[56] Lack of accountability ensures the absence of a deterrent for future violence. Also, as HRW notes, "This absence of accountability lends credence to allegations that this was a government-sponsored campaign of ethnic cleansing in which crimes against humanity were committed."[57]

Whether "ethnic cleansing," crimes against humanity, precursors to genocide, or outright genocide, it is clear that Rohingya have been targeted as such for violence owing to their ethnicity and religious beliefs. Nonetheless, Myanmar has been welcomed back into the fold of the international community, primarily based on recent political reforms. During the five decades prior to 2011, Myanmar was dominated by a series of military regimes.[58] "In 2011," writes Emanuel Stoakes, "Myanmar's reformist government launched a cautious process of liberalization that removed long-standing restrictions on opposition party activity, allowed for relative freedom of the press, and led to the release of many political prisoners."[59]

In 2010, Aung San Suu Kyi's National League for Democracy (NLD) boycotted elections. With political reforms underway, including the reintroduction of a multi-party parliamentary system in 2011, the NLD participated in by-elections in 2012, winning forty-three legislative seats, one of which went to Suu Kyi.[60] Then, in November 2015, the NLD won a landslide victory in Myanmar's first national vote since political reforms were introduced. With its victory, the NLD won control of Myanmar's parliament and the right to

The US relationship with genocide   185

choose Myanmar's president. Owing to a law preventing Suu Kyi from becoming president, the NLD nominated Htin Kyaw, a long-time confidante of Suu Kyi. On March 15, 2016, Kyaw was elected by Myanmar's bicameral legislature and began his term as president on April 1.[61]

Myanmar's political reforms have cast a long shadow over the egregious human rights violations perpetrated against the Rohingya. Suu Kyi, "while being feted in the West," [62] has participated in the marginalization of the plight of the Rohingya through her silence on the issue.[63] As Andrews and Sullivan note,

> Caught in the 'good news' narrative of a nation that has undergone significant reforms, including the release of Nobel Peace Laureate Aung San Suu Kyi and her election to Parliament…the world has been quick to declare the transformation of Burma a foreign policy success. In so doing the international diplomatic community has willfully ignored— or failed to adequately address—the warning signs of genocide and mass violence.[64]

The US has been one of the most active members of the international community in rewarding Myanmar for its political reforms, even as Rohingya have been victimized by crimes against humanity that include precursors to genocide. In 2011, then-Secretary of State Hillary Clinton traveled to Myanmar on a "goodwill mission." In 2012, the US reestablished a USAID mission to Myanmar, eased restrictions on the export of US financial services and new investment, and named the first ambassador to Myanmar in twenty-two years. Also, in November 2012, less than a month after violence against Rohingya resumed, President Obama visited Myanmar. This was followed by President Thein Sein's visit to Washington in May 2013.[65] Obama would visit Myanmar again in November 2014.[66]

In addition to reestablishing and strengthening diplomatic relations, the US has significantly reduced sanctions, such as the above-mentioned restrictions on the export of US financial services and new investment, that were originally enacted in 1988 following a military crackdown in then-Burma, and reinforced or increased during the subsequent presidencies. As a result, US exports to Myanmar grew by 121 percent to $146 million, and Myanmar's exports to the US jumped from zero to $30 million in 2013.[67] In May 2016, the Obama administration announced that it would lift additional sanctions. In remarks made at the Center for a New American Security on May 17, Deputy National Security Advisor Ben Rhodes highlighted these changes, including: (1) amending regulations to allow for most business transactions with Myanmar's financial institutions; (2) raising the threshold for the Responsible Investment Reporting Requirement from $500,000 to $5 million; (3) removing of seven state-owned enterprises and three state-owned banks from the Specially Designated Nationals list; and (4) possibly extending to Myanmar the US' Generalized System of Preferences, a

186 *The US relationship with genocide*

preferential tariff system that provides for a formal system of exemption from the general rules of the World Trade Organization.[68]

In his remarks announcing these policy shifts, Rhodes highlighted Myanmar's political reforms, while mentioning only in passing the plight of the Rohingya. With the dramatic increase in political and economic ties with Myanmar, however, comes a responsibility that the US has not fully embraced. As Andrews and Sullivan note, "The international community—and in particular the United States—is in a strong position to alter the course of these events. But, it is failing to do so."[69] The US has an obligation to employ all means reasonably available to it to prevent genocide in Myanmar. Though the violence in Myanmar may not have reached the level of "full blown" genocide, it has been well-documented that crimes against humanity, including precursors to genocide, have been perpetrated against the Rohingya with the acquiescence and the participation of representatives of the state. Yet, many of the sanctions that were lifted provide relief for state entities.

Can it really be said that the US has taken all measures within its power to prevent the egregious abuse of Rohingya in Myanmar? Clearly, the answer is no. Thus, the US has failed in its obligation, as established by the ICJ in Bosnia v. Serbia, to expend all available resources to prevent potential genocide by using its influence over those responsible. The reason for this is evident when one looks beyond the proclamations that portray US rapprochement with Myanmar as being motivated by a desire to support Myanmar's "efforts to modernize its laws and regulations so that the people of the country can seek economic prosperity."[70] In 2011, President Obama announced that his administration would be making a strategic "pivot" from the Middle East to East Asia.[71] A primary goal of this pivot was to challenge China's strategic and economic partnership with Myanmar,[72] and to take advantage of Myanmar's strategic location in Southeast Asia.[73] Myanmar has also become a destination for capital investment from the US.[74] For example, Coca-Cola, General Electric, and Apollo Towers have made significant investments in Myanmar since sanctions were lifted.[75]

In the conclusion to his remarks at the Center for a New American Security, Rhodes stated,

> The President has made Asia central to his foreign policy—and Southeast Asia central to his Asia rebalance. And the future of Burma is central to both objectives. Burma is a potential market for our goods; a potential partner on critical issues; and a potential example for how a country can transition from dictatorship to democracy, while pursuing effective development.[76]

None of the above addresses the egregious human rights violations being committed against the Rohingya in Myanmar except, perhaps, the transition from dictatorship to democracy. This transition actually increases the US' obligation to employ all reasonable means to prevent the potential genocide, because, in theory at least, a democratic Myanmar ought to be more responsive to such pressure than a military dictatorship. Nonetheless, the US has prioritized economic growth and competition with China ahead of the rights of the Rohingya. Significantly, in an interview, Maung Zarni, a former visiting fellow at both Oxford and Harvard Universities, and the founding director of the Free Burma Coalition, singled out UN Ambassador Samantha Power for ignoring the ongoing atrocities.[77]

Legal impunity

The culture of impunity that pervades US actions around the world is maintained in part by the US' legal impunity. Clearly, there is no lack of state crimes for which the US is directly responsible or shares responsibility. Rather, the US is simply unaccountable. A primary focus of this book has been on US state responsibility for genocide and its ancillary crimes. Using the Bosnia v. Serbia Precedent, I concluded that the US is responsible for conspiring to commit genocide in Indonesia; complicit in genocide in Bangladesh, Guatemala, Iraq, and Yemen; and responsible for failing to uphold its obligation to prevent genocide in Myanmar. Yet, the US has ensured that the ICJ will not be hearing any such cases or future cases. Of course, behind every US act there are responsible individuals. The US has also ensured its officials legal impunity by immunizing them in practice against international criminal accountability for their actions. This unaccountability contributes to a self-perpetuating perception that the US does not commit crimes.

Impunity from state responsibility for genocide

The ICJ is expressly named in the Genocide Convention as the arbiter of disputes pertaining to state responsibility for genocide. However, the US submitted a reservation to Article IX of the Genocide Convention when ratifying the treaty. The reservation states,

> That with reference to article IX of the Convention, before any dispute to which the United States is a party may be submitted to the jurisdiction of the International Court of Justice under this article, the specific consent of the United States is required in each case.[78]

In 2002, the Democratic Republic of the Congo (DRC) filed an application with the ICJ, instituting proceedings against Rwanda concerning its alleged role in "massive, serious and flagrant violations of human rights and of international humanitarian law" carried out on the DRC's sovereign territory.[79] Among other treaties, the DRC invoked Article IX of the

188 *The US relationship with genocide*

Genocide Convention to establish ICJ jurisdiction. Like the US, Rwanda maintains a reservation to Article IX. In its 2006 decision, the ICJ concluded that while "the rights and obligations enshrined by the Convention are rights and obligations erga omnes [for all]," the fact that the obligations under the Genocide Convention apply to all states does not in itself give the ICJ jurisdiction to entertain every dispute regarding the treaty's interpretation and application. Such jurisdiction is based on the consent of the parties involved.

Similar to its conclusion regarding *erga omnes* obligations, the ICJ found that the

> same applies to the relationship between peremptory norms of general international law (*jus cogens*) and the establishment of the Court's jurisdiction: the fact that a dispute relates to compliance with a norm having such a character, which is assuredly the case with regard to the prohibition of genocide, cannot of itself provide a basis for the jurisdiction of the Court to entertain that dispute.[80]

Therefore, the ICJ found that while Rwanda's reservation to Article IX of the Genocide Convention does not affect Rwanda's "substantive obligations relating to acts of genocide themselves," it does bear on the ICJ's jurisdiction.[81] In other words, Article IX reservations "exclude a particular method of settling a dispute relating to the interpretation, application or fulfilment of the Convention," but do not obviate a state's obligations under the treaty.[82]

With its Article IX reservation, the US can deny the ICJ jurisdiction over any case concerning its alleged role in acts prohibited by the Genocide Convention. It is clear in the ICJ's ruling that, because the prohibition of genocide is an *erga omnes* obligation and a peremptory norm of international law, the ICJ sees itself as only one forum at which disputes relating to the interpretation, application, or fulfillment of obligations under the Genocide Convention may be adjudicated. Like Rwanda, the US can reject the ICJ's jurisdiction, but it cannot reject its own responsibilities. However, there currently does not exist an alternative forum for the settlement of disputes; the jurisdiction of any such forum would similarly require the consent of state parties; and the US holds the power to veto any attempts to create an alternative forum via a Security Council resolution. Thus, the US has assured itself impunity with regard to its obligations under the Genocide Convention.

The same can be said regarding the role of the US in acts other than genocide that violate peremptory norms of international law, such as war crimes and crimes against humanity. The ICJ's jurisdiction is not limited to the Genocide Convention. Under Article 36(2) of its statute, state parties

> may at any time declare that they recognize as compulsory ipso facto and without special agreement, in relation to any other state accepting the same obligation, the jurisdiction of the Court in all legal disputes

concerning: the interpretation of a treaty; any question of international law; the existence of any fact which, if established, would constitute a breach of an international obligation; or the nature or extent of the reparation to be made for the breach of an international obligation.[83]

Once again, however, ICJ jurisdiction requires the consent of parties to a dispute.

While the US has maintained its albeit tenuous relationship with the ICJ, even consenting to participate in a number of cases before the court, as Sean Murphy notes,

> in reaction to decisions that were reached by the Court, the United States refused to participate in the proceedings on the merits of the case brought by Nicaragua in 1984, withdrew from the Court's compulsory jurisdiction in 1986, and recently terminated its acceptance of the Court's jurisdiction over disputes arising under the Vienna Convention on Consular Relations.[84]

Though its argument was rejected by the ICJ, the US argued that disputes involving armed conflict should be addressed at the Security Council, not the ICJ.[85] According to this argument, the United Nations Charter limits interference in questions of war and peace to the UN's political organs, the Security Council prime among them.[86] "This is," writes Theodore Lieverman, "of course, a satisfactory situation for the United States, which has a veto in the Security Council, but not in the ICJ."[87]

Between its reservation to Article IX of the Genocide Convention and its withdrawal from the ICJ's compulsory jurisdiction, the US enjoys practical impunity for its actions, including its participation in and facilitation of war crimes, crimes against humanity, and genocide. Thus, whether with regard to complicity in genocide in Pakistan, Guatemala, Iraq, and Yemen; conspiracy to commit genocide in Indonesia; genocide in Vietnam; or the failure to uphold its obligation to prevent genocide in Myanmar, the US has immunized itself against state responsibility for its actions.

Immunity from individual criminal responsibility

During the Genocide Convention's drafting process, Iran proposed an amendment to the treaty at the Sixth Committee that would have established a limited form of universal jurisdiction for the punishment of the crime of genocide. Iran argued that its amendment "was intended to remedy a deficiency in the system of punishment of genocide."[88] It contended that primary jurisdiction for trying someone suspected of planning and perpetrating genocide rested with the state on whose territory the alleged crimes were committed. However, according to Iran, "if it [the territorial authority] expressed no such desire, it thereby tacitly renounced its right to try him."[89]

190   *The US relationship with genocide*

Essentially, Iran was arguing that if the authority with jurisdiction over the territory on which genocide was committed was unable or unwilling to try genocide suspects, or was an alleged participant in the perpetration of genocide, a limited form of universal jurisdiction was needed.

Iran explained that its position struck the right balance between state sovereignty and the need to ensure that those who plan and perpetrate genocide are punished. It argued that opposition to subsidiary jurisdiction grounded in the principle of the sovereignty of states was misguided, because subsidiary jurisdiction allowed the state on whose territory the crime had been committed to seek the extradition of the alleged violator for trial. Thus, Iran questioned what would happen to a genocide suspect if extradition was not requested. Would the suspect simply go unpunished? This, Iran argued, must be avoided.[90]

Echoing Iran's argument in support of a limited form of universal jurisdiction, Matthew Lippman notes, "There is a contradiction between asserting that genocide is of international concern while relying on a system of territorial jurisdiction. Consider whether Nazi Germany would have voluntarily extradited or prosecuted those who had planned or implemented the Holocaust."[91] William Schabas adds,

> The fundamental difficulty with genocide prosecutions based on territorial jurisdiction is a practical one. States where the crime took place are unlikely to be willing to proceed, either because the perpetrators remain in power or influence, or perhaps because a post-genocide social and political *modus vivendi* is built upon forgetting the crimes of the past.[92]

Nonetheless, the US argued that Iran's proposed form of subsidiary jurisdiction for the punishment of genocide was "one of the most dangerous and unacceptable of principles."[93] According to the US, subsidiary jurisdiction would violate traditional principles of international law by allowing a state to punish a foreigner for crimes committed extraterritorially. Further, because states are often implicated in the commission of genocide, the Iranian position would allow the courts of one state to punish the leaders of another for crimes committed outside the punishing state. This, the US argued, could result in dangerous international tensions.[94]

While the US was correct that Iran's proposed form of subsidiary jurisdiction would have contrasted with accepted principles of international law, Iran made the case for treating the crime of genocide as a threat not only to particular groups, but to humanity as a whole. It stated,

> The source of the jurisdiction vested in national courts was the need for maintaining order in their respective territories. Genocide, however, involved not only the law and order of the State on whose territory the crime was committed, but also the law and order of all States constituting the family of nations.[95]

The US relationship with genocide 191

The Rome Statute of the International Criminal Court (ICC) was adopted by the United Nations General Assembly on July 17, 1998, with 120 votes in favor, 7 against, and 21 abstentions.[96] The ICC officially came into being on July 1, 2002, when the Rome Statute entered into force. As a court of complementarity, the ICC operates in part under a form of jurisdiction like that proposed by Iran for the crime of genocide. Iran sought with its proposal to fill the jurisdictional gap that would exist if a state whose national was suspected of committing genocide was unable or unwilling to prosecute the suspect, and no other organ or state had jurisdiction to do so. Similarly, former ICC President Philippe Kirsch explains that under the principle of complementarity, the ICC

> does not intervene if a domestic system is carrying out its responsibilities. A case is not admissible if it is being or has been investigated or prosecuted by a state with jurisdiction. The ICC will act only if a state is unwilling or unable genuinely to carry out an investigation or prosecution.[97]

However, an important difference between Iran's proposal, which included a form of limited universal jurisdiction, and the ICC's jurisdiction is that the latter is primarily contingent upon state consent. Article XII of the Rome Statute establishes that the ICC's jurisdiction is limited to parties to the Rome Statute. Therefore, the ICC may exercise jurisdiction when the state on whose territory the alleged crime was committed is a party to the Rome Statute, and when the individual accused of the crime is a national of a state party to the Rome Statute.[98] The US has yet to consent to ICC jurisdiction over its territory and its nationals, even though the US would maintain primary jurisdiction over both under the principle of complementarity.

By refusing to accept the ICC's jurisdiction, the US has significantly limited the avenues by which the ICC could gain jurisdiction over US officials for alleged criminal acts that fall within the court's jurisdiction, which include war crimes, crimes against humanity, and genocide. Under Article XIII of the Rome Statute, the Security Council has the authority to refer particular cases to the ICC.[99] It was through this process that the ICC gained jurisdiction over alleged crimes committed in Sudan and Libya, neither of which is party to the Rome Statute. However, unlike Sudan and Libya, the US could simply veto any Security Council resolution that includes such a referral.

Without the US being a party to the Rome Statute, and with its ability to veto a Security Council referral to the ICC, US nationals could still find themselves before the ICC if they are suspected of committing crimes within the court's jurisdiction on the territory of a party to the Rome Statute. Yet, once again, the US has sought to impede jurisdiction by exploiting a jurisdictional loophole. Article 98 of the Rome Statute states:

192 *The US relationship with genocide*

The Court may not proceed with a request for surrender or assistance which would require the requested State to act inconsistently with its obligations under international law with respect to the State or diplomatic immunity of a person or property of a third State, unless the Court can first obtain the cooperation of that third State for the waiver of the immunity.[100]

The US has justified a series of bilateral immunity agreements, the number of which currently stands at 102,[101] by asserting that the ICC itself allowed for the immunities under Article 98.[102] The purpose behind these agreements is to

assure that United States citizens would never be under the jurisdiction of the ICC, no matter where they lived or were stationed, no matter what international crimes they committed. In agreeing to the immunity agreements, foreign governments promised not to honor subpoenas or warrants issued by the ICC against Americans.[103]

In every one of the cases discussed in this book, there are US officials behind the actions carried out in the name of the state. Therefore, just as the US shares responsibility for some of the crimes discussed and is directly responsible for others, US officials are concurrently responsible for planning and implementing the policies that facilitated the crimes. However, for all practical intents and purposes, the US has immunized its officials against international criminal accountability for their actions.

This culture of legal impunity must change. The US should withdraw its reservation to Article IX of the Genocide Convention; resume acceptance of compulsory jurisdiction at the ICJ; ratify the Rome Statute; and dissolve its bilateral immunity agreements. If the US is unwilling to voluntarily hold itself and its officials accountable to the international community, which is likely, the international community must force accountability upon it. The ICJ must revisit the question of whether reservations to Article IX are compatible with the object and purpose of the Genocide Convention. Similarly, the ICJ should issue an advisory opinion regarding whether bilateral immunity agreements are consistent with Article 98 of the Rome Statute. In so doing, the ICJ ought to find that Article IX reservations and Article 98 agreements are incompatible with the objects and purposes of the Genocide Convention and the Rome Statute, because they directly impede accountability for criminal acts that violate peremptory norms of international law.

Ending scholarly impunity

Maintenance of the culture of impunity with which the US acts around the world is significantly aided and abetted by segments of academic scholarship. The general absence of US cases in the study of genocide cannot be justified by a lack of US responsibility for genocide. This failure to critically interrogate US policy contributes to a culture of impunity in which US actions are ignored, justified, or even celebrated.[104]

In this book, I presented evidence of US responsibility for genocide in three cases since 1948—cultural genocide against its indigenous peoples, genocide in Vietnam, and genocide in Iraq from economic sanctions. The US may also be responsible for two additional cases of genocide based on the means it employed during the Korean War and in its invasion of Iraq in 2003. I also provided evidence that the US conspired with Indonesia to commit genocide, and was complicit in genocide in Bangladesh, Guatemala, Iraq, and Yemen. Finally, evidence suggests the US has failed in its obligation to prevent genocide in Myanmar.

Even if other scholars disagree with some of the findings in this book, it cannot be denied that the US is more than a simple bystander to genocide. Both committing genocide and supporting those who do have been hallmarks of US policy. To try to explain away or justify these actions, without treating them in the same manner as those of the "usual suspects," helps maintain the culture of impunity. It lends legitimacy to acts that can never be legitimate. What context can possibly justify committing genocide, conspiring to commit genocide, and complicity in genocide? Imagine if Samantha Power, with her influence, had written a more critical account of the US relationship with genocide. What if she had addressed just some of the issues presented here?

The US may never stand before the ICJ on a charge of state responsibility for genocide, just as US officials will likely never be tried for their roles in genocide at the ICC. However, lack of legal accountability cannot be permitted to obscure the reality. Accountability must come from somewhere. Scholars have a responsibility that comes with the influence they wield. Those who contribute to the dissident strand of literature ought to be heard and celebrated; instead, they are marginalized, while those who contribute to the status quo or critique around the edges are the ones who are celebrated and welcomed in mainstream political and media discourse. US policy has significant, often deadly, consequences for people all over the world. If no one else, the US must be held to account by the people, but this can only happen with the support of those who currently act as the US' enablers.

Notes

1 Madeleine Albright and William Cohen, *Preventing Genocide: A Blueprint for U.S. Policymakers* (Washington, DC: United States Holocaust Memorial Museum, 2008), 57.
2 Samantha Power, *"A Problem from Hell": American and the Age of Genocide* (New York: Harper Perennial, 2002). Similarly, Peter Ronayne includes studies of Cambodia, Bosnia, and Rwanda. See Peter Ronayne, *Never Again?: The United States and the Prevention and Punishment of Genocide since the Holocaust* (New York: Rowman & Littlefield, 2001).
3 Power, *"A Problem from Hell"*, 172–173.

194 *The US relationship with genocide*

4 Albright and Cohen, *Preventing Genocide*, xxi.
5 Greg Grandin, "Politics by Other Means: Guatemala's Quiet Genocide," in *Quiet Genocide: Guatemala 1981–1983*, ed. Etelle Higonnet (New Brunswick, NJ: Transaction Publishers, 2009), 13.
6 Mehdi Hasan, "Why Do North Koreans Hate Us? One Reason—They Remember the Korean War," *The Intercept*, https://theintercept.com/2017/05/03/why-do-north-koreans-hate-us-one-reason-they-remember-the-korean-war/.
7 Leo Kuper, *Genocide: Its Political Use in the Twentieth Century* (New Haven, CT: Yale University Press, 1982), 46; Eric Markusen and David Kopf, *The Holocaust and Strategic Bombing: Genocide and Total War in the Twentieth Century* (Boulder, CO: Westview Press, 1995), 181.
8 In addition to the cases of Yemen and Myanmar, the US invasion of Iraq in 2003, especially when in combination with the previous twelve years of sanctions, displays the hallmarks of genocide. A Physicians for Social Responsibility (PSR) report published in 2015 supported a Lancet study that found that 655,000 Iraqis were killed between 2003 and 2006. Further, PSR notes, "should the number of Iraqis killed from the 2003 U.S. invasion until 2012 actually be around one million, as the analysis of the existing scientific studies presented in the present study suggests, this would represent 5% of the total population of Iraq—a number which additionally indicates the extent of the corresponding damage inflicted upon society and the infrastructure." See Physicians for Social Responsibility, "Body Count: Casualty Figures after 10 Years of the 'War on Terror,'" www.psr.org/assets/pdfs/body-count.pdf (accessed June 19, 2017). In addition to the people killed in the US war of aggression and those killed as a result of the war, cultural sites were destroyed. Iraq also experienced looting of cultural artifacts on a scale not seen since the "Mongol invasion of Baghdad in 1258." Quoted in Frank Rich, "And Now: 'Operation Iraqi Looting'," *New York Times*, www.nytimes.com/2003/04/27/arts/and-now-operation-iraqi-looting.html (accessed July 1, 2017).
9 Human Rights Watch, "Yemen: Embargo Arms to Saudi Arabia," www.hrw.org/news/2016/03/21/yemen-embargo-arms-saudi-arabia (accessed July 1, 2016).
10 Ibid.; Rasha Mohamed and Rawan Shaif, "Saudi Arabia Is Committing War Crimes in Yemen," *Foreign Policy*, http://foreignpolicy.com/2016/03/25/civilian-casualties-war-crimes-saudi-arabia-yemen-war/ (accessed July 1, 2016).
11 Ibid.; Human Rights Watch, "Yemen: US Bombs Used in Deadliest Market Strike," www.hrw.org/news/2016/04/07/yemen-us-bombs-used-deadliest-market-strike (accessed July 1, 2016); United Nations Human Rights Office of the High Commissioner, "Yemen: Zeid Calls for Investigation into Civilian Casualties," www.ohchr.org/EN/NewsEvents/Pages/DisplayNews.aspx?NewsID=15836 (accessed July 1, 2016).
12 Ibid.
13 United Nations Security Council, Resolution 2140 (2014) of 26 February 2014, www.un.org/en/ga/search/view_doc.asp?symbol=S/RES/2140(2014) (accessed May 15, 2016).
14 United Nations Security Council, "Final Report of the Panel of Experts on Yemen Established Pursuant to Security Council Resolution 2140 (2014)," www.securitycouncilreport.org/atf/cf/%7B65BFCF9B-6D27-4E9C-8CD3-CF6E4FF96FF9%7D/s_2016_73.pdf (accessed July 1, 2016), 39.
15 Ibid.
16 Ibid., 35.
17 Human Rights Watch, "Yemen: Embargo Arms to Saudi Arabia."
18 Amnesty International, "Yemen: Reckless Arms Flows Decimate Civilian Life a Year into Conflict," www.amnesty.org/en/latest/news/2016/03/yemen-reckless-arms-flows-decimate-civilian-life-a-year-into-conflict/ (accessed July 1, 2016).

19 Protocol Additional to the Geneva Conventions of 12 August 1949, and relating to the Protection of Victims of International Armed Conflicts (Protocol I), 8 June 1977, www.icrc.org/ihl/INTRO/470 (accessed July 1, 2016); Rome Statute of the International Criminal Court, July 1, 2002, www.icc-cpi.int/nr/rdonlyres/ea9aeff7-5752-4f84-be94-0a655eb30e16/0/rome_statute_english.pdf (accessed July 1, 2016).
20 Mohamed and Shaif, "Saudi Arabia Is Committing War Crimes in Yemen."
21 Gareth Porter, "The US Provided Cover for the Saudi Starvation Strategy in Yemen," *Truthout*, www.truth-out.org/news/item/40147-the-us-provided-cover-for-the-saudi-starvation-strategy-in-yemen (accessed July 1, 2017).
22 United Nations Human Rights Office of the High Commissioner, "Lift Blockade of Yemen to Stop 'Catastrophe' of Millions Facing Starvation, Says UN Expert," www.ohchr.org/EN/NewsEvents/Pages/DisplayNews.aspx?NewsID=21496&LangID=E (accessed July 1, 2017).
23 Ibid.
24 Porter, "The US Provided Cover for the Saudi Starvation Strategy in Yemen."
25 United Nations Human Rights Office of the High Commissioner, "Lift Blockade of Yemen."
26 Ibid.
27 Ibid.
28 United Nations International Children's Emergency Fund, "Malnutrition amongst Children in Yemen at an All-Time High, Warns UNICEF," www.unicefusa.org/press/releases/malnutrition-amongst-children-yemen-all-time-high-warns-unicef/31545 (accessed July 1, 2017).
29 Adam Jones, *Crimes against Humanity: A Beginner's Guide* (Oxford: Oneworld Publications, 2008), 6.
30 Rome Statute of the International Criminal Court. See Article 7.1(k).
31 Mohamad Bazzi, "Obama May Be Preaching 'Tough Love' to Saudi—But Arms Sales Tell Another Story," *The Guardian*, www.theguardian.com/commentisfree/2016/apr/22/us-saudi-arabia-weapons-arms-deals-foreign-policy (accessed July 1, 2016); William D. Hartung, "The Obama Arms Bazaar: Record Sales, Troubling Results, *LobeLog Foreign Policy*, http://lobelog.com/the-obama-arms-bazaar-record-sales-troubling-results/ (accessed July 1, 2016).
32 Bazzi, "Obama May Be Preaching 'Tough Love' to Saudi."
33 Human Rights Watch, "Yemen: Embargo Arms to Saudi Arabia."
34 Bruce Riedel, "The $110 Billion Arms Deal to Saudi Arabia Is Fake News," *Brookings*, www.brookings.edu/blog/markaz/2017/06/05/the-110-billion-arms-deal-to-saudi-arabia-is-fake-news/ (accessed July 1, 2017).
35 Elizabeth McLaughlin and Conor Finnegan, "The Truth about President Trump's $110 Billion Saudi Arms Deal," *ABC News*, http://abcnews.go.com/International/truth-president-trumps-110-billion-saudi-arms-deal/story?id=47874726 (accessed July 1, 2017).
36 Human Rights Watch, "Yemen: Embargo Arms to Saudi Arabia."
37 Samuel Oakford, "U.S. Doubled Fuel Support for Saudi Bombing Campaign in Yemen after Deadly Strike on Funeral," https://theintercept.com/2017/07/13/u-s-doubled-fuel-support-for-saudi-bombing-campaign-in-yemen-after-deadly-strike-on-funeral/ (accessed July 13, 2017).
38 Ibid.
39 United Nations International Children's Emergency Fund, "Malnutrition amongst Children in Yemen at an All-Time High."
40 Oakford, "U.S. Doubled Fuel Support for Saudi Bombing Campaign in Yemen."
41 Dan Kovalik. "The Obama Administration Should Be Found Guilty of War Crimes in Yemen," *Huffington Post*, www.huffingtonpost.com/dan-kovalik/obama-adminstration-guilt_b_8916380.html (accessed January 10, 2016).

196 *The US relationship with genocide*

42 United States Holocaust Memorial Museum, "'They Want Us All to Go Away': Early Signs of Genocide in Burma," www.ushmm.org/m/pdfs/20150505-Burma-Report.pdf (accessed June 1, 2016), 1.

43 Ibid., 2.

44 Thomas H. Andrews and Daniel Sullivan, *Marching to Genocide in Burma: Fueled by Government Action and a Systematic Campaign of Hate Aided and Abetted by the Diverted Eyes of the World*, United to End Genocide, http://endgenocide. org/wp-content/uploads/2014/03/marching-to-genocide-in-burma.pdf(accessed May 4, 2014), 1.

45 Ibid.

46 Human Rights Watch, *'All You Can Do Is Pray': Crimes against Humanity and Ethnic Cleansing of Rohingya Muslims in Burma's Arakan State*, www.refworld. org/docid/518230524.html (accessed May 4, 2014), 6.

47 Moshahida Sultana Ritu, "Ethnic Cleansing in Myanmar," *The New York Times*, www.nytimes.com/2012/07/13/opinion/ethnic-cleansing-of-myanmars-rohingyas.html?_r=0 (accessed July 1, 2016).

48 Ritu, "Ethnic Cleansing in Myanmar"; Human Rights Watch, *'All You Can Do Is Pray'*, 4.

49 Nehginpao Kipgen, "Conflict in Rakhine State in Myanmar: Rohingya Muslims' Conundrum," *Journal of Muslim Minority Affairs* 33, no. 2 (2013): 301.

50 Human Rights Watch, *'All You Can Do Is Pray'*, 7.

51 Ibid., 10.

52 Andrews and Sullivan, *Marching to Genocide in Burma*, 1.

53 Human Rights Watch, *'All You Can Do Is Pray'*, 12.

54 Ibid., 10.

55 Penny Green, "Islamophobia: Burma's Racist Fault-Line," *Race & Class* 55, no. 2 (2013): 95.

56 Human Rights Watch, *'All You Can Do Is Pray'*, 15.

57 Ibid.

58 Nicholas Farrelly and Chit Win, "Inside Myanmar's Turbulent Transformation," *Asia & Pacific Policy Studies* 3, no. 1 (2016): 38.

59 Emanuel Stoakes, "Monks, PowerPoint Presentations, and Ethnic Cleansing," *Foreign Policy*, http://foreignpolicy.com/2015/10/26/evidence-links-myanmar-government-monks-ethnic-cleansing-rohingya/ (accessed July 1, 2016).

60 Farrelly and Win, "Inside Myanmar's Turbulent Transformation," 41.

61 Zoltan Barany, "Myanmar's Shaky Transition: A Treacherous Path to Democracy," *Foreign Affairs*, www.foreignaffairs.com/articles/burma-myanmar/2016-03-30/myanmars-shaky-transition (accessed July 5, 2016).

62 Ritu, "Ethnic Cleansing in Myanmar."

63 Beina Xu and Eleanor Albert, "Understanding Myanmar," *Council on Foreign Relations*, www.cfr.org/human-rights/understanding-myanmar/p14385 (accessed July 5, 2016).

64 Andrews and Sullivan, *Marching to Genocide in Burma*, 7.

65 Xu and Albert, "Understanding Myanmar."

66 David Hudson, "President Obama Wraps Up Visit to China, Heads to Burma for Second Leg of His Trip," *The White House*, www.whitehouse.gov/ blog/2014/11/12/president-obama-wraps-visit-china-heads-burma-second-leg-his-trip (accessed July 5, 2016).

67 Ben Rhodes, "Remarks on Burma Policy," as Prepared for Delivery at the Center for New American Security, *White House*, www.whitehouse.gov/the-press-office/2016/05/18/remarks-deputy-national-security-advisor-ben-rhodes-burma-policy-center (accessed July 1, 2016).

68 Ibid.

69 Andrews and Sullivan, *Marching to Genocide in Burma*, 1.

The US relationship with genocide 197

70 Rhodes, "Remarks on Burma Policy."
71 Foreign Policy Initiative, "The Obama Administration's Pivot to Asia," www. foreignpolicyi.org/content/obama-administrations-pivot-asia (accessed July 5, 2016).
72 Xu and Albert, "Understanding Myanmar."
73 Barany, "Myanmar's Shaky Transition."
74 Ritu, "Ethnic Cleansing in Myanmar."
75 Rhodes, "Remarks on Burma Policy."
76 Ibid.
77 Usaid M. Siddiqui, "How Aung San Suu Kyi and Her U.S. Allies Deny Burmese Anti-Muslim Atrocities," *Alternet*, www.alternet.org/grayzone-project/how-aung-san-suu-kyi-and-her-us-allies-deny-burmese-anti-muslim-atrocities (accessed July 5, 2016).
78 Declarations and Reservations to the Convention on the Prevention and Punishment of the Crime of Genocide, *Prevent Genocide International*, www.preventgenocide.org/law/convention/reservations/ (accessed July 6, 2016).
79 Armed Activities on the Territory of the Congo (New Application: 2002) (Democratic Republic of the Congo v. Rwanda) Jurisdiction of the Court and Admissibility of the Application, Summary of the Judgment of 3 February 2006, www.refworld.org/cases,ICJ,43fb2f784.html (accessed August 17, 2017), 8.
80 Ibid., 3.
81 Ibid., 6.
82 Ibid., 27.
83 See Article 36 of the Statute of the International Court of Justice, www.icj-cij.org/en/statute (accessed August 17, 2017).
84 Sean D. Murphy, "The United States and the International Court of Justice: Coping with Antinomies," in *The Sword and the Scales: The United States and International Courts and Tribunals*, ed. Cesare P. R. Romano (Cambridge: Cambridge University Press, 2009), 46.
85 Theodore M. Lieverman, "Law and Power: Some Reflections on Nicaragua, the United States, and the World Court," *Maryland Journal of International Law* 10, no. 2 (1986): 298.
86 Andreas L. Paulus, "From Neglect to Defiance? The United States and International Adjudication," *European Journal of International Law* 15, no. 4 (2004): 789.
87 Lieverman, "Law and Power," 298.
88 Hirad Abtahi and Philippa Webb, *The Genocide Convention: The Travaux Préparatoires* (Leiden: Martinus Nijhoff Publishers, 2008), 1715
89 Ibid., 1716.
90 Ibid.
91 Matthew Lippman, "The Convention on the Prevention and Punishment of the Crime of Genocide: Fifty Years Later," *Arizona Journal of International and Comparative Law* 15, no. 2 (1998): 505.
92 William Schabas, *Genocide in International Law* (Cambridge: Cambridge University Press, 2000), 354.
93 Abtahi and Webb, *The Genocide Convention*, 1721.
94 Ibid.
95 Ibid., 1717.
96 William Schabas, *An Introduction to the International Criminal Court* (Cambridge: Cambridge University Press, 2004), 18.
97 Philippe Kirsch, "Applying the Principles of Nuremberg in the International Criminal Court," *Washington University Global Studies Law Review* 6, no. 3 (2007): 505.
98 Rome Statute of the International Criminal Court. See Article 12.

198 *The US relationship with genocide*

  99 Ibid.
100 Ibid. See Article 98.
101 Coalition for the International Criminal Court, "Status of US Bilateral Immunity Agreements (BIAs)," www.iccnow.org/documents/CICCFS_BIAstatus_current.pdf (accessed July 16, 2016), 1.
102 Samantha V. Ettari, "A Foundation of Granite or Sand? The International Criminal Court and United States Bilateral Immunity Agreements," *Brooklyn Journal of International Law* 30, no. 1 (2004): 251.
103 Ibid., 250–251.
104 Adam Jones, "Introduction: History and Complicity," in *Genocide, War Crimes & the West*, ed. Adam Jones (London: Zed Books, 2004), 11.

Bibliography

Abtahi, Hirad, and Philippa Webb. *The Genocide Convention: The Travaux Préparatoires*. Leiden: Martinus Nijhoff Publishers, 2008.

Alright, Madeleine, and William Cohen. *Preventing Genocide: A Blueprint for U.S. Policymakers*. Washington, DC: United States Holocaust Memorial Museum, 2008.

Amnesty International. "Yemen: Reckless Arms Flows Decimate Civilian Life a Year into Conflict." Accessed July 1, 2016. www.amnesty.org/en/latest/news/2016/03/yemen-reckless-arms-flows-decimate-civilian-life-a-year-into-conflict/.

Andrews, Thomas H., and Daniel Sullivan. *Marching to Genocide in Burma: Fueled by Government Action and a Systematic Campaign of Hate Aided and Abetted by the Diverted Eyes of the World. United to End Genocide*. Accessed May 4, 2014. http://endgenocide.org/wp-content/uploads/2014/03/marching-to-genocide-in-burma.pdf.

Armed Activities on the Territory of the Congo (New Application: 2002) (Democratic Republic of the Congo v. Rwanda) Jurisdiction of the Court and Admissibility of the Application, Summary of the Judgment of 3 February 2006. Accessed August 17, 2017. www.refworld.org/cases, ICJ, 43fb2f784.html.

Barany, Zoltan. "Myanmar's Shaky Transition: A Treacherous Path to Democracy." *Foreign Affairs*. Accessed July 5, 2016. www.foreignaffairs.com/articles/burma-myanmar/2016-03-30/myanmars-shaky-transition.

Bazzi, Mohamad. "Obama may be Preaching 'Tough Love' to Saudi—But Arms Sales Tell Another Story." *The Guardian*. Accessed July 1, 2016. www.theguardian.com/commentisfree/2016/apr/22/us-saudi-arabia-weapons-arms-deals-foreign-policy.

Coalition for the International Criminal Court. "Status of US Bilateral Immunity Agreements (BIAs)." Accessed July 16, 2016. www.iccnow.org/documents/CICCFS_BIAstatus_current.pdf.

Declarations and Reservations to the Convention on the Prevention and Punishment of the Crime of Genocide. Accessed July 6, 2016. www.preventgenocide.org/law/convention/reservations/.

Ettari, Samantha V. "A Foundation of Granite or Sand? The International Criminal Court and United States Bilateral Immunity Agreements." *Brooklyn Journal of International Law* 30, no. 1 (2004): 205–255.

Farrelly, Nicholas, and Chit Win. "Inside Myanmar's Turbulent Transformation." *Asia & Pacific Policy Studies* 3, no. 1 (2016): 38–47.

Foreign Policy Initiative. "The Obama Administration's Pivot to Asia." Accessed July 5, 2016. www.foreignpolicyi.org/content/obama-administrations-pivot-asia.

Grandin, Greg. "Politics by Other Means: Guatemala's Quiet Genocide." In *Quiet Genocide: Guatemala 1981–1983*, edited by Etelle Higonnet, 1–16. New Brunswick, NJ: Transaction Publishers, 2009.

Green, Penny. "Islamophobia: Burma's Racist Fault-Line." *Race & Class* 55, no. 2 (2013): 93–98.

Hartung, William D. "The Obama Arms Bazaar: Record Sales, Troubling Results." *LobeLog Foreign Policy*. Accessed July 1, 2016. http://lobelog.com/the-obama-arms-bazaar-record-sales-troubling-results/.

Hasan, Mehdi. "Why Do North Koreans Hate Us? One Reason—They Remember the Korean War." *The Intercept*. Accessed June 24, 2017. https://theintercept.com/2017/05/03/why-do-north-koreans-hate-us-one-reason-they-remember-the-korean-war/.

Hudson, David. "President Obama Wraps Up Visit to China, Heads to Burma for Second Leg of His Trip." *The White House*. Accessed July 5, 2016. www.whitehouse.gov/blog/2014/11/12/president-obama-wraps-visit-china-heads-burma-second-leg-his-trip.

Human Rights Watch. *'All You Can Do Is Pray': Crimes against Humanity and Ethnic Cleansing of Rohingya Muslims in Burma's Arakan State*. Accessed May 4, 2014. www.refworld.org/docid/518230524.html.

Human Rights Watch. "Yemen: Embargo Arms to Saudi Arabia." Accessed July 1, 2016. www.hrw.org/news/2016/03/21/yemen-embargo-arms-saudi-arabia.

Human Rights Watch. "Yemen: US Bombs Used in Deadliest Market Strike." Accessed July 1, 2016. www.hrw.org/news/2016/04/07/yemen-us-bombs-used-deadliest-market-strike.

Jones, Adam. *Crimes against Humanity: A Beginner's Guide*. Oxford: Oneworld Publications, 2008.

Jones, Adam. "Introduction: History and Complicity." In *Genocide, War Crimes & the West*, edited by Adam Jones, 3–30. London: Zed Books, 2004.

Kipgen, Nehginpao. "Conflict in Rakhine State in Myanmar: Rohingya Muslims' Conundrum." *Journal of Muslim Minority Affairs* 33, no. 2 (2013): 298–310.

Kirsch, Philippe. "Applying the Principles of Nuremberg in the International Criminal Court." *Washington University Global Studies Law Review* 6, no. 3 (2007): 501–509.

Kovalik, Dan. "The Obama Administration Should Be Found Guilty of War Crimes in Yemen." *Huffington Post*. Accessed January 20, 2016. www.huffingtonpost.com/dan-kovalik/obama-adminstration-guilt_b_8916380.html.

Kuper, Leo. *Genocide: Its Political Use in the Twentieth Century*. New Haven, CT: Yale University Press, 1982.

Lieverman, Theodore M. "Law and Power: Some Reflections on Nicaragua, the United States, and the World Court." *Maryland Journal of International Law* 10, no. 2 (1986): 295–320.

Lippman, Matthew. "The Convention on the Prevention and Punishment of the Crime of Genocide: Fifty Years Later." *Arizona Journal of International and Comparative Law* 15 (1998): 415–514.

Markusen, Eric, and David Kopf. *The Holocaust and Strategic Bombing: Genocide and Total War in the Twentieth Century*. Boulder, CO: Westview Press, 1995.

McLaughlin, Elizabeth, and Conor Finnegan. "The Truth about President Trump's $110 Billion Saudi Arms Deal." *ABC News*. Accessed July 1, 2017. http://abcnews.go.com/International/truth-president-trumps-110-billion-saudi-arms-deal/story?id=47874726.

200 *The US relationship with genocide*

Mohamed, Rasha, and Rawan Shaif. "Saudi Arabia Is Committing War Crimes in Yemen." *Foreign Policy.* Accessed July 1, 2016. http://foreignpolicy.com/2016/03/25/civilian-casualties-war-crimes-saudi-arabia-yemen-war/.

Murphy, Sean D. "The United States and the International Court of Justice: Coping with Antinomies." In *The Sword and the Scales: The United States and International Courts and Tribunals,* edited by Cesare P. R. Romano, 46–111. Cambridge: Cambridge University Press, 2009.

Oakford, Samuel. "U.S. Doubled Fuel Support for Saudi Bombing Campaign in Yemen after Deadly Strike on Funeral." *The Intercept.* Accessed July 13, 2017. https://theintercept.com/2017/07/13/u-s-doubled-fuel-support-for-saudi-bombing-campaign-in-yemen-after-deadly-strike-on-funeral/.

Paulus, Andreas L. "From Neglect to Defiance? The United States and International Adjudication." *European Journal of International Law* 15, no. 4 (2004): 783–812.

Physicians for Social Responsibility. "Body Count: Casualty Figures after 10 Years of the 'War on Terror'." Accessed June 19, 2017. www.psr.org/assets/pdfs/body-count.pdf.

Porter, Gareth. "The US Provided Cover for the Saudi Starvation Strategy in Yemen." *Truthout.* Accessed July 1, 2017. www.truth-out.org/news/item/40147-the-us-provided-cover-for-the-saudi-starvation-strategy-in-yemen.

Power, Samantha. *"A Problem from Hell": American and the Age of Genocide.* New York: Harper Perennial, 2002.

Protocol Additional to the Geneva Conventions of 12 August 1949, and relating to the Protection of Victims of International Armed Conflicts (Protocol I), 8 June 1977. Accessed July 1, 2016. www.icrc.org/ihl/INTRO/470.

Rich, Frank. "And Now: 'Operation Iraqi Looting'." *New York Times.* Accessed July 1, 2017. www.nytimes.com/2003/04/27/arts/and-now-operation-iraqi-looting.html.

Riedel, Bruce. "The $110 Billion Arms Deal to Saudi Arabia Is Fake News." *Brookings.* Accessed July 1, 2017. www.brookings.edu/blog/markaz/2017/06/05/the-110-billion-arms-deal-to-saudi-arabia-is-fake-news/.

Ritu, Moshahida Sultana. "Ethnic Cleansing in Myanmar." *The New York Times.* www.nytimes.com/2012/07/13/opinion/ethnic-cleansing-of-myanmars-rohingyas.html?_r=0.

Rhodes, Ben. "Remarks on Burma Policy." Prepared for Delivery at the Center for New American Security. *White House.* Accessed July 1, 2016. www.white-house.gov/the-press-office/2016/05/18/remarks-deputy-national-security-advisor-ben-rhodes-burma-policy-center.

Rome Statute of the International Criminal Court. Accessed July 6, 2016. www.icc-cpi.int/nr/rdonlyres/ea9aeff7-5752-4f84-be94-0a655eb30e16/0/rome_statute_english.pdf.

Ronayne, Peter. *Never Again?: The United States and the Prevention and Punishment of Genocide since the Holocaust.* New York: Rowman & Littlefield, 2001.

Schabas, William. *An Introduction to the International Criminal Court.* Cambridge: Cambridge University Press, 2004.

Schabas, William. *Genocide in International Law: The Crime of Crimes.* Cambridge: Cambridge University Press, 2000.

Siddiqui, Usaid M. "How Aung San Suu Kyi and Her U.S. Allies Deny Burmese Anti-Muslim Atrocities." *Alternet.* Accessed July 5, 2016. www.alternet.org/grayzone-project/how-aung-san-suu-kyi-and-her-us-allies-deny-burmese-anti-muslim-atrocities.

Statute of the International Court of Justice. Accessed August 17, 2017. www.icj-cij. org/en/statute.

Stoakes, Emanuel. "Monks, PowerPoint Presentations, and Ethnic Cleansing." *Foreign Policy*. Accessed July 1, 2016. http://foreignpolicy.com/2015/10/26/evidence-links-myanmar-government-monks-ethnic-cleansing-rohingya/.

United Nations Human Rights Office of the High Commissioner. "Lift Blockade of Yemen to Stop 'Catastrophe' of Millions Facing Starvation, Says UN Expert." Accessed July 1, 2017. www.ohchr.org/EN/NewsEvents/Pages/DisplayNews. aspx?NewsID=21496&LangID=E.

United Nations International Children's Emergency Fund. "Malnutrition amongst Children in Yemen at an All-Time High, Warns UNICEF." Accessed July 1, 2017. www.unicefusa.org/press/releases/malnutrition-amongst-children-yemen-all-time-high-warns-unicef/31545.

United Nations Security Council. "Final Report of the Panel of Experts on Yemen Established Pursuant to Security Council Resolution 2140 (2014)." Accessed July 1, 2016. www.securitycouncilreport.org/atf/cf/%7B65BFCF9B-6D27-4E9C-8CD3-CF6E 4FF96FF9%7D/s_2016_73.pdf.

United Nations Security Council. Resolution 2140 (2014) of 26 February 2014. Accessed May 15, 2016. www.un.org/en/ga/search/view_doc.asp?symbol=S/RES/2140(2014).

United States Holocaust Memorial Museum. "'They Want Us All to Go Away': Early Signs of Genocide in Burma." Accessed June 1, 2016. www.ushmm.org/m/pdfs/20150505-Burma-Report.pdf.

Xu, Beina, and Eleanor Albert. "Understanding Myanmar." *Council on Foreign Relations*. Accessed July 5, 2016. www.cfr.org/human-rights/understanding-myanmar/p14385.

Index

30 September Movement 80

"A Problem from Hell": America and the Age of Genocide 8–11
accountability: Myanmar genocide 184; state responsibility 40–2
acts of aggression: UN General Assembly resolutions 157; US against Vietnam 157–8
acts of barbarity 57
acts of cultural genocide 56
acts of vandalism 57
Ad Hoc Committee draft: cultural genocide inclusion 32; political group inclusion 22; US exclusion of cultural genocide 61
Agent Orange 159–60
aggression 37–40; acts of aggression resolutions 157; definitions 156–7; intent requirement 156; US acts of aggression against Vietnam 157–8
Albright, Madeleine: *Preventing Genocide: A Blueprint for U.S. Policymakers* 175–6
allied bombings during World War II 38
al-Majid, Ali Hassan 124
Amnesty International: Yemen genocide investigations 178–9
Anfal Campaign 2
Anti-French Resistance 162
Arakenese Buddhists *see* Myanmar genocide
armed members of targeted groups as victims 24–6
Article 2(4) of United Nations Charter 156
Article IX reservation 187–9
Articles of Responsibility of States for Internationally Wrongful Acts 41

assimilation: cultural genocide 35; Native Americans 65–70
Awami League genocide *see* Bangladesh genocide
Axis Rule in Occupied Europe 57–8

Bangladesh genocide 97–8; acknowledgment of violence 104; "Blood Telegram" 102; complicity by US 105–6; India intervention 103; material support to Pakistan 101–2; Samantha Power effect 10; US prevention of genocide 105; US solution of withdrawing forces from foreign territories 103–4
barbarity 57
Bedau, Hugo Adam: Vietnam genocide 160, 165–6
bias: study of genocide 7–8
bilateral immunity agreements 192
biological genocide: cultural genocide separation from 32, 61
"Blood Telegram" 102
boarding schools: Native American children 65–9
bombings in Vietnam 159
Bosnia v. Serbia precedent 42–6; prevention, complicity, conspiracy 83–4

Cambodia bombings: Samantha Power effect 9–10
CCC (Commodity Credit Corporation) program 126
CEH (Commission for Historical Clarification): Guatemala genocide 10, 98–9
Charter of the International Military Tribunal: aggression definition 37, 156

204　*Index*

Chemical Ali 124
chemical weapons: Iraq 124, 128–9; UN
　Security Council resolutions 130–2;
　Vietnam genocide 159–60
Cherokee Indians 65
chronic conflict in Iraq 123
civil war *versus* genocide 26
civilian destruction 24
civilizing effects of education 68
Cohen, William: *Preventing Genocide: A
　Blueprint for U.S. Policymakers* 175–6
combatants as victims 24–6
Commission for Historical Clarification
　(CEH): Guatemala genocide 10, 98–9
Commodity Credit Corporation (CCC)
　program 126
communists *see* Indonesia genocide;
　Vietnam genocide
complicity in genocide: East Pakistan
　105–6; Guatemala 111–12; Indonesia
　mass murder of communists 90;
　Kurdish population 134–5; state
　responsibility 84; Yemen 178–82
concentration camps in Vietnam 159
Conlon, Paul 138
conspiracy to commit genocide;
　Indonesia 90–1; state responsibility 84
constraints: Genocide Convention 19–20
Convention on the Prevention and
　Punishment of the Crime of Genocide
　see Genocide Convention
Court of Indian Offenses 66
crimes against humanity 30–1; *versus*
　genocide 31; Yemen genocide 179–81
cultural genocide 3, 32–6; acts 56;
　attacks against the life of the group
　other than mass killing 58; definition
　32, 56; exclusion from Genocide
　Convention 9, 60–4; indigenous
　communities 34–5; Lemkin's
　conception 57–60; physical genocide
　58–9; separation from physical/
　biological genocide 32, 61; US
　responsibility 64–70
culture of impunity 7–8; Samantha
　Power effect 8–11; *see also* legal
　impunity
Cushman, Thomas 24

*The Deaths of Others: The Fate of
　Civilians in America's Wars* 123
Declaration of Emancipation: Awami
　League 97

defensive engagement in war 38
definition of genocide 4–7, 21
degenerate war 38
deliberately imposing conditions likely
　to kill members of a group 30–2
democide 7–8; Vietnam 167
Democratic Republic of the Congo
　(DRC): Genocide Convention Article
　IX 187
"democrisy" 7
diplomatic support: Arkan government
　185–6; Guatemala 2; Iraq 2, 133;
　Pakistan Searchlight 2; Saudi
　Arabia 181
dispersal: cultural genocide 35
dissident strand of literature on US
　foreign and domestic policies 11–12
distinction between war and genocide
　161–2
DRC (Democratic Republic of the
　Congo): Genocide Convention Article
　IX 187
dual-use commodities: providing to Iraq
　126–7

East Pakistan genocide *see* Bangladesh
　genocide
economic sanctions against Iraq
　136–7; attribution to US 138–40;
　cause of death and human suffering
　137–8; effect on public health 136–7;
　genocidal intent 142–5; method of
　genocide 140–1
economic support: Guatemala 107–8;
　Iraq 126, 132–3; Myanmar army
　185–6
education: civilizing effects 68; Native
　Americans 66–8
"ethnocide" 66
exclusion of cultural genocide from
　Genocide Convention 9, 60–4

First Indochina War 162
free-fire zones in Vietnam 159

gender groups: inclusion as social group 22
General Assembly: acts of aggression
　resolutions 157
Geneva Agreement: partitioning of
　Vietnam 162–3
genocide: *versus* crimes against humanity
　31; definition 4–7, 12; distinction from
　war 161–2

Index 205

Genocide Convention: Article IX reservations 187–9; constraints 19–20; definition of genocide 4; exclusion of cultural genocide 9; Samantha Power effect 8; US exclusion of cultural genocide 60–4

"Genocide or Civil War?: Human Rights and the Politics of Conceptualization" 26

genocide *versus* civil war 26

global poverty: inhumane intentional acts causing 31

Gordon, Joy: genocidal intent in Iraq 142–3

group identity: culture role 63

Guatemala genocide 2, 98–100; complicity of US 111–12; destruction of villages 107–8; economic support from US 107–8; "Guatemala Memory of Silence" report 10; Mayans declared enemies of the state 99–100; military support from US 106–8; Operation Sofía 99; political cover 108; Reagan's support of Ríos Montt 109; US Embassy portrayal of human rights situation 108–9; US prevention 109–11

"Guatemala Memory of Silence" report 10, 99

Guided Democracy 79

Gulf of Tonkin events 157–8

Halabja attack 125

Houthis 178

HRW (Human Rights Watch): Kurdish genocide intent 124; Yemen genocide investigations 178–9

Human Rights Review: "Genocide or Civil War?: Human Rights and the Politics of Conceptualization" 26

ICC (International Criminal Court): Rome Statute 30, 191

ICJ (International Court of Justice): *Bosnia v. Serbia* precedent 42–6

ICTR (International Criminal Tribunal for Rwanda): intent requirement 27

IDPs (internally displaced persons) 183

ILC (International Law Commission): aggression definition 156–7; Articles of Responsibility of States for Internationally Wrongful Acts 40–1

immunity *see* legal impunity

implied intent 27

impunity of US 7–8; Samantha Power effect 8–11

India intervention in East Pakistan genocide 103

Indian Child Welfare Act 69

Indian Wars 65–6

indigenous communities: cultural genocide 34–5; US physical genocide 64–5

indirect genocide 30–2; economic sanctions as method 140–1

individual criminal responsibility 189–92

Indonesia genocide of communists 2, 79–82; 30 September Movement 80; anti-communism rumors and propaganda 81; complicity of US 90; conspiracy to commit genocide 90–1; exclusion of political groups from Genocide Convention protection 24; Guided Democracy 79; Indonesian Army General Staff 79; mass killings 81–2; NASAKOM 79; political genocide 82–3; US–Indonesia relations 84–9; US prevention of genocide 89–90

Indonesian Army General Staff 79

intent requirement 26–9; aggressive war and genocide 156; economic sanctions on Iraq 142–5; Korean War 162; Kurdish genocide 124; Vietnam genocide 160–6

intergenerational effects of cultural genocide 35

internally displace persons (IDPs) 183

International Court of Justice (ICJ): *Bosnia v. Serbia* precedent 42–6

International Criminal Court (ICC): Rome Statute 30, 191

International Criminal Tribunal for Rwanda (ICTR): intent requirement 27

International Law Commission *see* ILC

international law violations: state responsibility 41, 70

Iran–Iraq War: chemical weapons 128–9; complicity of US 134–5; dual-use commodities from US 126–7; economic support of Iraq 126; intelligence sharing 127–8, 134; Iraq political cover by US 129–30; Samantha Power's analysis of US role 135–6; US prevention of genocide 132–4; US–Iraq relations 126

206   *Index*

Iraq: Anfal Campaign 2; chronic conflict 123; Operation Desert Storm 3; US–Iraq relations 126–32; war with US 123; *see also* Iraq's economic sanctions

Iraq Kurdish genocide 124–6; chemical weapons 128–9; chemical weapons attacks 124; complicity by US 134–5; dual-use commodities from US 126–7; economic support of Iraq 126; Halabja attack 125; intelligence sharing 127–8, 134; intent 124; Samantha Power effect 11; Samantha Power's analysis of US role 135–6; UN Security Council resolutions on chemical weapons 129–32; US prevention of genocide 132–4

Iraq's economic sanctions 3, 136–7: attribution to US 138–40; cause of death and human suffering 137–8; effect on public health 136–7; genocidal intent 142–5; method of genocide 140–1; Sanctions Committee 139

Khmer Rouge: Samantha Power effect 9–10

killing members of a group 30

Korean War: genocidal intent 162; US aggression 1

Kurdish genocide 124–6; chemical weapons 128–9; chemical weapons attacks 124; complicity of US 134–5; dual-use commodities from US 126–7; economic support of Iraq 126; Halabja attack 125; intelligence sharing 127–8, 134; intent 124; Samantha Power effect 11; Samantha Power's analysis of US role 135–6; UN Security Council resolutions on chemical weapons 129–2; US prevention of genocide 132–4

Kuwait: Operation Desert Storm 3

leadership on language of Genocide Convention 8–9

legal definition of genocide 4; compared to scholarly definition 20

legal impunity 187; individual criminal responsibility 189–92; state responsibility for genocide 187–9

legitimation of war 161–2

Lemkin, Raphael: cultural genocide 57–60

Leupp, Francis 68

limited universal jurisdiction 189–92

malnutrition of children in Yemen 182

material support: Guatemala 2, 106–8, 112; Indonesian Army 88–9; Iraq 2, 132–3; Pakistan 2, 101–2; Saudi Arabia 181

Mayan genocide 98–100; complicity by US 111–12; declared enemies of the state 99–100; destruction of villages 107–8; economic support from US 107–8; military support to Guatemala 106–8; Operation Sofía 99; political cover 108; Reagan's support of Ríos Montt 109; US Embassy portrayal of human rights situation 108–9; US prevention 109–11

methods of genocide 29–36; cultural genocide 32–6; deliberately imposing conditions likely to kill members of a group 30–2; killing members of a group 30

military support: Guatemala 112; Indonesian Army 84–6; Iraq 132–3; Saudi Arabia 181

My Lai massacre 159

Myanmar genocide 182–7; absence of accountability 184; beginning of violence 183; open commission of violence 183–4; political reforms 184–5; US political/economic ties 185–6; US prioritization of economic growth/competition with China 186–7

NASAKOM (nationalism, agama, communism) 79

Native Americans cultural genocide 65–70; education 66–8; forcibly removed from lands 65; saving them 66

Netherlands: cultural genocide 62

NLD (National League for Democracy) 184–5

NLF (National Liberation Front) 158, 163–6

Nuremberg Principles 40

Oil for Food program 139–40

Operation Desert Storm 3

Operation Searchlight 2, 97

Operation Sofía 99

outing system: Native American children 69

Index 207

Pakistan genocide in East Pakistan 97–8; acknowledgment of violence by US 104; "Blood Telegram" 102; complicity by US 105–6; cultural genocide 62; India intervention 103; material support from US 101–2; Operation Searchlight 2; US prevention of genocide 105; US solution of withdrawing forces from foreign territories 103–4

Panel of Experts on Yemen 178

partitioning of Vietnam 162–3

Pell, Senator Claiborne: Prevention of Genocide Act 135

Pentagon Papers 165

physical genocide 58–9; cultural genocide separation from 32, 61; US treatment of indigenous populations 64–5; Yuki Indians 65

physical violence: killing members of a group 30

PKI (Partai Komunis Indonesia) mass murders 79–82; 30 September Movement 80; anti-communism rumors and propaganda 81; complicity of US 90; conspiracy to commit genocide 90–1; Guided Democracy 79; Indonesian Army General Staff 79; mass killings 81–2; NASAKOM 79; political genocide 82–3; US prevention of genocide 89–90; US–Indonesia relations 84–9

political definition of genocide 5

political genocide: Awami League and supporters 97–8; Indonesia mass murder of communists 82–3; *see also* Vietnam genocide

political groups: inclusion in definition 23–4; Soviet argument for exclusion 22–3

political support: Iraq 129–33; Pakistan 106; *see also* diplomatic support

politicide 36

Power, Samantha 8–11; analysis of US role in Iraq 135–6

preventing genocide: East Pakistan 105; Guatemala 109–11; Indonesia mass murder of communists 89–90; Kurdish population 132–4; Rohingya genocide 182–7; state responsibility 84

Preventing Genocide: A Blueprint for U.S. Policymakers 175–6

Prevention of Genocide Act 135

prioritizing economic growth over human rights 186–7

protected groups 21–4

public health: economic sanctions on Iraq 136–7; Saudi blockade in Yemen 180

Public Law 959 69–70

Reagan's support of Ríos Montt 109

redefining genocide 19–21; intent requirement 26–9; methods of genocide 29–36; protected groups 22–4; relationship between aggressive war and genocide 37–40; state responsibility 40–2; victims 24–6

religious groups: inclusion as cultural group 22

Relocation Act 69

Resolution 96(I) of United Nations General Assembly 59

Resolution 582 130

Resolution 598 131

Resolution 612 131

responsibility for genocide 175–8

responsibility in East Pakistan genocide: acknowledgment of violence 104; "Blood Telegram" 102; complicity 105–6; India intervention 103; material support 101–2; prevention of genocide 105; US solution of withdrawing forces from foreign territories 103–4

responsibility in Guatemala genocide: complicity 111–12; destruction of villages 107–8; economic support 107–8; military support 106–8; political cover 108; prevention of genocide 109–11; Reagan's support of Ríos Montt 109; US Embassy portrayal of human rights situation 108–9

responsibility in Indonesia genocide: complicity 90; conspiracy to commit genocide 90–1; prevention of genocide 89–90; US–Indonesia relations 84–9

responsibility in Kurdish genocide: prevention 132–34

responsibility in Vietnam genocide: acts of genocide 158–60; destroying communism 164–6; intent requirement 160–6; partitioning of Vietnam 162–3; victims 167–8

responsibility of economic sanctions on Iraq 136–7; attribution to US 138–40; death and human suffering

208 *Index*

137–8; effect on public health 136–7; genocidal intent 142–5; sanctions as method of genocide 140–1

Ríos Montt: Reagan's support 109

Rohingya genocide 182–7; absence of accountability 184; beginning of violence 183; open commission of violence 183–4; political reforms 184–5; political/economic ties to US 185–6; US prioritization of economic growth/competition with China 186–7

Rome Statute of the International Criminal Court 30, 191

Rwanda 27–8

SAM (Sever Acute Malnutrition) 182

Samantha Power effect 8–11; omission of genocide cases 9–11; US leadership in drafting Genocide Convention 8–9

sanctions on Iraq 3, 136–7; attribution to US 138–40; cause of death and human suffering 137–8; effect on public health 136–7; genocidal intent 142–5; method of genocide 140–1

Sartre, Jean-Paul: genocidal intent in Vietnam 161

Saudi Arabia genocide of Yemenis 178–82; arms support 181; bombings against Houthis 178; crimes against humanity 179–81; HRW/Amnesty International investigations 178–9; logistical/diplomatic support 181; Panel of Experts on Yemen findings 178; war crimes 179

scholarly definition of genocide 5–6; compared to legal definition 20

scholarly impunity 192–3

scorched-earth policy 109

Secretariat Draft: cultural genocide inclusion 32; political group inclusion 22

Serbia: Bosnia precedent 42–6

settler-colonial brutality against Native Americans 65

Severe Acute Malnutrition (SAM) 182

Sixth Committee: US exclusion of cultural genocide 61–2

Soviet argument for political group exclusion 22–3

state obligations to Genocide Convention 43–4

state responsibility 40–2; Articles of Responsibility of States for Internationally Wrongful Acts 41; *Bosnia v. Serbia* precedent 42–6; international law violations 70; legal impunity from genocide 187–9; prevention, complicity, conspiracy of genocide 83–4; US and genocide 175–8

structural violence 31

subsidiary jurisdiction proposal 190–1

tactical herbicides: Vietnam genocide 159–60

taming Native Americans 67

targeted groups: armed members as victims 24–6

Termination Acts 69

Tirman, John 123

Trail of Tears 65

Tutsi genocide 28

Twenty Years' War 123

UN (United Nations): acts of aggression resolutions 157; Charter Article 2(4) 156; genocide is an international crime resolution 59; "Guatemala Memory of Silence" report 10; Iran–Iraq war use of chemical weapons 129–32; *see also* economic sanctions against Iraq

unaccountability *see* legal impunity

UNICEF (United Nations Children's Fund): deaths of Iraqi children 137

United States Indian Industrial School 66

United to End Genocide: Myanmar fact-finding mission 183

US: exclusion of cultural genocide from Genocide Convention 60–4; foreign policy and responsibility for genocide 175–8; responsibility for cultural genocide 64–70

USHMM (United States Holocaust Memorial Museum): Rohingya genocide 182–7

US–Indonesia relations 84–9; awareness of killings 87; covert assistance to Indonesian Army 85–6; material support 88–9; military aid 84; PKI threat to US interests in Southeast Asia 85; US supplied PKI leader list to Indonesian Army 89

US–Iraq relations 126–32; chemical warfare 128–9; dual-use commodities

Index 209

126–7; economic support 126; intelligence sharing 127–8, 134; political cover 129–32; removal of Iraq from state sponsors of terrorism list 126; Samantha Power's analysis of US role 135–6; *see also* economic sanctions against Iraq

vandalism 57
victims of genocide: armed members of targeted groups 24–6; Iraq 136–8; Vietnam 167–8
victims of politicide 36
Viet Cong 158, 163–6
Vietnam democide 8
Vietnam genocide: acts of genocide 158–60; destroying communism 164–6; Gulf of Tonkin false flag events 157–8; intent requirement 160–6; partitioning of Vietnam 162–3; US acts of aggression 157–8; US aggression 1–2; victims 167–8

WANA (West Asia-North Africa) Institute 123
war crimes: Saudi Arabia in Yemen 179

war of aggression on Vietnam: acts of genocide 158–60; destroying communism 164–6; genocidal intent 160–6; Gulf of Tonkin events 157–8; partitioning of Vietnam 162–3; victims 167–8
wars: distinction from genocide 161–2; rules 39
wars of aggression: relationship with genocide 37–40
West Asia-North Africa (WANA) Institute 123
WHO (World Health Organization): deaths of Iraqi children 137
WMD program in Iraq 3
Worcester v. Georgia 65

Yemen genocide 178–82; arms support 181; bombings against Houthis 178; crimes against humanity 179–81; HRW/Amnesty International investigations 178–9; logistical/ diplomatic support 181; Panel of Experts on Yemen findings 178; war crimes 179
Yuki Indians 65

 Taylor & Francis eBooks

Helping you to choose the right eBooks for your Library

Add Routledge titles to your library's digital collection today. Taylor and Francis ebooks contains over 50,000 titles in the Humanities, Social Sciences, Behavioural Sciences, Built Environment and Law.

Choose from a range of subject packages or create your own!

Benefits for you
- » Free MARC records
- » COUNTER-compliant usage statistics
- » Flexible purchase and pricing options
- » All titles DRM-free.

Benefits for your user
- » Off-site, anytime access via Athens or referring URL
- » Print or copy pages or chapters
- » Full content search
- » Bookmark, highlight and annotate text
- » Access to thousands of pages of quality research at the click of a button.

 REQUEST YOUR FREE INSTITUTIONAL TRIAL TODAY

Free Trials Available
We offer free trials to qualifying academic, corporate and government customers.

eCollections – Choose from over 30 subject eCollections, including:

Archaeology	Language Learning
Architecture	Law
Asian Studies	Literature
Business & Management	Media & Communication
Classical Studies	Middle East Studies
Construction	Music
Creative & Media Arts	Philosophy
Criminology & Criminal Justice	Planning
Economics	Politics
Education	Psychology & Mental Health
Energy	Religion
Engineering	Security
English Language & Linguistics	Social Work
Environment & Sustainability	Sociology
Geography	Sport
Health Studies	Theatre & Performance
History	Tourism, Hospitality & Events

For more information, pricing enquiries or to order a free trial, please contact your local sales team:
www.tandfebooks.com/page/sales

 Routledge
Taylor & Francis Group

The home of Routledge books

www.tandfebooks.com

Printed in the USA
CPSIA information can be obtained
at www.ICGtesting.com
LVHW020034080224
771239LV00001B/160